WHERE ECONOMICS WENT WRONG

Where Economics Went Wrong

Chicago's Abandonment of Classical Liberalism

David Colander and Craig Freedman

PRINCETON UNIVERSITY PRESS

PRINCETON AND OXFORD

Published by Princeton University Press
41 William Street, Princeton, New Jersey 08540
6 Oxford Street, Woodstock, Oxfordshire OX20 1TR

press.princeton.edu

LCCN: 2018942713
ISBN 978-0-691-17920-9

British Library Cataloging-in-Publication Data is available

Editorial: Joe Jackson and Samantha Nader
Production Editorial: Nathan Carr
Jacket/Cover Design: Chris Ferrante
Jacket/Cover Credit: World's Columbian Exposition, 1893. C.D. Arnold, photographer.
World's Columbian Exposition Photographs by C.D. Arnold, Ryerson & Burnham Archives,
The Art Institute of Chicago. Digital File #198902.E20807
Production: Erin Suydam
Publicity: Tayler Lord and Caroline Priday
Copyeditor: Karen Verde

This book has been composed in Adobe Text Pro and Gotham

Printed on acid-free paper. ∞

Printed in the United States of America

10 9 8 7 6 5 4 3 2 1

To Craig's daughters, Emily and Nicola, who have wisely chosen to abstain from reading a single word he has written, and to Dave's granddaughter, Adelaide, who, as a one year old, also won't be reading this book anytime soon.

CONTENTS

PREFACE

This book's origin can be traced back to a somewhat dreary ASSA meeting in 2010 where, over dinner and with the help of some good wine, we came to agreement on what was wrong with the Chicago School and what was wrong with modern economics. Although our training and approaches to economics were quite different, we were surprised that we were in close agreement on the Chicago School and on what's wrong with modern economics. The problem was not Chicago beliefs and ideology, as it was in the standard narrative; the problem was connected more to the Chicago pit bull attitude toward argumentation. Instead of trying to find common ground, its argumentation style was designed to win debating points. That, blended with some loose expression of ideas in what we later termed the Samuelsonian theoretical policy framework, led to a polarization of views within economics, both in economic policy analysis and in economics theory because the Samuelsonian policy discussion had connected the two.

We both have an interest in the history of economic thought and we agreed that the modern approach was a quite different approach to economic theorizing and argumentation than could be found in the best of Classical economics, such as that of John Stuart Mill. Mill's argumentation style, which we called argumentation for the sake of heaven, was designed to explore philosophical truths, not to win debates in the eyes of some outside observer. In changing that argumentation style, Chicago had lost the Classical Liberal methodology.

Debating with the goal of discovering shared truths, not with the goal of winning, is difficult. To make the debate somewhat easier, Classical economists separated out economic policy analysis from economic theory and science. That separation was a key element of their methodology because it allowed them to distinguish differences about policy—where disagreement was to be expected and would have to be addressed through friendly debate exploring issues that went far beyond economic science, and differences about theory and science, where debates would be resolved by appeal to logic and empirical evidence within economics. In the science of economics, it would be expected that all well-trained economists would agree. But that science would have no direct implications for policy which involved values that went far beyond what science dealt with. With this methodological approach, economists of all political views could share the same theory but could differ significantly on policy.

Our telling of the story started as an article, but the story quickly expanded beyond article length and turned into a book. As we developed it, we decided that the story was about Classical Liberalism and how the economics profession lost its Classical Liberal groundings. Chicago was useful in telling that story because it was the last holdout, a bit like the Alamo, not because Chicago was unique. Long before Chicago abandoned it, the broader economics profession had as well. When the Chicago School coalesced in the 1950s, Classical Liberal methodology as the reigning economic methodology was dead.

The reader will detect a real sense of loss in our telling of the story. In our view, by giving up Classical Liberalism, the economics profession went down the wrong track in its policy analysis. That injured both its scientific theory and its policy analysis. The problem is not that economic scientists attempt to keep values out of their science. That's what good science does. The problem is that they don't sufficiently separate out science from policy analysis. That separation is necessary because the appropriate methodology of policy analysis is quite different from the appropriate methodology of science. Classical liberal methodology solved the problem by placing a firewall between science and policy. Modern economics removed that firewall, and in doing so removed Classical economics' method of keeping a consensus on theory and simultaneously dealing with differing sensibilities and values. Thus, while we agree with both right and left heterodox economists that modern economics has problems, we differ from most of them because they also do not maintain a firewall. Economic science and theory do not and cannot tell us whether the right or the left is correct. Both the right and the left heterodox economists have insights, as do mainstream economists. The problem is that those insights get lost by their joint use of a methodology that doesn't distinguish between science and policy, and thus doesn't direct them to the most useful methods to resolve, or at least to agree to disagree, on inevitable policy differences.

The goal of the book should be clear upon reading. It is to fan some of these embers that remain of the Classical Liberal methodology, and to create an environment in which the Classical Liberal attitude toward methodology can reign once again within the economics profession.

We worked hard to keep the book short, and one of the ways we did that was to put many of our ideas into endnotes. There are a lot of them, and the average reader can skip them without loss of our central points. But they are there for the interested reader to consume. We encourage readers to think of the endnotes as a book within a book, and to explore the tangents they discuss. One strategy might be to read them consecutively after finishing the relevant chapter.

As always, there were lots of people who contributed to this book. First, we've presented the ideas herein at a variety of workshops, seminars, and conferences and have received useful comments whenever we did. We thank all of those who provided comments. Second, as part of other books he has written and is working on, Craig interviewed numerous Chicago economists, and quotations from them can be found scattered throughout the text, especially in the endnotes. All these economists were very forthcoming and we thank them sincerely. Third, we would like to thank the reviewers, who sent us helpful comments, and improved the manuscript significantly. Fourth, we would like to thank Joe Jackson, our editor at Princeton University Press, for guiding the manuscript, Nathan Carr,

Samantha Nader, and Theresa Liu who assisted him, and our copy-editor, Karen Verde. Fifth, we thank our families, who gave us the time and space to work on the book.

And finally, we'd like to thank each other—for the patience necessary to put up with one another. We both recognize that we are idiosyncratic pains in the neck requiring the forbearance of a saint to put up with us. How two non-saints actually managed to write a book together is, in our view, somewhat miraculous. In that spirit of generosity, all the mistakes and incorrect arguments that remain are to be attributed entirely to the other author.

DC and CF

WHERE ECONOMICS WENT WRONG

1

Sweet Science

ENGINEERING A NEW APPROACH
TO ECONOMIC POLICY

Economic policy does not follow from economic theory. Instead, policy needs to be drawn from a complicated blend of judgments about ambiguous empirical evidence, normative judgements, and sensibilities that may be framed, but are not determined, by scientific theory.[1] Put another way, economic policy is a blend of engineering and judgment—an "art and craft," not a scientific endeavor that follows from economic theory.[2] Debates about policy are best treated as debates about the art and craft of economics, using a methodology appropriate for an art and craft. Policy debates should not be treated as debates about science, and should not be governed by a methodology more appropriate to science.

Unfortunately, modern economics doesn't treat policy in this way. Instead, it conceives of policy as an applied science, and uses the methodology of science to study policy issues. To some degree, that makes sense. Clearly, one wants evidenced-based, objective analysis of policy. An art and craft methodology uses theory and science whenever it can, meaning to the extent it is appropriate. But when dealing with the messy issues of policy, an art and craft methodology takes seriously the fact that statistical evidence needs interpretation and that one's views and analysis are inevitably influenced by one's normative judgments.[3] An art and craft methodology recognizes that policy is intrinsically entangled and must be dealt with using a methodology designed to guide in such ambiguous, messy, and uncertain situations. To pretend otherwise undermines both the science of economics and economic policy discussions.

Early on, economists struggled with this policy/science divide. Advocates of various policy positions all claimed to have science and theory on their side. They inevitably attacked their opponents for being non-scientific. This struggle led Classical Liberal economists to embrace a methodological tradition that interpreted the science of economics narrowly and created a firewall between scientific pursuits and policy endeavors. This tradition is best found in the policy methodology of Classical Liberals such as John Stuart Mill and his followers. That methodology recognized the messiness of policy compared to the elegance of the theory underlying science.

To deal with that messiness, the policy methodology needed a branch of economics that was free of scientific certainty. One way to handle that problem would be to accept that no part of economics was a science.[4] The second way—the path adopted by Classical Liberals—was to divide economics into different branches—a scientific branch concerned with agreed-upon empirical facts and logical implications of assumptions, in which normative values played as minimal a role as possible, and a policy branch in which values were seen as essential elements of the analysis. The policy branch of economics would use a different methodology than the scientific branch, and its conclusions would not be considered scientific conclusions.

Since our goal in this book is to talk about the methodology appropriate for applied policy, we do not distinguish between the "economics is not a science" and the "economic policy branch of economics is not a science" alternatives. The reason is that our interest is in applied policy, not the science of economics. We interpret the "no economic science" alternative, such as that proposed by some philosophers, for example, Hillary Putnam (2002) or Alexander Rosenberg (Rosenberg 1992), as being included in the Classical "separate branch" alternative. The "no economic science" alternative simply makes the further assumption that the science branch of economics is empty, an assumption we do not accept. But for our purposes these come to the same conclusion since, if there is no part of economics that is a science, then the applied policy branch of economics will not be guided by scientific methodology. If one believes, as Putnam and Rosenberg believe, that no part of economics is a science, it does not change our argument that applied policy should not be thought of as applied science—it strengthens it, since if there is no economic science, our argument—that applied policy economics should not be seen as applied science—becomes tautologically true.[5]

Most classical economists accepted that there was a scientific branch of economics.[6] But they also believed that policy did not follow from scientific theory, and they built that belief into their applied policy methodology. By doing so, Classical Liberalism sought to discourage the conflicting advocates of any policy issue from claiming the authority of scientific justification. Only a powerful firewall between theory and policy could accomplish that. For John Stuart Mill, policy was not based on science, and science did not concern policy. Instead, science was about a search for the truth. In pursuit of that truth, in order to see the scientific truth more clearly, one should ideally harbor no policy considerations whatsoever. Since that was practically impossible, one should attempt to guard, as much as possible, against a tendency to claim too much from science. Policy construction was meant to be about the search for answers to specific policy questions. That search required one to go far beyond the limits imposed by science. The objective was to integrate into the argument judgments that had no scientific basis, but that might have a philosophical basis. To keep the two separate, an economist needed to always lean over backward to confess that, in his or her role as an economic scientist, he or she had nothing to say about policy. That doesn't prevent him or her, when operating in a "statesman" role, from expressing views, and if he or she has expertise in that area, from offering them as the views of a special-ist. But that expertise has to be broader than that of an economic scientist, and it must involve knowledge that goes far beyond sci-ence. Given the complexity of the economy it is an expertise that will emphasize its fallibility and view that often the best we can do in a complex world is to muddle through without definitive answers (Colander 2003).

The Abandonment of Classical Liberal Methodology

In the 1930s, the economics profession began to abandon the pol-icy methodology of Classical Liberalism by removing the firewall between economic science and policy. This book is an exploration of that abandonment and a call for the profession to return to a more Classical Liberal methodology in policy matters. In our con-sideration of the abandonment of Classical Liberal methodology, we use the University of Chicago as a case study of this largely post-war phenomenon. We focus on Chicago, not because of the politi-cal inclinations or ideological leanings that characterized Chicago in this era, nor because Chicago was unique in abandoning this Classical firewall separating scientific theory from policy. Instead, we choose it because the stalwarts of the postwar Chicago School actually imagined themselves to be, and were seen by most econo-mists as being, defenders of Classical Liberalism.[7] In our view, the Chicago School failed to defend what was important in Classical Liberalism, namely its art and craft policy methodology.

The Chicago School was intent instead on maintaining a narrow interpretation of a laissez-faire policy precept.[8] Chicago adopted a viewpoint which insisted that economic science effectively under-pinned the conclusion that the market is capable of solving its own problems. Consequently, government policy interventions should be strongly discouraged. There were two problems with this. The first is that, in Classical Liberal thought, no policy precept followed directly from economic science. In this regard, the Chicago School failed to adhere to that Classical Liberal position. The second issue was the failure to recognize that the laissez-faire policy precept of

Classical Liberalism was far more ambiguous than its Chicago interpretation. The Classical laissez-faire understanding could be held by economists with a wide disparity of views of government policy, ranging from John Maynard Keynes's policy activism to Frederick von Hayek's pro-market policy. Moreover, because it was a policy precept, it could change over time, as the problems faced by society changed, as sensibilities changed, and as government structures in turn changed. It was not for economic scientists to settle this debate about policy since the issues debated were, to a large extent, non-economic.

What we are saying is that at the core of Classical Liberalism was a methodology that required separating out, as much as possible, one's consideration of scientific research from one's policy views. One could, and inevitably would, hold ideological and policy views, but, using a Classical Liberal methodology, debates about such matters were best separated from debates about science. As the economics profession progressively abandoned Classical Liberal policy views in a process extending from the 1930s to the 1960s, they simultaneously abandoned the corresponding methodological approach to policy.

The abandonment of these methodological views started with the development and acceptance of what would come to be called welfare economics. Welfare economics provided a formal scientific economic framework for thinking about policy. That framework proved extremely useful in shedding light on many policy questions and incorporating insights from economic thinking. The problem of coordinating responses to scarcity could be captured in a mathematical general equilibrium model and applied to a wide variety of situations. The power of this mathematical model was recognized by the profession, and it became central to the teaching of economics. It was subsequently supplemented by empirical work applying the theory, which could be carried out more rigorously due to developments in statistical analysis. These advances led many economists to believe that economics had become engaged in a series of scientific breakthroughs that would rescue economics from what many considered to be the realm of pseudoscience. Instead, the discipline would be invested with the much more welcomed foundation of formal science.

The general equilibrium model framed policy within a mathematical optimal control structure. The model implicitly assumed that a perfectly competitive market would optimally organize economies in most situations, but that government intervention would be needed to correct for market failures, such as externalities. This approach resulted in what was considered a scientifically based policy conclusion implying some need for government intervention if an economy was to run smoothly. The theory proceeded to develop formal marginal conditions that were capable of guiding policy makers. Laissez-faire was correspondingly non-optimal.

This welfare economics policy framework caught on like wildfire. Since the best way to understand the framework was to understand the mathematical structure of the general equilibrium system, adopting this framework changed the way economics was taught. Students were taught more math and statistics and less moral philosophy and institutional insights. With that change in place, the general equilibrium welfare policy framework eliminated the previously acknowledged firewall. What was considered scientific economic theory was connected directly to policy.

The change to a mathematical general equilibrium welfare economics framework occurred throughout the profession. It started slowly, but resistance decreased as new mathematically and statistically trained economists replaced those trained in the broader Classical Liberal discursive tradition. The art of policy was lost, and the craft of policy became synonymous with scientific theory. The policy/science firewall was fundamentally violated by this change.

Classical Liberals objected, arguing that thinking about policy in too rigid a mathematical fashion eliminated all types of issues that were important components of the policy debate. The general equilibrium model wasn't wrong, but it wasn't "the" sole economic model that should be employed. It was a model based on assumptions that for some issues was useful, but for others was not. Different assumptions could lead to different results. The problem with the model was that it didn't appropriately capture many of the debatable issues relevant to policy, and thus inappropriately limited the scope of policy discussion. Those objections were vigorous at first, and then tended to fade away. Economists advancing those arguments were attacked as being old-fashioned and unscientific. They were dismissed as lacking mathematical knowledge and skills. This change in methodology occurred throughout the English-speaking economics profession, but was led by economists at LSE (Hicks and Lerner), Cambridge (Pigou), as well as Harvard and MIT (Samuelson).

The Chicago Response

The incipient Chicago School (George Stigler, Milton Friedman, Aaron Director, and their associated colleagues) objected to the development of this general equilibrium welfare frame as a basis for policy. They saw it as a rejection of Classical precepts guiding both microeconomic and macroeconomic policy. Particular ire was directed at what they viewed as the malignant travesty encapsulated by the developing Keynesian (collective) policy.[9] These Chicago economists insisted that the Keynesian model was a Trojan horse being used to advance statist ideology and collectivist ideas. They chose, however, not to argue in favor of Classical Liberal methodology. Nor did they reject the implicit contention that policy must follow from mathematically rigorous models. Instead, they responded to this challenge by developing an alternative "scientific" pathway that would lead to the desired laissez-faire policy precept. Specifically, they developed an alternative model demonstrating that the types of government intervention supported by the welfare economic framework, as well as the Keynesian macro framework, were fundamentally flawed theories. In their alternative scientific model, an economy would work best when left to its own devices.

Because of their impressive rhetorical and intuitive marketing skills, the Chicago economists eventually managed to engineer a successful partial counterrevolution against this general equilibrium welfare economics framework. But, in engineering that counter-revolution to save the Classical Liberal policy precept of laissez-faire, they abandoned the most essential part of Classical Liberalism—its methodological foundations. In doing so they, like the advocates of the general equilibrium welfare policy framework, abandoned the Classical Liberal firewall that had previously separated science from policy. Once they accepted that policy necessarily followed from a scientific model, the economic policy debate became inextricably focused on whose science was correct. The bone of contention no longer survived as a debate focused on judgments and sensibilities, which is where Classical Liberal methodology placed it. Serious discussion concerning the subtleties and judgments underlying these differing views became impossible. Each side characterized the other as ideology masquerading as science. These pointed accusations were precisely the type of futile debate that the Classical Liberal firewall had been designed to avoid.

Our concern in this book is not focused on which policy view is correct. Instead, our interest lies in the manner in which the debate about those policy views should be conducted. Should it be primarily a debate about science, formal models, and statistical tests of empirical evidence? Or should it be primarily a debate about sensibilities and judgments that are informed, but not determined, by science? Our argument is that Classical Liberal support for the market was a precept upon which good economists could disagree. It was not a fundamental conclusion based on economic science. Although science and theory can provide some guidance about policy, resolution of such debates is not to be found in theory, but rather in vigorous "argumentation for the sake of heaven," a term that designates a process of cordial argumentation that attempts to seek out the best estimate of truth that is possible.[10] It is not argumentation that focuses primarily on winning policy debates.

Had the fight been about Classical Liberal methodology, not policy, the battle lines would have been drawn quite differently. For example, in terms of policy, the Chicago School vehemently opposed John Maynard Keynes. But in terms of methodology alone, Keynes was an ally of Classical Liberalism. Throughout his career he steadfastly stayed within the Classical Liberal methodological tradition. He questioned mathematical models, econometric models, and tended to use discursive arguments to make his key points.[11] While in terms of specific policies, Frank Knight, a guiding light of Chicago in the 1930s, was often diametrically (and vehemently) opposed to Keynes, methodologically Knight had much more in common with Keynes than he did with either Samuelson or Arrow (or Friedman for that matter). That methodological connection between Keynes and Knight was lost when policy (and ideological) fidelity trumped methodological fidelity as the litmus test for Classical Liberalism. By surrendering Classical Liberal methodology, the economics profession steered the policy debate to its current sterile state.

Talk Is Cheap: Paying Lip Service to the Science/Policy Firewall

Even as economists were tearing down the firewall erected between theory and policy, they implicitly recognized what they were doing. They even paid lip service to maintaining that traditional separation, as they were busily blending the two. For example, Milton Friedman, who most observers saw as constructing scientific arguments supporting the superiority of the market, states:

> I have tried to influence public policy. I have spoken and written about issues of policy. In so doing, however, I have not been acting in my scientific capacity but in my capacity as a citizen, an informed one, I hope. I believe that what I know as an economist helps me to form better judgments about some issues than I could without that knowledge. But fundamentally, my scientific work should not be judged by my activities in public policy. (Friedman quoted in Overtveldt 2007: 91)

His counterpart, Paul Samuelson, similarly acknowledged this need (as well as the difficulty anyone would have in preserving it), writing:[12]

> I could disagree 180 degrees with his [Milton Friedman's] policy conclusion and yet concur in his diagnosis or the empirical

observations and inferred probabilities. Yet such is the imperfection of the human scientist, an anthropologist studying us academic guinea pigs will record the sad fact that our hearts do often contaminate our minds and eyes. The conservative will forecast high inflation danger on the basis of the same data that leads the do-gooder to warn against recession. (Conscious of this unconscious source of bias, as the subsequent discussion will elaborate on, I make a special effort toward self-criticism and eclecticism—with what success, the record must testify to.) (Samuelson 2011: 888–889)

Our argument is that, while recognizing the need for a firewall when forming policy arguments, as well as the use of economic theory to support that policy, MIT economists such as Samuelson, Chicago economists such as Friedman, and Keynesian economists such as Abba Lerner and Jim Tobin[13] continually violated the science/policy firewall.[14] Doing so forced the opposing side to feel as if it had to do the same. Neither side could bring itself to hold firmly to the Classical Liberal position that the basis for their policy recommendations did not, and could not, directly follow from economic theory or science. Instead, their policy conclusions should have followed from a much more complex set of contestable arguments, reasoning, and sensibilities. Policy involves matters on which reasonable people, who share the same deep understanding of scientific economic theory, can differ and which cannot be resolved satisfactorily in terms of economic theory or science. The best we can hope for is resolution through "argumentation for the sake of heaven," which requires good faith efforts from both sides to communicate.[15] So, while both sides instinctively comprehended the gulf dividing economics as a science from its role in guiding policy, they also found following these instincts almost impossible.[16] Expediency, as it often does, triumphed. In a suitable phrase that one can imagine being employed over lunch at the University of Chicago's Quadrangle Club, the gulf existing between intentions and actions can be summed up by an all-purpose dismissal, namely that "talk is cheap."

In the postwar struggle for the soul, or at least the lungs of the discipline, most of the niceties separating the rough and tumble of policy hawking from the more imposing heights of economic science became blurred. The application of economics would come to be seen as grounding policy on a firmer and more scientific foundation. Doing so involved replacing discursive economic analysis, which touched on the sensibilities and judgments underlying policy differences, with the supposed rigor of "scientific" analysis. Math replaced words whenever possible. Statistical studies replaced case studies, and empirically tested theory replaced reasoned discursive argument. Economic policy analysis evolved into an applied science that was no longer seen as an art and craft. Discursive argument, dealing with judgments and sensibilities, no longer had a featured place in the applied science of policy economics.

Seeking a scientific basis for policy was by no means a radical procedural departure that definitively separated the Chicago School from the broader swath of the more mainstream economics profession of that era. As we have emphasized, it was a movement that transcended the confines of Chicago. As previously mentioned, throughout the Classical period of economics, there had been continual attempts by one side or the other to claim a scientific foundation for its policy views. The evolving acrimony in dealing with those competing claims led Classical Liberal economists to develop their science/policy firewall. Precisely because the temptation to assert such a scientific basis for one's policy views was so powerful, that claim had to be continually challenged and contained.[17] However, in the rising optimism characterizing the postwar era, economic policy seemed to present no more of a challenge to a rising set of engaged professionals than did the previous daunting tasks of mobilizing resources to conquer the Great Depression or to successfully vanquish wartime foes. The solution to any policy problem simply involved the appropriate application of measured scientific methods.[18] To manage this task, a new cohort of young economists achieved positions of increasing prominence,[19] implicitly promising to shift away from the sort of judgment-making and ill-defined interpretative skills required by the older, Classical Liberal economists still trapped by the past.[20] The prevailing conviction was that by employing scientific methods, ambiguity-ridden policy pronouncements would be significantly reduced if not eternally banished.

What developed in the postwar period was in essence a transformation in the approach economists accepted when formulating economic policy. This book explores that transformation and argues that it contained within it a fatal flaw. In an attempt to achieve a more scientific foundation for its policy analysis, economics violated Hume's Dictum that a "should" cannot follow from an "is." By doing so, this highly touted scientific approach shifted policy debate away from the nuanced understanding that policy required, namely a subtle blend of theory, moral philosophy, and judgment. Instead, the discipline maneuvered itself into an untenable corner where differences in policy unswervingly followed from differences in scientific theory. Consequently, they could only be resolved by using scientific methodology.

Why Did the Profession Abandon Classical Liberal Methodology?

Classical Liberal methodology developed in response to a recognition of the problems created by too closely linking science with policy. This methodology was a correction of a misconceived reaction. Initially, for example, Adam Smith's broad-ranging discursive style failed to lead to any definite policies. Instead, he seemed to provide qualifications, which allowed for different views and interpretations. He supported the market, and laissez-faire, but the support was highly qualified. As a counterpoint to Smith's approach, later economists felt compelled to construct more definitive formulations. David Ricardo proved more than willing to oblige. But, as Classical economists discovered, doing so came with attached problems. For example, as Alfred Marshall noted:

> Their [Ricardian economists'] agreement with one another made them confident, the want of a strong opposition made them dogmatic; the necessity of making themselves intelligible to the

multitude made them suppress even such conditioning and qualifying clauses as they had in their own minds. Therefore, although their doctrines contained a vast deal that was true, and new, and very important, yet the wording of these doctrines was often so narrow and inelastic that, when applied under conditions of time and place different from those in which they had their origin, their faults became obvious and provoked reaction. (Marshall 1923: 759–760)

In response, subsequent Classical Liberal economists vowed to do better. They developed a firewall separating policy from economic science to help them keep their vows. Since a key argument in our book is that Classical Liberal economists were correct in erecting and preserving a firewall, a natural question is: Why was that methodology abandoned by the profession? We argue that the abandonment was related to, but not synonymous with, the movement from classical to neoclassical economics. Neoclassical economics could be quite consistent with Classical Liberal methodology as long as the neoclassical economist treated the model as a suggestive tool, to be used as only one of many inputs into policy, and not as a direct guide.[21] Through the 1930s, and even into the 1950s and 1960s, vestiges of that Classical Liberal methodology survived despite the onslaught of a newer, more scientific approach. For example, Alfred Marshall, the leading neoclassical economist throughout the 1920s, remained committed to Classical Liberal methodology, although, to be honest, Marshall waivered depending on how the political winds were blowing, as did other supporters of that methodological persuasion. The temptation to claim science as being on your side is often almost overwhelming.[22]

Marshall conceived of economics as operating most successfully when it performed as an applied discipline, in the sense of a tool or way of thinking that allowed insight and understanding of common problems and situations. He termed this formulation the study of commonplace business of everyday life. The reason for studying the subject was not merely to gain an understanding of how the economy worked, but more importantly to provide the basis for sound policy measures. Similarly, John Maynard Keynes also maintained a Classical Liberal methodology, which separated him from those that came to be labeled as his neo-Keynesian followers. They readily abandoned Classical Liberal methodology and entered almost without exception into the scientific policy debate.[23]

As we discussed above, the Classical Liberal method had its origins in Adam Smith's studied and educated commonsense approach to problem-solving. His recognition of the need to yoke the moral to the economic originated in the linkage between his two great works, *The Theory of Moral Sentiments* and *The Wealth of Nations*. In his grand schema, economic analysis and policy provisions were necessarily interwoven with ethics and moral philosophy. He intertwined the two by employing the viewpoint of a hypothetical impartial spectator who was able to serve as the basis for evaluating proposed policies. Consequently, the goal posed by any discussions or written monograph was to convince such a spectator that the advocated policy offered a preferable, rather than an ideal, option.[24] From this perspective, no aspect of the argument was incontestable or off the table.

To move from the realm of theoretical argument to that of policy, one required this notion of a hypothesized impartial spectator. This imagined umpire would be capable, by means of appeal, of arbitrating and sorting out conflicts and differences attached to the relevant issues. Smith's argumentation was directed at those impartial spectators. The qualifications he placed on his laissez-faire policy precepts were ones that any group of reasonable people could be expected to place on such proposed policies.[25] Formal mathematical and theoretical arguments would not serve the purpose. They might inform the thinking of an advocate of a particular policy position, while still failing to be decisive. All reasonable qualifications about a given policy would be part of the debate. Equally, the question of what precisely was meant by designating a privileged "impartial spectator" to perform this essential role remained far from settled and should itself be subject to debate. Ultimately resolving such debates was distinctly not the job of the economist, but rather of the statesman or of the economist acting in the role of statesman, not scientific economist.

Whereas Smith concretely grounded his policy analysis in *The Theory of Moral Sentiments* as we stated above, Ricardo did not. Joseph Schumpeter would later characterize the resulting outcome as reflecting the "Ricardian Vice."[26] Smith's approach, clothed in much more sophisticated garb, would later be reinstated by John Stuart Mill, the philosopher/economist who best represents the Classical Liberal methodology we advocate. Mill curbed Ricardo's overly optimistic, and quite immodest, enthusiasm by insisting on the inherent limitations constraining theoretical and scientific policy conclusions. Policy was not an exact science but could be more productively thought of as an art that demanded judgment and skill. Theory did not imply specific policies but might prove useful in thinking about them. That would only hold true as long as one had a deep understanding of all the other necessary dimensions involved in arriving at policy conclusions.

Smith's impartial spectator device provides insight into understanding Classical Utilitarianism, an approach that defined the normative goal of economic policy as "the greatest good for the greatest number."[27] Classical utilitarianism was a normative touchstone that one could reasonably argue would be arrived at by employing the impartial spectator perspective.[28] Classical economists saw the utilitarian rules of thumb they developed as the appropriate ways to make needed interpersonal comparisons when engaged in policy analysis. Those rules of thumb did not follow from science (or theory), and an economist accordingly was well advised not to pretend that they did. They were just useful reference points in the inevitable debates arising during policy discussions.

This normative version of utilitarianism was in no sense science, nor was the "utility" it referred to a concept that could be encapsulated by empirical measurements of preferences. Utility was not a concept that could be made empirically observational, as some later neoclassical economists would attempt to accomplish.[29] As Vilfredo Pareto pointed out, what might be measured by scientific methods was something quite different than the normative concept of utility. What could be measured, and what might be shown by revealed preference, was a concept that captured people's choices, which Pareto called ophelimity to distinguish it from utility.[30]

The Classical Liberal Laissez-Faire Precept

If economic theory does not lead to policy results, how did Classical Liberal methodology come to achieve its close association with laissez-faire policy? The answer is that Classical Liberal's laissez-faire policy was based on a set of debatable judgments about the working of the political process, as well as a normative commitment to individual freedom.[31] Classical Liberals did not claim that these judgments were based on science or economic theory. Instead, they were based on observations of how governments and the market actually worked, including their sensibilities about the normative beliefs that were most important to them. Both judgments were recognized as debatable, and given to change.[32] Nonetheless, they were largely shared by Classical Liberals of varying normative and ideological persuasions. They were judgments that many Classical Liberals believed a relatively neutral person would likely arrive based on all the arguments, not just a subset of economic arguments.

These shared normative and institutional judgments were the reason Classical Liberals often came to similar policy conclusions. Many at that time shared the belief that policy of real-world governments would generally not achieve the ends that policy advocates claimed.[33] (It can be argued that governments then were even less transparent, and more controlled by vested interests, than they are now because democracy was only in its beginning stages.) This perspective strongly implies that their support of laissez-faire policy *was not based on economic theory*. It was based on shared judgments about the difficulties connected with how government policy worked, and should be presented as such. Jacob Viner, a neoclassical economist who firmly embraced a Classical Liberal methodology, points this out.[34] He writes:

> Adam Smith was not a doctrinaire advocate of laissez faire … He had little trust in the competence or good faith of government. He knew who controlled it, and whose purposes they tried to serve … He saw, nevertheless, that it was necessary, in the absence of a better instrument, to rely upon government for the performance of many tasks which individuals as such would not do, or could not do, or could only do badly. (Viner quoted in Overtveldt 2007: 90)

These critical judgments underlying policy were based on historical and empirical judgments upon which reasonable people might differ. The arguments for laissez-faire might refer to theorems developed in economic theory as a framework to capture insights that were not apparent at first sight, but laissez-faire was not based on such theorems. Viner serves as a striking representative of those neoclassical economists who strongly insisted on the need to maintain an imperturbable classical methodology. He writes:

> I do not think it is practical to write an elaborate work on the working of economic process in modern society on a completely "objective" basis … Anyone who could do so would be pathological and the pathology would be likely to extend to his selection of premises—it is always necessary to begin somewhere, but where one begins can have great influence on where one ends up—and on his decisions as to what are facts and what myths. In so far as is possible, value-judgments should be labelled as such, but their systematic exclusion is, I am convinced, not in practice either possible or desirable. They should not be concealed, they should not be eccentric, and they should not be elaborated or didactically pressed. (Viner quoted in Van Horn 2011: 291fn)

Viner followed the lead of Classical Liberal economists in believing that price-coordinated markets held both advantages and costs when observed in the actual world. Markets were necessarily embedded in institutional and social structures subject to unforeseen transformations. Both markets and the governments within which they must necessarily operate evolved over time and were consequently co-dependent rather than opposing forces. What Adam Smith and his subsequent followers understood specifically was that questioning whether governments should retain an active role within the operations of a market economy was not a theoretical issue. The effective contestable terrain, one that nourished fruitful debate, encouraged opposing sides to argue the nature, rather than the existence, of that role.

Accordingly, policy debate from a Classical Liberal viewpoint was not about the existence, but rather about the nature of a government's role. The adoption by the profession of the general equilibrium welfare policy model, as well as the neo-Keynesian macroeconomic model, violated this precept because these models were designed to directly lead to answers about the policy role of governments. Classical Liberal economists didn't believe any specific model could answer such questions. At best, a model might shed some useful light. True, when interpreted by more sophisticated economists, the limited relevance of formal models to policy would be admitted, but that was not the way such models were used in practice. In the immediate postwar texts, and in the relevant policy discussions, models directly supported government intervention into a market economy. However, the users of that general equilibrium policy model and the Keynesian model claimed to be ideologically neutral despite such unvarying conclusions.

Lost in the use of these models were the concerns voiced by Classical economists that the policy levers of government were controlled by vested interests, not by benevolent public engineers. Inevitably, these vested interests would use policy to advance their objectives in subtle and devious ways. It was primarily this concern about vested interests and the working of governments, not economic science or theory, that led Smith and later Classical Liberal economists to drift toward supporting a relatively laissez-faire policy. Therefore, their sensibility was that policies, when formulated and enacted, would be dominated by the powerful, which makes the fruit of such policies highly tainted. Those in power could not be trusted to design programs in the public interest unless they faced an effective countervailing power. Consequently, every policy proposal had to be met with unbridled skepticism. True, Chicago voiced a similar skepticism, but theirs appeared to be more an ideological conviction outfitted with the benefit of scientific justification. In contrast, the Classical Liberal position was grounded, not in science, but in judgment from experience. They found that generally, hidden in the footnotes and subclauses of any such policy act, lurked an intention at odds with its more publicized objectives. Given such inherent limitations, rather than engaging in active economic planning and restructuring, government policy should preferably focus on maintaining competition. Intervention by government remained an option of last resort. But long-term policy success depended on creating competitive institutions that managed to use selfishness to counterbalance selfishness.

Conclusion

In summary, the story we tell in this book about policy is one of how economists lost what might be called the "least worst" justification for markets and replaced it with competing scientific justifications. These substitutions alternatively supported either laissez-faire or government intervention. One side claimed that though markets were efficient, government intervention was needed to correct imperfections, thus enabling markets to work even better. The other side claimed that markets were efficient and that government intervention would only precipitate cascading problems. What both sides lost by shunning the Classical Liberal approach was the acknowledgment that scientific inputs into policy form only a limited part of any economic policy debate. A fruitful debate would necessarily address a wide array of issues that go far beyond traditional economic concerns.

2

A Classical Garden of Liberal Economics

POLICY VERSUS ABSTRACTION

A central hypothesis of this book is that modern economics abandoned its Classical Liberal roots. In this chapter we spell out and explore what we mean by that Classical Liberal methodology. For us, Classical Liberal methodology reflects an approach to economics as first developed by Smith (from earlier strands). This framework was later refined and advanced by John Stuart Mill.[1] A key element of the Classical Liberal tradition can be found in this quotation from Mill:

> No one who attempts to lay down propositions for the guidance of mankind however perfect his scientific acquirements, can dispense with a practical knowledge of the actual modes in which the affairs of the world are carried on, and extensive personal experience of the actual ideas, feelings, and intellectual and moral tendencies of his own country and his own age. (Mill quoted in Bronk 2009: 54)

The Limited Value of Abstract Theory

Abstract theory, which formed a central element of Classical economic science, will only provide limited policy guidance.[2] Economic policy requires an integral knowledge of the practical, including issues that go far beyond the confines of economic science. Given these constraints, economic scientists should refrain from using scientific rhetoric to link policy conclusions with constructed theory unless their expertise extends far beyond that bounded space.

Classical Liberal methodology was deeply embedded within the Classical tradition. As Myrdal remarks:

> John Stuart Mill wanted to restrict the scope of economic science to the study of the factual and the probable. Senior had forcibly argued for the same view in his inaugural lecture when he succeeded to the newly created Oxford professorship in economics, and he never tired of reiterating the same thesis in his later writings. He expressly stated that the economist's "conclusions, whatever be their generality and their truth, do not authorize him in adding a single syllable of advice." (Myrdal 1954: 3)

Classical Liberal methodology was not fixed; it evolved over time. A consistent strain of this approach was grafted onto the subsequent development of economics in the decades following Mill's approach, and aspects of this methodology continued to be maintained by many economists throughout the 1940s and into the 1950s. Thus, a branch of what is often denominated as neoclassical economics (taking its guidance from Alfred Marshall) can fall comfortably within our Classical Liberal classification. Individual economists of this era, operating in much the same fashion as would befit a disciplined cohort of myrmidons, fought to retain these principles.[3] They methodically engaged in a process of professionalization along these lines, a strategy they viewed as being intrinsic to any future success of the discipline. Leaders of this movement, who attempted to transform economics into an exclusively academic-based discipline, included such notable figures as Marshall and

Sidgwick. Both insisted on preserving the Classical Liberal tradition (at least in a configuration consistent with their aims) while initiating a transformation of these techniques. They succeeded in guiding a portion of the thinking that framed political economy through much of the first half of the twentieth century. These relevant departures from the previous accepted tradition are now recognized as the beginnings of what would later blossom into neoclassical economics.[4]

The point brought into a state of almost bas relief here is that the Classical Liberal approach was, and remained, sufficiently flexible to accommodate the evolution and formalization of economic theory. Its very ambiguity and lack of multiple dictated norms allowed a wide range of views and techniques to prosper within its sheltering shade.[5] Consequently, the responsibility for any general dismissal of this perspective lies not with any intrinsic methodological inconsistencies, but with the movement to formalize or mathematicize economics. Thus, the onus lies in the way in which the resulting formalized version of economics was used to evaluate and shape policy. In the Classical Liberal method, formal theory was something to be conscious of, to be kept in the back of one's mind as difficult policy issues were confronted. But it was secondary to educated common sense, and the method required one to be clear about the judgments one was making in applying a particular model, and in deciding which assumptions were reasonable and which were not. Applied policy economics had to explicitly deal with all such issues, which meant that no firm policy conclusion followed from scientific theory. In policy, science played only a supporting role. However, in what would increasingly become associated with the neoclassical method, that would change and scientific theory would occupy center stage within the realm of policy thinking.

Classical Liberalism's Moral Philosophical Foundations

Classical Liberalism composed a philosophy transcending the relatively narrow boundaries defined by economics. Economics provided only a limited portion of a broader exploration occurring within the borders characterizing social science. Consequently, economic science, if strictly defined, represented an even smaller subset of a broader social science. The core material of economic science was necessarily restricted to limited investigations that pertained only to those questions that related directly to material welfare. Since policy considerations went beyond these relatively narrow constraints, scientific economic analysis composed only a small part of policy formation. The implication flowing from this necessity required that any applied methodology had to be broadly inclusive of factors extending beyond the narrow grasp of economics as a scientific pursuit. Formulating policies that could yield potentially productive results involved developing principles grounded in a blend of moral philosophy and cultural sensibilities that could be combined with practical and institutional knowledge.

Within the Classical Liberal cosmology, certain key objectives and principles defined this approach. Individual freedom, bolstered by the constraining pull of rights and responsibility, formed the unarguable core of a constructed moral and philosophical perspective. Judgments went beyond simple fact or the limits imposed by what could be scientifically proven. In this Classical methodology, only decisions that were sufficiently consensual could form a workable policy basis. However, the very method by which these agreements were reached rendered such judgments time- and place-specific. A successful policy was almost inevitably incapable of being effectively generalized, or of being extended indefinitely.

Because the field seemed defined by these impenetrable barriers, successful professionalization was viewed as requiring separate and different divisions of the subject. For these Classical Liberal economists, the actual science of economics extended no further than the limits defined by a number of developed theories, along with associated empirical findings. This realm could be carefully differentiated from a more normative division of economics grounded in moral philosophy and statesmanship. Last, an art of economics involved the deft use of judgment, allowing for contextually specific policy recommendations. These applied outcomes reflected viable results from the other two branches without involving any immediate or explicit connections. This tri-partite perspective quite naturally existed only as a target for aspiring economists of the nineteenth century. In actual practice, the tendency to stray from any strict adherence could be realistically expected, but the acknowledged goal involved straying as little as possible from this designated path.[6]

Since policy was so interconnected with differing aspects of life, positions could not be legitimately justified by any conclusions drawn directly from the science of economics. For example, systematic support for an entrenched laissez-faire policy, and any other mounted defense of markets, could not be based on theoretical tenets that dissected market mechanics. Rather, their legitimacy was grounded in philosophical and historical principles. These tenets were in turn laced with judgments dependent upon the observed nuts and bolts of practical experience. Markets were neither a divine dispensation nor were they deemed inherently infallible. Accordingly, displaying a preference for markets could not depend upon, or be argued from, theoretical conclusions.[7]

Laissez-Faire as a Precept

In Classical terminology, laissez-faire was a precept—a judgment about policy based on issues that went far beyond economics and thus was not capable of being determined by economic scientists. Precepts, by definition, were inherently debatable. In fact, intellectual honesty compelled such issues to be debated regularly in a manner that helped those involved reach some level of understanding and agreement. Insight, rather than the directed demolition of opposing standpoints, reflected the compelling objective defining Classical economists. Limited precepts rested on the observed operative case, grounded upon the best available evidence. This understanding was dependent on the closest estimate of what an impartial spectator would be most likely to conclude. Thus, the Classical Liberal justification for relying on market mechanisms is very close to the way that commentators have historically justified the institution of democracy. Markets cannot be expected to achieve anything resembling optimal results. They are simply preferable given the even less salubrious available alternatives.[8]

> Cannan attributed his support for the market mechanism to skepticism about the available alternatives rather than any ardent enthusiasm for its workings. "Modern civilization, nearly all civilization, is based on the principle of making things pleasant for those who please the market and unpleasant for those who fail to do so," he observed in *An Economist's Protest*, "and whatever defects this principle may have, it is better than none." (Burgin 2012: 18)

Classical Liberal thought escaped the accrued perils of either deifying or fetishizing markets. Similarly, within this framework, laissez-faire derived its justification in much the same fashion. Support for laissez-faire was not a theoretically derived policy resulting in anything resembling an optimal outcome. Instead, it reflected a viewpoint that took into account the limitations and inherent difficulties of satisfactorily accomplishing certain objectives through the intermediation of the state. Judgments levied were necessarily specific to the era in which they were made. Based on prior experience, there loomed the distinct possibility, as conceived by these formulators of practical policy, that state action, whatever its professed intentions, would deviate considerably from its proposed beneficial objectives. This empirically grounded version of policy formation, as perceived by these economists, accorded all too closely with the past historical record.[9] The conclusions to be drawn from that record encouraged extreme caution when confronted by any form of government intervention. However, the perceived need to exercise such caution did not automatically mutate into a discernible imperative to provide markets with a dangerous sheen of infallibility. Mill makes this point clearly:

> There is, in fact, no recognized principle by which the propriety of government interference is customarily tested. People decide

according to their personal preferences. Some, whenever they see any good to be done, or evil to be remedied, would willingly, instigate the government to undertake the business; while others prefer to bear almost any amount of social evil, rather than add one to the departments of human interests amenable to governmental control. (Mill 1947 [1859]: 9)

As previously indicated, Classical Liberals dealt with the ambiguous nature of prescriptive economics by strictly separating a branch of economics that might fit the classification of a science from the remainder of their research and investigation. That branch focused on developing a deductive model of the economy based on assumptions of rationality and self-interest. It was a model that could not be proven, nor was it a model that they believed fit reality, which was far more complicated. But since it was based on logic, it was a model that could be debated in terms of its logic, hence separating it from discussions that were more value-driven. That strategy worked only as long as the scientific model was not applied directly to reality. Doing so allowed someone who opposed any model-drawn policy conclusion to say—your logic is correct, but your assumptions are wrong, or your empirical evidence is faulty. By focusing on assumptions limiting the scientific model's applicability to policy, economists with different values were conceded the right to debate economic policy issues in relation to these models. They were excused from embedding their debates about the models within broader debates concerning values.[10]

Policy analysis was to be done in the branch of economics that Mill referred to as the "art of economics."[11] The attempt to bifurcate policy in this manner was intended to insulate the science of economics (and its search for the truth) as much as was humanly possible, from the inevitable intrusion of values when theory confronted reality. Even though they recognized that it was impossible to perfectly separate individual values from scientific analysis, they believed that, with some focused finesse, the problem could be significantly reduced. Employed as a working methodological heuristic, this pragmatic approach might be able to better move the debate forward. Classical Liberal methodology was accordingly designed to encourage and maintain that separation.

In developing a separate policy branch that went far beyond the boundaries limiting economic science, these early Classical economists recognized the irrefutable fact that relevant events unfolded within an historical context. Economic principles required careful judgment, demanding insight honed through experience, if it was to be applied with any degree of success. Policy was necessarily historically and geographically based. Thus, it exuded an intrinsic unpredictability. "The usefulness of history is not in giving us rules which can be made the basis of inference and prediction, it is not in this respect a science but rather an art" (Knight quoted in Stapleford 2011: 26). The science of economics was infused with logic. It involved a search for truth and, given the undeveloped state of empirical and statistical techniques of the time, was essentially a matter of logical deduction. "Economic laws, like other scientific laws, state a tendency, a result which would follow if certain conditions are present" (Knight quoted in Medema 2011: 154). Essentially, theory failed to provide a path to any specific policy position whatsoever. As Myrdal noted in our earlier discussion, Nassau Senior, one of the earliest Classical Liberal economists to specifically consider methodology, emphatically made this point. He wrote:

> (An economist's) conclusions, whatever be their generality and their truth, do not authorize him in adding a single syllable of advice. That privilege belongs to the writer or statesman who has considered all the causes which may promote or impede the general welfare of those whom he addresses, not to the theorist who has considered only one, though among the most important of those causes. The business of a Political Economist is neither to recommend nor to dissuade, but to state general principles, which it is fatal to neglect, but neither advisable, nor perhaps practicable, to use as the sole, or even the principle, guides in the actual conduct of affairs. (Senior [1836] 1951: 2–3)

For Senior, as well as for most early Classical economists concerned with methodology, the economic science of the time evolved as a branch of deductive logic.[12] The pure science of economics, at least during that period, involved the development of theorems from almost self-evident first principles. But, as Senior makes clear, economic theory was not meant to provide a *direct* link to policy prescriptions.[13] To move with any discernible justification from the theorems developed by the scientific branch of economics to the principles useful for the policy-relevant branch, Classical economists generally subscribed to the belief that in this regard, one essentially had to rely on the limits imposed by the type of judgment provided by an educated common sense, at least insofar as it was honed by logical application.[14] Since institutional knowledge was required to apply theory to the real world, and since institutions changed over time and place, it was impossible to devise time- and place-specific recommendations. Policy recommendations had to be contextual. Discussing a given policy in an applicable manner involved different, and not necessarily transferable, skills than those required when constructing economic theories.

The Classical Liberal Argument against Paternalism

Another aspect defining Classical Liberalism was its assumption that an individual was intrinsically more qualified to recognize what lay in his or her best interest than some outside, vested authority.[15] The foundation for this assumption was introspection. Thus, the approach was based on normative judgments evaluating those who could make decisions about what was good for someone else. It was not seen as some scientifically proven fact, but rather existed as a judgment that could, and should, be debated. But, to move forward to policy formulation, some individually specific decision based on self-knowledge had to be made. In Classical Liberal thought, self-interest was not viewed as reflective of revealed preferences. The concept of self-interest to be employed in formulating policy was conjectural. It was what someone who had specialized in moral philosophy would arrive at, if placed in that person's shoes. Thus, it could differ from what people wanted for themselves. But since the impartial spectator mechanism was highly imperfect, whenever this conception of self-interest differed from that defining a given individual, policy makers needed to exercise caution.

Thus, Classical Liberal economists hesitated before accepting any strong form of paternalism, the lingering belief that an outside power could somehow surmise what was best for others.[16] They held that, generally, actual policies based on such paternalistic views were almost inevitably hiding, perhaps unknowingly, ulterior, and often far from beneficent, motives. Adam Smith refused to mince his words or qualify his objections in this regard. Responding to arguments from businessmen that markets necessarily require regulation, Smith did not say that they were categorically wrong and such actions should never be implemented. Instead, he argued that such proposals "ought never to be adopted, till after having been long and carefully examined, not only with the most scrupulous, but with the most suspicious attention" (Smith 1937: 250). The problem attached to such proposals is that they "come ... from an order of men, whose interest is never exactly the same with that of the public, who generally have an interest to deceive and even oppress the public, and who accordingly have, upon many occasions, both deceived and oppressed it" (ibid.). Whether markets were efficient or optimal in any precise sense that could be sufficiently captured by empirical or theoretical models held only a minimal degree of importance when evaluating the proposed justifications for markets and market solutions. Such considerations generally failed to greatly sway the direction of policy proposals provided by Classical Liberal economists.

As noted, the working assumption that designated individuals as the best judges of their own welfare and advantage remained inherently a subject of debate. Such claims could not by their very nature be ultimately resolved. Perhaps unfortunately, assumptions of that ilk necessarily formed an intrinsic component of policy formulation. Any resolution of this perplexing impasse could never claim to be optimal or scientifically grounded. The best one could hope for was a practical, pragmatic solution. Ultimately, the approach disavowed any definitive or scientific certainty when it came to policy. This allowed several generations of economists the chance of not supporting broadly generalizable policies, which might be viewed as flowing directly from the tenets of economic theory.[17]

> The theorist not having definite assumptions clearly in mind in working out the "principles," it is but natural that he, and still more the practical workers building upon his foundations should forget that unreal assumptions were made, and should not take the principles over bodily, apply them to concrete cases, and draw sweeping and wholly unwarranted conclusions from them. (Knight 1971: 11)[18]

Clearly these Classical Liberals did not subscribe to any unqualified and unwavering set of beliefs. Instead, they simply insisted that whatever people favored was that which they felt left them better off. However, vices by definition could not lead in that direction. Consequently, Classical economists were quite willing to classify some levels of activities as being better than others.[19] A good life involved much more than just consuming as much as possible. Classical Liberals saw their policy role not as insisting on, or even compelling, people to follow prescribed behavior, but rather convincing people by means of incisive argumentation to choose certain goals.[20]

Thus, Classical Liberals would clearly recognize the need for arriving at a composite social welfare function. However, they would insist that the one proposed should not subsequently be imposed by any group on any others. Such a clear violation of individual liberty would be apparent and unacceptable. Arguing for an optimal, one-size-fits-all, outcome would be in direct contradiction to their fundamental faith in supporting individual choice whenever possible. From a Classical Liberal perspective, a formal social welfare function could never become operational. This particular formalization clearly *was not* an acceptable way to add values to economists' policy analysis. The best that economists could hope for was to develop a more informal set of judgments relating to an impartial spectator's view of social welfare. Such a result would be arrived at through discursive argumentation for the sake of heaven. Agreements arrived at through philosophical, rather than scientific, debate should form an essential component of economic policy analysis. That philosophical debate would require going beyond selfish interest. Instead, participants would consider issues from as impartial a perspective as possible.

It is similarly the case with policy. Setting up impartial rules of the game required impartial political groups. When following self-interest, groups would almost always attempt to structure policy in a fashion that was self-beneficial. They would justify it as being impartial even while levying a distinct cost on others.[21] That could be expected from all concerned. Consequently, one needed some way of insuring that decision makers would be following social goals that an impartial spectator might support. Alternatively, one needed rules that provided checks and balances in political fights that corresponded to the checks and balances competition provided in economic fights. The goal was to create constitutional rules governing policy that pitted one selfish interest against another. Doing so would drive people to compromise on a policy that reflected what an impartial spectator might support. Where such rules could not be established, then the reasonable option was to create rules that limited government policy intervention.[22] It was such judgments that led Classical Liberals to support a laissez-faire approach as their default policy. The case for intervention had to be strongly argued and the probabilities of a desirable outcome sufficiently proven. The difficulty attendant in determining policy goals, and the intricacies involved in their application, caused these Classical Liberals to adopt a correspondingly more circumspect position.[23]

The Rationality Assumption

Instead of comprehending rationality as leading to a position that provided unequivocal support for market mechanisms, and a corresponding opposition to government intervention, Classical Liberals considered the rationality assumption to be useful as a logical tautology that helped to structure their thinking. Whatever people did could be classified as logical, as long as the model allowed a sufficiently wide range of preferences.[24] Where actions might not fit narrow interpretations of self-interest, these were replaced with a broader interpretation that encompassed the achievement of social goals. Psychic income, under this consideration, was not only allowed to drive actions, but was expected to do so. Consequently, motivation was not restricted to monetary income alone. Empirical monetary measures would not be an acceptable measure of welfare or of rationality except for a small subset of issues. Maximizing individual monetary income or societal GDP was not synonymous with acceptable policy goals. Any action could be interpreted as fitting this broad-based rationality assumption. This wider interpretation transformed the rational homo-economicus model from a scientific construct that could be empirically tested with market data to an all-encompassing analytical framework. It definitely no longer was a model that could be used as the main gear in a machine for grinding out policies.

As Classical economics evolved into Neoclassical economics, the mantle adorning John Stuart Mill, who in many ways defined the tradition, was passed on to Alfred Marshall, the dominating figure in the world of British economics from the 1890s to the 1920s.[25] In his primer on the subject, Marshall (1890) attempted to blend a Classical Liberal methodology with what could be considered to be more progressive, scientific developments in the realm of theory. In doing so, he remained ultra-cautious about making any strong claims or drawing any conclusions concerning the implications of theory for policy from these newly developing analytic techniques. These breakthroughs were providing insights into complicated problems of constrained optimization. Most early Neoclassical economists in the United States, including many Chicago economists of that time, identified with Marshall and followed his more tentative approach.[26] This Marshallian method viewed economic theory as simply one among a number of tools to assist thinking. It remained a tool that was incapable of delivering much in the way that conveyed direct policy relevance. Decisions of such complexity inevitably involved issues that transcended economics.[27] For his part, Marshall did offer a subtle mixture that blended Classical methodology with newly developed Neoclassical tools, theories, and techniques. As we will see in later chapters, the Marshallian Classical Liberal approach would eventually be abandoned. By the late 1940s, it would be dismissed as outdated by the then cutting-edge economists.

Marshall died in 1924. His disciples and successors, while still following his general methodological approach, were clearly less committed to it. For example, Arthur C. Pigou, who assumed Marshall's Chair at Cambridge, developed a more technical analysis that integrated general equilibrium issues into an analytic framework. Pigou started drawing broad general policy implications (such as concluding that decreasing cost industries should be subsidized) from his technical analysis. In his *Economics of Welfare*, Pigou (1920) presented his analysis while drawing out its policy implications. However, a careful reading of this work reveals that he specifically pointed out the enormous qualifications upon which his arguments were based.[28] He emphasized that his efforts were realistic or fruit-bearing science, not the pure or light-bearing variety. This caused him to add significant qualifications to his welfare policy principles. But these qualifications tended to be forgotten. Soon, many economists began treating welfare economics as a formal guide for policy. As the 1940s ended, a new modern era in policy analysis had arrived, as reflected in this comment by George Stigler.

> It should be a cause for self-congratulation, no doubt, that we modern economists find so little to learn from the classical economics. In our apprenticeship we are still sent back to read Smith, with pleasure, and Ricardo, with torment, and Mill, with less predictable feelings. But the classical economics seems now to have become some sort of substitute for the classical languages. We may or may not acquire erudition, but usually we acquire the conviction that we can learn little about our working technique from the classical economists. (Stigler 1949c: 25)[29]

As a guide for policy, Pigou's welfare economics suggested a much larger role for government than would have made most of the earlier Classical Liberal economists comfortable. That larger role was not necessarily inconsistent with Classical Liberal precepts, which accepted that the role played by government within the marketplace did not follow directly from theory but was derived from broader social judgments. These could change over time, and they did change in the 1930s. Faith in markets waned as the Great Depression took hold. Faith in government waxed as government structures were improved upon, becoming more closely aligned with democratic ideals. Governments appeared to be doing more good, or at least trying to do more good, than had previously been conceded. Moreover, some of the more egregious uses of government power by vested interests seemed likely to decrease or be effectively contained. Governments appeared to be listening to economists, which economists naturally interpreted as a positive sign. Consequently, the sensibility of economists with regard to government gradually shifted in tandem with changes appearing in the general sensibility of society itself.

This change placed the Classical Liberal laissez-faire precept out of sync with the prevailing environment. Ideally, Classical Liberalism should have been able to adjust its prevailing precepts since its methodological approach imposed no theoretical straightjacket in terms of permissible policy positions. Laissez-faire was only an accepted precept upon which reasonable people could disagree. It was not a scientific theorem. This sense that Classical Liberalism was not bonded to laissez-faire policies goes back at least to the time of Adam Smith. As Steven Medema (2009) and others have pointed out, Classical economists were not inherently anti-government in their policy positions. The later visceral reaction to Smith by ideologically motivated market advocates such as Murray Rothbard underlines this point. Within this narrow framework, Rothbard felt justified in labeling Adam Smith as some sort of proto-socialist. Though noticeably skeptical about the effectiveness of market meddling and what officials could hope to accomplish, Smith recognized that situations and instances must be evaluated for what they are. Transforming perceived circumstances into desired prescriptions by the employment of strictly ideological lenses would not prove productive.[30] Therefore, when perceptions of government changed in the 1930s and 1940s, one would expect Classical policy precepts to change as well. These perceived alterations would reflect shifting sensibilities, rather than scientific truths. However, as we will see, during the 1930s and 1940s, Classical Liberal methodology was increasingly abandoned. Instead, policy became connected to science, transforming policy debates into scientific controversies.

3

Planting the Seeds of a Chicago Tradition

Beginning sometime in the 1930s, the economics profession essentially abandoned the Classical Liberal methodology that we explored in the last chapter. In this and the next four chapters we consider that abandonment by using the University of Chicago as a case study. In this chapter we return to the beginning of economics at the University of Chicago in order to explore the development of a Chicago tradition. Then in the next chapters we consider how that original Chicago tradition evolved into the postwar Chicago School of economics.

The Germination of the Chicago Tradition

The Chicago tradition begins with James Laughlin, the first chair and founder of the department in 1892.[1] He put his stamp on Chicago economics in ways that would serve to nurture future generations but would also prove to be regrettable.[2] Laughlin, during his sometimes controversial career, placed himself well within the boundaries defining Classical Liberalism. Individuals such as Laughlin seem to harbor a proclivity to be contrarian, almost by reflexive reaction to their environment. They are instinctively suspicious when confronted with any received, or unquestioned, wisdom. The consciousness of such individuals lies in an almost automatic refusal to accept any claim at face value.[3]

Laughlin demonstrated this trait to an almost startling degree. He seemed to seek out controversy, hoping to somehow unearth opposition even when and where none seemingly existed. Laughlin was one of those often irritating but also useful people who enjoyed stirring up the status quo, thriving on the reactions and the controversy he managed to provoke.[4] But he was nevertheless consistently committed to an unstinting openness of inquiry, no matter through what uncharted paths such efforts might lead. Thus, when filling positions in Chicago's newly created department, Laughlin sought out those he viewed as possessing the potential to evolve into the select shining lights that would adorn the profession. Talent tended to trump ideology or even perspective. Holding religiously to this principle led him to largely ignore the distinct contours, economic viewpoints, or discernible ideological leanings of those he hired. Many who found shelter, if only temporarily, at Chicago could easily be classified as outside the prevailing mainstream of the profession, the rebels who were often eyed with gimlet-like suspicion by the East Coast bastions of authoritative wisdom.[5] Accordingly, Chicago's reputation for honoring maverick opinions and heterodox viewpoints seemed to be imprinted on the department at birth.

Laughlin helped create the persistent, but at times quite misleading, appearance that identified the Chicago department as a virulent breeding ground of ultra-conservative thought, tarred by a predilection for ideologically tinged policy prescriptions.[6] Laughlin, an inveterate stirrer, also embodied the second element that would become implanted within a developing Chicago tradition. This tendency might best be labeled the *dog and fire hydrant* approach to scholarship. The Chicago contingent, no matter what their underlying viewpoint or treasured beliefs, demonstrated an almost irresistible urge to treat all existing institutional structures and tenets as nothing more than targeted rows of convenient fire hydrants. Consequently, they accorded these supposedly unassailable foundations the corresponding and requisite degree of respect they were perceived to have earned. This meant that within their academic sphere of action, nothing was truly sacred, nor would any theory, principle, or assumption be accorded an undeserved degree of irreproachable reverence. Debates and discussions were laced with an almost unwarranted level of ferocity where the objective would appear to be the total demolition of any and all entrenched positions and opposing viewpoints. With academics descending into tactics more characteristic of combat sports than sedate seminars, little was done to actively encourage rays of reasoned insight or prudent harmony to enlighten the proceedings.

As the guiding spirit of this hatchling department during its formative years, Laughlin seemed to live for and breathe controversy with an ease natural to his disposition. His tenure at Chicago displayed a consistency of temperament. Almost instinctually, he skillfully managed to alienate much of the professional establishment by publicly scorning the recently initiated American Economic Association, while having the concomitant gall to set up his own upstart house organ, the *Journal of Political Economy* (1892). He did so in deliberate defiance of, and in competition with, the legitimately acknowledged American voice of economics, the *Quarterly Journal of Economics* (1886). This oldest of economic journals was produced by the members of the undisputed American giant of the profession, Harvard, a university manned by its orthodox choir of irreproachable gentlemen scholars. Thus, the seeds of the contest between the Eastern Establishment and the upstarts manning this Provincial Outpost were planted and nurtured from the very first years, defining the new Chicago department.[7]

Laughlin sought to gain instant notoriety, as well as widespread recognition, for his fledging department. Part of that strategy, as pointed out previously, entailed the deliberate positioning of Chicago as an academic sanctuary for the inveterate mavericks of the profession. In accord with his own Liberal values, he ensured that this new department would be open to the profession's outsiders, especially those with somewhat unacceptable leanings. Rather than paying a requisite obeisance to orthodoxy, insight and merit ruled when making appointments. Where other institutions might be reluctant to give such scholars their necessary recognition, Laughlin valued originality and innovative thinkers. Thorsten Veblen, among the department's early members, was a classic example, encapsulating in a multidimensional way what it meant to be on the outside looking in. Laughlin is described as having "a genuine interest in his students, passion for scholarship, a gift for recognizing distinction even in persons with whose views he disagreed and a wide cultural knowledge extending far beyond the frontiers of his subject" (Nef 1967: 780).

Because of his contrarian nature, Laughlin constructed his new Chicago department to be a school of outsiders with an ingrained critical stance toward orthodoxy. Over the years, that sense of Chicago as a brotherhood of outsiders[8] would develop and evolve, but it would remain as a defining feature.[9] Chicago became a department in which such luminaries as Wesley Mitchell and Thorsten Veblen could equally thrive during their Midwest sojourns.[10] Once Laughlin left, the same perspective continued to survive, having been thoroughly entrenched during those initial decades. This unique enclave would later embrace a Polish socialist, Oscar Lange, as well as a cantankerous and garrulous backwoods Tennessee boy like Frank Knight.[11] "[Laughlin] assembled around him many of the best economists of his day regardless of their political or theoretical leanings" (Emmett quoted in Overtveldt 2007: 25). Laughlin's openness to uncongenial ideas was accompanied by a notably cantankerous aspect to his own character (as is often the case) which spilled over into his professional behavior. He found it difficult to avoid the dubious pleasure of quarreling with, and defeating in armed rhetorical combat, his erstwhile peers in the economics discipline. While remaining open to other viewpoints in his appointments, a finely honed competitive spirit led him to battle to win debates in a pointedly opportunistic fashion, whether justified or not.

Laughlin's approach to argumentation differed substantially from Mill's "argument for the sake of heaven" approach. In Mill's approach, argumentation was meant to further understanding. If opponents couldn't clearly state their thinking logically, one was obliged to assist them in clarifying their thoughts by making the associated argument as strong as possible. The ultimate goal of argumentation from this standpoint was collaborative, rather than competitive. The objective was to facilitate the emergence of the best idea, which may or may not have been the idea one supported when initially entering into the argument. Argumentation was a means that could be employed to find a reasonable approximation of truth, not a means of marketing a known and incontrovertible truth to a resistant opposition.

> In the case of any person whose judgment is really deserving of confidence, how has it become so? Because he has kept his mind open to criticism of his opinions and conduct. Because it has been his practice to listen to all that could be said against him, to profit by as much of it as was just, and expound to himself, and upon occasion to others, the fallacy of what was fallacious. Because he has felt, that the only way in which a human being can make some approach to knowing the whole of a subject, is by hearing what can be said about it by persons of every variety of opinion, and studying all modes in which it can be looked at by every character of mind. No wise man ever acquired his wisdom in any mode but this; nor is it in the nature of human intellect to become wise in any other manner. The steady habit of correcting and completing his own opinion by collating it with those of others, so far from causing doubt and hesitation in carrying it into practice, is the only stable foundation for a just reliance on it: for, being cognizant of all that can, at least obviously be said against him, and having taken up his position against all gainsayers— knowing that he has sought for objections and difficulties, instead of avoiding them, and has shut out no light which can be thrown upon the subject from any quarter—he has a right to think his judgment better than that of any person, or any multitude, who have not gone through a similar process. (Mill 1947: 20)[12]

Laughlin's approach to argumentation was never intended to be collaborative. Confrontational and stubbornly marked out positions informed his implicit strategy of turning academic differences into something best settled in a bear pit. The negative sum thinking of the courtroom seemed to dominate over the more positive sum type of exchange encouraged by Mill. What mattered was one's success in entirely demolishing and embarrassing a targeted opponent. As described by one of his younger colleagues (Harold G. Moulton):

> [Laughlin's] real shortcoming both as a writer and a teacher lay in the fact that he employed debating tactics which were unfair to those whose theories he was attacking. He never stated the other fellow's case in a genuinely sympathetic way ... He usually stated it at its worst and then attacked the logic. (Bornemann 1940: 19)[13]

This confrontational approach to argumentation would be adopted by subsequent Chicago School economists. Much more than mere rhetorical posing, these strategic tactics would play their part in undermining any remnants of the once dominant Classical Liberal methodology at this Midwestern outpost. Specifically, the elements that would coalesce during the postwar period to become the Chicago School[14] reflected this stormy bit of history. These links with the past implied a decided tendency to replace an openness to different ideas and heuristics with a style of lawyer-like rhetoric designed to win arguments. Chicago advanced this approach even at the cost of overwhelming any attempt to advance knowledge, whether accomplished systematically or not.

Chicago between the Wars

The University of Chicago economics department, like Gaul, was divided into parts. Knight and Viner were the theorist patriarchs and rivals. Paul Douglas was the more-than-token liberal. Henry Schultz represented the wave of the future in econometrics and mathematical economics. Henry Simons, critic of the regulated state and advocate of redistributive income taxation, was in Knight's camp. Although Aaron Director began in the

Douglas workshop, his heart was with Knight. Indeed Frank Knight was the irresistible Pied Piper. For five years—from the time I [Paul Samuelson] was sixteen until I was twenty-one—I was bewitched by Knight. The cream of the graduate school—a Stigler, Friedman, Wallis, Homer Jones, or Hart—downplayed the Vinerian sagacity and erudition. Schultz, an earnest pioneer who lacked in self-confidence and brilliance, was in the rear, patronized by the arrogant youth of the day; that did not add to his serenity or sureness of judgment. (Samuelson 2011: 590)

Key intellectual leaders at Chicago during the interwar period included, but were not limited to, Frank Knight and Jacob Viner. Both navigated comfortably beneath a broad Classical Liberal tent without staking out the same, identical neighborhood. Knight maintained a verbal philosophical approach that eschewed the theories widely propagated in the 1930s. In fact, he refused to place any substantial value on empirical work.[15] Viner willingly embraced certain aspects of the theoretical breakthroughs of that period (though certainly not the work of Keynes and those allied with him). Although an early user of statistical and empirical work, he remained skeptical regarding its reach.[16] Viner never claimed that his theoretical work acted as a direct bridge to policy conclusions. Neither one of these two economists could fruitfully be classified as a simple conservative or ideologue.

In contrast to the postwar Chicago School, it would require a stretch of the imagination to assert that in the 1930s the Chicago department marched in lockstep or anything resembling unison, whether concerning matters of theory or of policy. But, as a vestige of its previous hold on thinking, in interwar Chicago, Classical Liberalism remained a methodological approach devoid of any litmus test as far as politics or policy extended.[17] Interwar Chicago was by design eclectic, allowing its members to find their own paths. If anything, the department's vitality and diversity in the 1930s were eagerly fed by streams of refugee academics escaping Hitler's encroaching Reich and Jews otherwise hemmed in by the more pronounced anti-Semitism at eastern redoubts such as Harvard, Yale, or Princeton.[18]

I think the way he [George Stigler] worked was more similar to Jacob Viner than to Frank Knight. The sort of economics he did was more like Viner's custom theories and so on, which were empirically based. Knight would not look at any data. In fact, Frank could hardly be convinced by any data. Like inequality. Knight always thought inequality was growing in the United States while all the evidence up until 1970 said it was falling. And Stigler and Friedman and others would point this out to Knight, and George told me this, Knight would say "yes, yes" but next time he'd say the same thing. So, I guess, he differed with Knight in this regard but that was not unusual. He began to differ with Knight in a lot of respects. I'm saying he becomes more like Viner. Look at Viner, early on in Viner's own dissertation on international trade, he is already testing the Canadian and American data. George became a big, empirical testing guy. As with Friedman, Viner was the greater influence. Not Knight. (Conversation with Gary Becker, October 1997)

The initial abandonment of Classical Liberal methodology occurred primarily outside Chicago, starting in the 1930s.[19] Graduate students and other young economists, perhaps emboldened by the unsettled times, embraced the cause of science-based theory and policy as providing the only reliable basis for either one.[20] At that time of revolutionary thought, only Chicago and the London School of Economics (where Hayek and Robbins still ruled) provided any semblance of a sustained resistance to that abandonment in the postwar era.[21] But the change did not occur quickly. Rather, it occurred only as economists trained in a Classical Liberal methodology were replaced by younger, "scientifically trained" economists. Not until there was an effective replacement of the old guard in Chicago could there be a substantial shift in the approach practiced throughout the department.[22]

The more discernible change occurred during the 1950s and '60s. By the 1960s, at least at a superficial level, it was believed that little remained to be gathered from the thoughts of those who had founded the discipline of economics. Thus, to these modern economists (circa 1949), knowledge of their thoughts and their approach could yield nothing of value other than a tiresome display of erudition. The past, in this understanding, offered little that could assist the young cohort of newly coined economists seeking to change the world. Stigler (1949a), in his own inimitable fashion, manages to pinpoint, at least indirectly, the way in which the profession had clearly shifted away from the tenets of their economic ancestors. In doing so, they fancied that they were productively eliminating the welter of bare assertions that had heretofore plagued the profession. These pronouncements, no matter how vigorously articulated, had lacked any sturdy theoretical base or empirical foundation. The World War, washing away the false accretions of the past, had seemingly ushered in a brave new world in which economists would finally be capable of fashioning economics, and the policy dependent on its findings, into a true science.

It was within this setting that the Chicago School of Economics emerged. Led initially by Milton Friedman and later joined by his close friend George Stigler, this noticeably younger cohort rapidly endorsed the movement that sought to place economics, including derived policy, on a scientific footing. For economics at this particular historical juncture, the choice presented was one of whether or not to wholeheartedly embrace the future.

Chicago Rising: A School Is Formed

> I sometimes think some of the Chicago people are hopeless. Well, I wouldn't include Milton as among the hopeless because he was smart enough to punch his way out of a paper bag sometimes. But in the end he didn't want to do so. (Conversation with Paul Samuelson, October 1997)

Chicago's eclecticism, and certainly its openness during the interwar period, would change after the war.[23] All three key architects of the postwar Chicago School (Milton Friedman, George Stigler, and Aaron Director),[24] were students at Chicago during these formative interwar years. As a result of their graduate experience, they were influenced to a nearly terminal degree by such figures as

Knight, Simons, and ultimately Viner.[25] However, as time wore on, they had no qualms in discarding the Classical Liberal methodology of their teachers and to varying degrees substituting scientific certainty for the more pragmatic philosophical uncertainties and ambiguities emphasized by their predecessors.[26] "I think it is misleading to connect Knight with Marx . . . for I do not think of Knight as a rigid ideologue, jealously imposing conformity on his disciples and colleagues" (Letter from Don Patinkin to George Stigler, November 20, 1972). The Chicago School version of economics that developed in the 1960s did not reflect what those preceding them had consciously constructed, or what they had tried to impress upon their students.

However, Knight's skepticism, along with Laughlin's wont to play the self-styled iconoclast, did create something of an arch connecting prewar Chicago with its postwar image. Yet the real living thread between these periods might be more precisely specified by noting the combative nature of the positions they assumed and the tenacity with which they conducted their battles. At times it seemed that they were forerunners of the Vince Lombardi philosophy. "Winning was not the most important thing, it was the only thing."

> MILTON FRIEDMAN: I think you are getting something that is (a) the atmosphere at Chicago, and (b) intensified by Knight. That an academic is concerned not with being diplomatic, not with trying to avoid hurting people's feelings, but an academic is concerned with saying what's right. Telling the truth, or trying to get at it. And if you disagree with somebody you don't say "well, now there may be something in what you say."
>
> ROSE FRIEDMAN: You may be right.
>
> MILTON FRIEDMAN: You say that's a bunch of nonsense.
>
> AARON DIRECTOR: Exactly. That's not surprising. (Conversation with Milton Friedman, Rose Friedman, and Aaron Director, August 1997)

However, neither shared skepticism nor venomous language did a distinguishable School make. As noted, the department was a mixed medley of various and sometime conflicting methodologies, ideologies, and techniques. Moreover, the immediate postwar department also failed to represent a truly separate and recognizably coherent school for a number of decades. The concept itself of a distinct Chicago School can best be traced back to Laurence Miller's 1961 article (Miller 1961). However, George Stigler, now ensconced at Chicago after returning in 1958, felt compelled to brusquely dismiss the piece and question the legitimacy of publishing it in the *Journal of Political Economy*. However, by the time Stigler (1988) was coaxed (or possibly strong-armed) by Aaron Director to write his own intellectual autobiography, perhaps he had either recognized the value of the burgeoning brand, being the savvy marketer he had become, or had bowed to what by then was the acknowledged consensus of the economics profession.[27] By the 1960s, and certainly with the shift into the 1970s, avoiding the existence of a unified Chicago School holding a defining view regarding theory, policy, and ideology, as well as an almost unique ability to package and market their identifiable brand of economics, would be a marked example of willful blindness. Chicago by that time had clearly mounted the ramparts to repel and push back the postwar forces of Keynesianism. The department had also taken deliberate aim at, and acted as a reliable counterweight to, an emerging consensus of microeconomic analysis attempting to place Walrasian general equilibrium analysis at the very center of economic thinking and policy analysis.[28]

Economics Outside the Cozy Confines of Chicago

In the profession as a whole, Paul Samuelson unarguably became one of the early and most influential voices impatient to dump Classical Liberalism and replace it with a scientifically based policy view. He had flourished as an undergraduate student at Chicago, noted for having the temerity to correct Jacob Viner in his famous graduate course on price theory. However, his bravura performance displayed in his Harvard PhD dissertation (*Foundations of Economics*) and his subsequent reconceptualization of the mainstay introductory economics textbook,[29] transformed him into the champion of what quickly became the new postwar consensus. This perspective would deftly don the mantle of modernism, shedding a more scientifically focused light onto what had previously been an impenetrable thicket of policy issues.

Chicago formulated the most significant and effective opposition to this modern postwar consensus, but by staging that opposition the school demonstrated that it was deliberately out of step with the rest of the profession. The reason was not because they eschewed the scientific tide that was demolishing all other approaches to policy as well as theory. Chicago may have lagged a step or two behind the pioneers of the new modernism, but they displayed few qualms in dispensing with the Classical Liberal approach. Instead, they formulated and embraced their own version of economic science, which opposed and countered the version of economic science being promulgated at Harvard and MIT.[30] Like their opponents, those at Chicago didn't explicitly deny the older approach to policy. They just proceeded to ignore the practice, as did most of the profession swept up in the spirit of the times.

Specifically, what would become known as the Chicago School, whether through a deliberate, conscious strategy or not, abandoned a central element, intimately connected, at least in an implicit sense, to the Classical Liberal method.[31] They saw little cost in doing so, or if they did see a cost, they viewed it as overshadowed by a perceived need to save society from a surging tide of anti-market obstructionism and collectivist ideology. Such dangers, it was believed, would inevitably undermine the essential Classical Liberal commitment to individual freedom. Given this viewpoint, the policy activism and Keynesianism, based on a version of economic science, had to be effectively countered at all costs. This transgression, supported by many economists, was viewed as the first step down a slippery slope of government intervention, which would lead to the totalitarianism foretold by Hayek's *Road to Serfdom* (1944).[32]

Like its predecessor, this newly hatched version of Chicago continued to claim Marshallian roots by holding onto a partial equilibrium framework, as if this singular tool satisfactorily encapsulated

Marshall's intent and purpose.[33] Yet their prescribed alternative to the scientific framework proffered by a Samuelson or an Arrow was to substitute a regime of rigorous testing of any and all theory through a process of empirical analysis. What became known as the Chicago method insisted that any theory must incorporate a testable hypothesis, which could then, by a judicious application of statistical methods, be empirically grounded in terms of its validity.[34] This allowed the Chicago School economists to confront their opponents with what they argued was a more precise and scientific approach.

This ever-evolving Chicago School, while adamantly insisting that they had remained steadfastly within a clearly defined Marshallian tradition, professed little interest in maintaining Marshall's corresponding Classical Liberal methodology.[35] Instead, they perceived the core values of Classical Liberalism to be resident within a given set of policy conclusions, specifically those they viewed as unequivocally supporting individual choice and freedom. The need to protect liberty against the postwar onslaught of collectivism left little room for concern over methodological niceties. This aspect, at least from their own constructed vantage point, allowed these economists to anoint themselves as the rightful heirs of John Stuart Mill, the acknowledged defenders of individual freedom. In the postwar era, as the Cold War intensified, maintaining this cherished degree of liberty against the depredations of collectivism was deemed to be more central to sustaining Classical Liberalism than an old-fashioned and out-of-date methodology. Liberalism called out for scientific modernization and Chicago easily responded to this widely acknowledged imperative.

Consequently, what makes the case of the postwar Chicago School such a striking example of a fundamental abandonment of Classical Liberal Economics is the sense in which this tradition was to some extent entrenched within the Chicago department during the interwar years. This subsequently burnished framework reflected a characteristic imperative defining the preferred approach of some of Chicago's most eminent economists.[36] Those who broke from this tradition to form the subsequent Chicago School were some of the very same people that had been nurtured by this older approach during the 1930s. The previous Chicago department, featuring such luminaries as Knight, Viner, and Simons, had fundamentally incubated those who during the postwar period claimed to be recasting and saving traditional Liberal thought by dispassionately jettisoning the methodology that formed its backbone. However, by the time Chicago moved discernibly away from this older strain of Classical Liberal methodology, the vast majority of the profession had already preempted its subsequent break from the Liberalism of the previous Chicago guiding light, Frank Knight. This unalloyed triumph, vaunting a scientific view of policy over the older art and craft view, was by then complete within the mainstream which then defined the profession. Consequently, those populating the staunchly pro-market encampment, entrenched at Chicago, would be steadfastly opposed by the more interventionist economists headquartered at the strategic duopoly of Harvard and MIT.

Interwar Classical economics then seems at one level consistent with what Melvin Reder (1982), in his analysis of the Chicago School, has defined as forming a "tight prior" approach, which provides the basis for arriving at policy precepts. The core of this idea holds that individuals are capable of handling their own problems as well as is feasibly possible, basically constructing a fundamental "consumer sovereignty" foundation for economics. But, as previously indicated, for old-style Classical Liberals, this broad assertion stopped far short of deteriorating to the level of mindless fetishism.[37] Liberalism in this framework refuses to idealize market exchange. It remains a particularly useful governance structure, not only in concordance with individual choice, but also as a flexible starting point from which to begin policy analysis.

Interwar Chicago economics fit that Classical Liberal approach to a productive degree. The postwar Chicago School did not. The "tight prior" transmuted into something much stronger and became almost unrecognizable from the original notion. In place of a rational choice competitive model serving as a convenient starting point, the new approach used the rational choice competitive model as an ending point—the only truly scientific way to analyze policy. It was an irrefutable principle of analysis.[38] The Classical Liberal nuance or embracing of limitations methodology was abandoned.

George Stigler, for instance, consistently failed, or perhaps substantially refused, to recognize the ad hoc nature of the rational choice competitive model and the possibility of it not being the correct model for analyzing policy. He could never bring himself to accept that Adam Smith's *The Theory of Moral Sentiments* was not an outright anomaly, nor that it served in any sense as a foundation for *The Wealth of Nations*.[39] Stigler held that Smith's moral philosophy was distinguishable and distinct from his economic treatise (*Wealth of Nations*), whereas the volume is actually more comprehensible as a definitive attempt to detail the aspects of human nature that not only complement the advancement of self-interest, but underlie it.[40]

> Nature, when she formed man for society, endowed him with an original desire to please, and an original aversion to offend his brethren. She taught him to feel pleasure in their favourable, and pain in their unfavourable regard. She rendered their approbation most flattering and most agreeable to him for its own sake; and their disapprobation most mortifying and most offensive. (Smith 1976: 116)

The Chicago School and the Classical Liberal approach did manage to share an intrinsic skepticism about the unequivocal value of government intervention into a market economy. But from this point of agreement, the two methodologies diverged significantly. They arrived at this similar destination by taking discernibly different paths.[41] Classical economists recognized government intervention as a reluctant last resort, though decidedly not as anything resembling a deduced conclusion flowing directly from a tight analytical framework. Theory, for such Classical Liberals, failed to demonstrate the inevitable superiority of laissez-faire theory. For the newly hatched Chicago School, theory provided unequivocal scientific support for laissez-faire.

4

Ashes and Diamonds

THE RISE OF THE CHICAGO SCHOOL

Understanding the transformation that defined the Chicago School, and the way in which that transformation slots into broader changes within the profession, requires an accurate sense of the mood prevailing in the postwar era.[1] Namely, what needs to be investigated are the contours of the emerging economic consensus of that period, as well as the concomitant changes in theory and methodology. Paul Samuelson captures that consensus in the following quotation:

> The generation of my teachers found mathematics a sore cross to bear. In their presidential addresses they inveighed against it as pretentious and sterile, seeking comfort by quoting the views of Marshall, Pigou, and Keynes on the triviality of mathematical economics. But that wolf at their door just would not go away. Funeral by funeral they lost their battle. (Samuelson 2011: 939)[2]

Policy Becomes Scientific

By the 1940s, a group of ambitious young economists, led by polymaths such as Paul Samuelson, had developed a conducive and appealing façade covering the less assessable aspects of mathematical economics. The widespread acceptance of the need for mathematical technical tools allowed an alternative theoretical path to be blazed. This approach to applied policy gained strength and eventually overwhelmed all contenders.[3] In many instances, the method came to dominate the theory it was intended to support.

A driving force in this new approach was Paul Samuelson, who had moved from Chicago to Harvard.[4] Whereas Marshall, and Classical economists before him, had deliberately eschewed long chains of reasoning, this new Samuelsonian approach handled it by employing higher level mathematics. Samuelson adroitly welded a Pigovian-style logic to a mathematically specified Walrasian general equilibrium framework. The resulting model shed significant light on some economic policy problems, but also pushed other policy problems into the background.[5]

Without the Classical Liberal critics pointing out the limitations of that model and of all mathematical models for policy, the model became more and more important in policy analysis. The sensibility of not taking theoretical models too seriously as the basis for policy, which Knight had built into Chicago, was no longer limiting. This departure freed Samuelson and the emerging mainstream of neoclassical economists from the methodological tenets of Classical Liberalism.[6] In this fashion, the move to Harvard freed Samuelson from these hypersensitive concerns about the limitations of science and math for policy analysis.[7]

Chicago economists, such as Simons and Knight, had clearly subscribed to this more traditional methodological approach and imparted this sensibility to their students.[8] The Samuelson framework, braced by the rigor of a mathematized economics, essentially replaced the Classical Liberal approach to policy analysis with an approach connecting scientific theory to policy. The attempt by neoclassical economists, operating within a more Marshallian persuasion (such as Jacob Viner), to maintain and nurture this more traditional approach came to a virtual end.[9] Marshall had assiduously endeavored to develop and deploy the bones and sinews provided by neoclassical tools and concepts, while remaining stoutly Classical in appropriating the methods of his predecessors. As a result, the policy views he proposed could not be drawn directly from his economic models, but only from a broader array of reasoning that avoided direct reliance on economic models. For Classical Liberals, all theoretical constructs were only building blocks, which along with other essential material composed a larger and more complex policy edifice. Making sweeping claims for economic models, buttressed solely, or even primarily, by theoretical apparatus, was clearly anathema to Marshall's approach, his thinking, and his natural disposition.[10]

Under the sway of this postwar methodological upheaval, economic policy strayed decisively from its Classical Liberal abode in moral philosophy. Instead, it eagerly attempted to forge a more glamorous alliance with the newly refurbished, and rigor-saturated, realm of economic theory. The older, Classical approach, which had acknowledged that "policy is very messy and in large part non-economic" and hence policy advice could not reasonably flow directly from theory, became a relic of the past. Given the progress of mathematics, quantification, and the increasing application of statistical analysis, theories were now thought to be validated through careful econometric testing.

Following this methodological imperative, those theories capable of generating hypotheses, a specific formulation which lay at the heart of this approach, would be carefully constructed and rigorously challenged by employing the best available data. For George Stigler, this methodology would effectively eliminate the Classical reliance on subjective judgment when applying theory to specific instances. "I don't believe that empirical work owes much to either institutionalism or historicism" (Letter from George Stigler to Donald Patinkin, June 28, 1976).[11] Possibilities, at the dawn of what was widely perceived to be a bright new era of scientific clarity with regard to policy, seemed to be almost unlimited.

As pointed out, this idea of adhering strictly to a scientific policy approach, although presented in opposing fashions and battled over by those with clashing ideologies, defined the emerging postwar generation of economists, especially those enrolled within the cadre of young academics. Under this modern dispensation, policy had been transformed into simply another occasion to practically apply precise scientific methods. Any approach imbued with the spirit of more traditional Classical thinking met with studied indifference. This resolve prevailed despite the fact that the pitched contests waged at the theoretical level remained unresolved. Seeming impasses were reduced to the limiting form of technical questions. An almost unconstrained optimism reassured these ambitious young academics into believing that any such stumbling blocks could be efficiently resolved.

> Most of us younger people think that the macroeconomic problem has been solved by the generation of Samuelson, Modigliani and Arrow. Our students have never seen a cycle. If there are cycles, it's because the governments are stupid enough not to follow the advice of the economists. (Lester Thurow quoted in Levi 1973: 103)

Following the government's role in directing a successful war effort, and by doing so lifting the nation out of the depths of a seemingly endless depression, the ruling spirit of this postwar era viewed government as equivalent to a resourceful master planner, a benevolent and resourceful "Mr. Fixit." The attendant bureaucracy evolved from a traditional role, one that was steeped in indifference or even the source of self-seeking antagonism, into that of a friendly helpmate. Bureaucracy was now capable of embodying an essential component of the postwar "can do" methodology. A newly embraced scientific theology could not fail to find a way to resolve even the most perplexing dilemmas.[12] If X was identified as a problem, the government would wage a war on X. If Y posed an additional problem, war would be waged against Y. X and Y could represent whatever the concern of the time might be, whether it be poverty, crime, or corruption.

Providing a defining justification for the self-labeled Keynesians, this newly ordained economic mainstream was focused on repairing any shortcomings posed by the world of market exchange as highlighted by the theoretical model.[13] In a sharply delineated reaction to the ingrained pessimism holding sway during the interminable years of the Great Depression, accomplishment in these more vibrant postwar years largely appeared to depend on a simple willingness to roll up one's sleeves and apply the appropriate scientific approach to unlock the solution to any problem.

> One of George's [George Stigler's] main emphases was that developments in theory are partly a reaction to surrounding circumstances, partly an outgrowth of things within theory itself, internally generated and not necessarily by external events. But in this case, I would say that the external event, which was generative, was the Great Depression and the difficulties of the Thirties. That created a real problem, about which there was a puzzle and great interest which drove people to be concerned with it. That I think was the driving force. The internal factor was the development of the new mathematical tools. That wasn't the outside world, that was the inside world. (Conversation with Milton Friedman, August 1997)

In much that same spirit, applied statistics in the form of econometrics offered a transformed economics profession the hope of a re-energized world. The discipline could finally turn away from a dubious reliance on assertion, discursive argumentation, and deductive logic and forge a new path paved with the unarguable bedrock of empirical science. Armed with such a powerful theoretical and empirical foundation, the social sciences would henceforth be empowered with the means to successfully improve society systematically. Doing so was consistent with the way in which the physical sciences had successfully transformed many of the other aspects of everyday life.[14] According to the popularly accepted view of that era, economics, more than any of the other contenders, uniquely possessed a vital capacity to pioneer a new direction in reorganizing and improving society.

Economics was the only social science discipline that could, and did, dare to lay claim to the required rigorous foundations that formed the bedrock defining the scientific method. The rising power and financial heft of flourishing independent and non-profit foundations, formed to disburse private fortunes, led the foundations to be irresistibly drawn to underwriting this vision of an ever brighter economic tomorrow.[15] Grants became tokens signifying a broader and intrinsically more optimistic viewpoint, a social engineering scientific framework that was widely shared by many of the major foundations. The Ford Foundation, for one, actively engaged in methodically underwriting research intended to reconstruct the world in quite a literal fashion (Goodwin 1989).

The Challenge to Classical Liberal Sensibilities

In this postwar era, military and economic success had fostered a widespread belief in the power of scientifically directed government projects to achieve just about any imaginable objective.[16] As a result, the Classical Liberal sensibility, which traditionally had been grounded in a strong distrust, or at least a highly developed level of skepticism of government solutions, was being fundamentally challenged, even turned upside down, when not openly scorned. Government spending during World War II clearly had not only defeated a serious threat to an "open society," but had also pulled the economy out of the seemingly intractable slough of the Great Depression. In stark contrast, markets in the 1930s, when measured on most scales of achievement, had failed dismally to deliver. Consequently, government intervention, along with planning and increased control over economic activity, were now seen as the requisite sources capable of producing essential goods and beneficial services.[17] The Samuelson "market failure" foundation for policy fit this sensibility to a tee.

As an understandable response, activities formerly ceded to the marketplace steadfastly shifted geography; they were relocated to government agencies and to their associated functionaries. These politicians and bureaucrats were implicitly assumed, almost universally, to be neutral facilitators, appropriately skilled and trained to achieve consensus objectives.[18] Individual risk and responsibility was significantly downgraded. A universal government safety net, in the form of social security and other welfare measures, became integrated within the social fabric. An intrinsic role for increased government policy was additionally furthered by Cold War fears of a Communist menace. Foreign threats, complete with incessant charges of traitorous numbers of often unnamed domestic moles, engendered booming, and at times seemingly unrestrained, levels of defense spending. Enriching this sprouting industrial-military complex was a subsidized and concomitant rising tide of complementary "scientific" economic research.[19]

As a result, government budgets began to stretch almost elastically, along with the concomitant taxes. Part of this new necessity was due to sustained efforts that hoped to maintain an acceptable level of postwar economic optimism, despite the chilling effects of Cold War anxiety. Resulting in poorly founded hopes, society's newly formed expectations, and its unalloyed hopes for a brighter future, proved to be more demanding than a series of engineering patches were able to sustain. The sunny belief that the instrument of government planning, newly based on scientific methods and research, could achieve any set of stated goals, began to appear problematic. Nonetheless, through the 1950s and '60s, government funding for scientific research of this nature, including mathematically rigorous economic analysis, continued to flow with minimal discussion or opposition.

Corresponding to this postwar fixation on managerial approaches to the economy was the distinct rise of a theoretical move toward a mathematical "economics of control" foundation for policy. This innovative framework allowed for a government that was theorized to be capable of "controlling" a market economy and through that control to be able to maximize social welfare. Maximizing a social welfare function became the goal of government, even though it was unclear whether a social welfare function could be defined or arrived at. Within this carefully constructed scaffolding, it was assumed that the market was doing a reasonably acceptable job, except for those highlighted areas that had been flagged by the theoretical model as bordering on market failure. The policy focus consequently had shifted to spotlight possible avenues leading to a government correction of such market failures.

This movement in economic thinking, which aimed to improve the market mechanism, had its origins in the 1930s and continued unabated through the 1940s. This framework was successfully buttressed by a secondary support encapsulating a basically new set of beliefs. As previously mentioned, in the aftermath of World War II, people's perception of government effectiveness changed. Prior to that war, a world economy mired in depression had seemed to conclusively contradict the pragmatic Classical argument that had opted to champion strong support for market solutions. This decided preference might accurately be termed as reflecting a pragmatic laissez-faire approach to economic issues.[20] Such a perspective focused intently on the limitations of intervention. This inherent hesitancy to meddle was based, not on any formal theory, but on the accumulated experience of having observed government in action. That Classical concern did not fit easily within the framework provided by scientific mathematical modeling. Such hesitancy almost automatically fell to the wayside in the postwar policy considerations.

The New Policy Framework

In this new policy framework, it was assumed that government was able to know its objectives and to achieve its objectives effectively. In this postwar era, bureaucratic planners were seen as saviors, based on the still sharply remembered, depression-riddled economy of the 1930s. This supposition was further fortified by the rescue of democratic countries from the cataclysmic threat posed by the totalitarian Axis countries. This unalloyed success appeared to stem largely from the leadership and planning provided by bold government action, stepping in to avert a looming disaster. Thus, the foundational support underpinning Classical Liberal notions of prosperity and freedom were now publicly attributed to the bounty flowing from government intervention. These virtues were no longer conjoined to entrepreneurial individuals operating within largely unregulated markets. Consequently, public sentiment had decidedly shifted. No longer would a government personified as a somewhat passive night watchman be generally accepted as constituting an acceptable status quo.

The conversion to more mathematical economic theories also had the effect of moving the emphasis away from a focus on the ambiguities of policy nuance. Within the emerging postwar neoclassical method, these concrete territories defining the process of policy formation were no longer informed by the various shades of gray that had artfully defined the Classical Liberal topography. The more pragmatic and intuitive approach characterizing the Classical laissez-faire tradition had permitted divergent policy views to find a home beneath a constantly expanding tent. This Classical Liberal method, now found to be hopelessly old-fashioned, was summarily dismissed from the discipline's mainstream endeavors. Substituted as a replacement was a noticeably more constricted, and often ideologically defined, series of very separable silos in which carefully constructed theories served to produce specific policy outcomes. Little, if any, crossover of ideas occurred among the painstakingly fabricated silos, whether consciously motivated or not.

Within this more modern carnival of sideshow specialties, to disagree on policy became equivalent to rejecting commonly held, even "proven" theory. Given this approach, policy debates between economists could often best be understood as masking a fundamental disagreement over contending theories. Within the realm of this new methodology, the subtleties of Classical Liberal arguments supporting laissez-faire became transmuted (and often casually dismissed) as simple-minded pro-market passivism, protecting the status quo against a flood of indisputable improvement. In contrast, successful government activism seemed firmly rooted in the very best scientific models that economics had to offer. A common ground developed during this period, one that redefined scientific discourse. Entry into this privileged arena needed to be delicately finessed before opposing theories could be granted the imprimatur of legitimacy.

Given this radical reversal, the traditional Classical Liberal approach to policy, championed by Mill and carried forward by Sidgwick and Marshall, fell into disuse.[21] What essentially vanished in policy discussion was a type of laissez-faire economics predicated on a permissible array of government activism. This older perspective considered such interventions on a case-by-case basis, though usually with the onus falling on those promoting government action to make their case, essentially a "suspect till proven worthy" mechanism. As George Stigler recognized, for Mill, "the claims of laissez-faire were tentative and provisional, and major, even radical, changes in the functions of government might come readily with important changes in the circumstances of a society or in its ability to use government effectively" (Stigler 1988a: 9). In its place there appeared a generalized economic methodology that was interpreted, in an unduly facile manner, as providing a sound, theoretical rationale for expanded government intervention.[22] This spreading postwar perspective encouraged less subtle economists (of whom there is never a lack) to dismiss those still entranced by the market as ideologically biased and hopelessly out of date. This perspective then structured the ground that served to nurture the ideas and objectives ultimately composing the Chicago School. This oppositional thought subsequently percolated and solidified.

The Foreseeable Reaction

Claims such as these, tinged as they were with an almost irritating shade of arrogance, provoked a foreseeable reaction from staunch laissez-faire advocates such as Director, Hayek, von Mises, and others. They perceived the dominant status of mainstream economics as having arrived at a calamitous and potentially dire stage. Their concern was not limited to the theoretical niceties of the discipline but extended to a clash of antagonistic ideologies. These self-professed Liberals felt the urgent need to shift the terms of debate to more friendly territory. They believed that the current state of affairs left them no other viable option than to mount an expeditious response as quickly as possible, before matters, in their opinion, took an even more calamitous turn. Hesitating would risk the likelihood that intellectual debate would deteriorate even more precipitously and conclusively.[23] To succeed, recalcitrant Liberal thinkers had to reconstruct the Classical Liberal argument and reoccupy the intellectual high ground of academic discussion.

Despite discernible, and often heated, differences among themselves, these self-proclaimed postwar Liberals had become convinced that the economics profession was explicitly embracing unsubstantiated ideas that were intrinsically dangerous. These newly dominant positions were accordingly labeled as being precipitously ill-advised. They erred by reflecting, if even implicitly or unconsciously, a decidedly collectivist turn of mind. This group of self-styled Liberal and politically right-wing activists were quite naturally aware of what they conceived to be Hayek's (1944) prescient analysis of the incipient dystopia being constructed almost unwittingly, even if sometimes undertaken with the best of intentions.

The feared but almost inevitable result, in their judgment, could only be a cancerous growth in government activity that would subsequently undermine the vision of a civil society that Classical Liberals preferred. Their aspiration had at its core an irrefutable dedication to individual choice and liberty. This fiercely entrenched view evaluated freedom as being currently under a parallel danger from the threats posed by left-wing totalitarianism as it had previously been imperiled by the fascist version of collectivism. Framed in this manner, such a perceived, and largely unanswered, leftward intellectual drift effectively spurred this oppositional group to develop the equivalent of a crusade, one that was organized and pitted against this perception of a pending and imminent danger.

The initial meeting of the Mont Pelerin Society would provide these incipient policy views with the requisite space for them to effectively crystallize. The first such gathering (1947) essentially defined the imminent totalitarian threat, arming the newly associated members with a determination to combat the transgressions of the intellectual left and the associated alarming shift to collectivism. Bonding at this initial gathering, Director and his recently cultivated protégés, Friedman and Stigler, came to believe that mounting and winning arguments supporting markets, while raising serious doubts about the efficacy of any government intervention, had now become ever more exigent.[24]

The Mont Pelerin Society was definitely not constructed as a group devoted to a Millian search for philosophical "truths" through argumentation for the sake of heaven. Rather, it was constructed to further an energized crusade to rescue the public's intellectual soul. The battle necessitated the strategic development of a path by which they could gain and continue to hold sway in ideological debates. Their underlying objective was to move society from a *fait-au-mieux* view of government policy to one that favored a decidedly laissez-faire approach. To do so, they needed to depart from Mill's more measured attitude toward argumentation and instead embrace an attitude conducive to a winner-take-all struggle, one more reminiscent of the perennially aggressive James Laughlin. The fixed-upon strategy acted more as a blunt weapon, with a combative nature being fundamental to its success. The ultimately effective strategy adopted was a carefully crafted reduction of opposing arguments into strawman-like replicas. The combatant proceeded to douse the resulting construction with opprobrium and flammable derision. The resulting deliberately combustible construction was then ignited with an almost loving degree of care. The ensuing destruction would create the space for alternative ideas to flourish, namely those advocating an entrenched, laissez-faire mentality.

> So to succeed, you've got to be able to sell your ideas somehow. How do you do that? I don't really know. Maybe you do attack other people. That's been done over the years, but it doesn't always work. It doesn't work if there's nothing behind your attack. (Conversation with Sherwin Rosen, October 1997)

The Chicago Counterrevolution

For the economists joining together to form the Chicago School, those prevailing mathematical models, providing the justification for this newly accepted condoning of government activism, needed to be strenuously interrogated, tested, and ultimately rejected. The underlying, pro-government rhetorical bias was perceived as an inherent and irritatingly prevalent filter clinging stubbornly to economic theory. That theory itself, propagated far too broadly in their opinion, had gained an unfounded degree of influence. In this Chicago view, economists, under the sway of these mathematical theorists, had provided an unwarranted and dangerous level of support for expanding the already perilous degree of government interference into what was otherwise a self-regulating market process. The legitimacy of such intellectual arguments needed to be rigorously countered and their intellectual flimsiness decisively exposed.

At the commencement of this counterrevolution, which took lethal aim at the prevailing postwar economic consensus, the formative odds facing this small core of Chicago economists appeared overwhelming, if not insurmountable. These economists, who would form the nucleus of the Chicago School, were almost forcibly relegated to the very periphery of the discipline. As the battle lines formed, one of the stalwarts of the Classical Liberal faith, grounded in the Chicago of the interwar years, summed up postwar prospects in decidedly bleak tones.

> The outlook at Chicago, if better than elsewhere, is not very promising. Our divisional dean has no apprehension of economic liberalism and a distinct hostility toward it and the same is true of most persons in the other social science departments.... In the Department [of Economics] we are becoming a small minority. (Henry Simons quoted in Coase 1993: 245)

In a similar vein, James Buchanan described how another Chicago-trained economist, Warren Nutter, had virtually surrendered to the postwar tide of "collectivist" ideas. He had abandoned the forlorn hope of saving Classical Liberal ideas and argued instead for a valiant attempt to "save the books" (Buchanan 2000). Even the irrepressible Milton Friedman, newly hired at Chicago in 1946, was unable to see any hope for a believable redemption arising out of the dark passage of those postwar years. The Cowles Commission, in which many of the members of the Chicago department also held positions, seemed to threaten to overwhelm and swallow up all other legitimately approved academic research. The department itself seemed to be shifting irrevocably to a Keynesian perspective. Academics such as Paul Samuelson were deliberately pursued, with definitive offers being made. Certainly, in the late 1940s, Milton Friedman would have had no inkling of being on the verge of a distinctly new regime, which would subsequently become blended into the mainstream.

Under these circumstances, a small group of true believers, who would come to congregate at the University of Chicago, could only see the future of a free society as hanging perilously in the balance. At this juncture, Milton Friedman and George Stigler (as well as others) who saw themselves as the intellectual heirs of Knight and Simons rose to the challenge, refusing to stand idly by. They desired to shape, rather than to be shaped by, events. But, in their fight, they failed to express any discernible concern for the Classical Liberal methodology of their predecessors. They viewed the more pressing need to lie in exposing the false basis of collectivist policy claims. They shared, along with the more mainstream supporters of the Samuelsonian (economics of control) policy framework, a willingness to place economic policy on an unambiguous scientific foundation. In this sense, they were as modern in their embrace of science as their counterparts at MIT and Harvard. With so much at stake, almost any method that helped achieve such a fundamental goal could, at least hypothetically, be easily justified in this struggle for freedom and liberty.[25]

While one could see this abandonment of Classical Liberal methodology as a strategic move, it is easier to see it as a natural evolution in their own thinking.[26] They required neither pressure nor encouragement to forsake the older Chicago tradition. They saw themselves as restoring what they considered to be the essential basis of Classical Liberalism while necessarily shedding those components no longer applicable to a more modern era.

This emerging Chicago School would match the prevailing dose of scientific rigor promoted by pro-government activists with an even stronger variant. This alternative foundation would require not only the development, but also the testing of models which conclusively demonstrated that free markets inevitably led to desirable results. By doing so, these Chicago economists irrevocably abandoned a defining methodological basis of Classical Liberal applied policy, namely the separation of policy from theory.

5

What Has Chicago Wrought?

PAINTING POLICY BY THE NUMBERS

A major difference between the Chicago Economics Department of Frank Knight and the postwar Chicago School of Friedman and Stigler involved their views of economic theory.[1] The interwar department was highly skeptical of the direct relevance of all theory for policy. The succeeding Chicago School lost much of that skepticism. For example, Stigler envisioned an all-encompassing theory with the potency to resolve any social science policy question or issue, no matter what its nature. This unwavering assurance reflected his adamant conception that theoretical developments were almost completely compelled by debates internal to the profession. By definition, such contests were largely impervious to any battering posed by external events. Economics as science, at least when seen from Stigler's resolute perspective, was essentially a closed and hermetic pursuit. Adhering to this path required an intensely focused methodology, one capable of abstracting away from specifics in order to discover the hidden universals.

> The main explanation for the power of an abstract theory is that it has not specified a lot of factual content. If I specify factual

content, if I get descriptive in my assumptions, there is a great danger that while I can tell a very good story, it doesn't tell me anything about the world. (Stigler 1988a: 1)

Accordingly, the appeal of categorizing, and reducing all markets to a common essence, based on a shared theory of human choice (rational decision making), would become increasingly impossible to forswear, if the underlying and imperative truth was to remain inviolate.[2] This understanding of theory provided the Chicago School with a heavy dose of confidence which, combined with its embrace of renegade positions, would work to Chicago's advantage in the years immediately following World War II. The relative tolerance exhibited by Chicago during the years preceding and following the War (as opposed, for instance, to the anti-Semitism openly displayed by many universities such as Harvard[3]) enabled Chicago to snare European refugees, as well as somewhat gauche, but sharp-witted, and pointy elbowed, provincial young men of enormous talent and ability.[4]

Much of the strength of the Chicago tradition continued to be built upon the importance of openness and the near imperative of providing a home to outsiders of all stripes. These defining characteristics imply that the department, rather than preordained to traverse a narrowly defined path, could have veered off to follow instead a variety of byways in the postwar era. As Reder (1982) points out, many members of the Chicago faculty through the 1940s were not particularly pro-market or ideologically single-minded.[5] Chicago academics supported a variety of policies during this period, by no means unified by a consistent ideological bent. Veblen and Mitchell exemplified the range of economists, approaches, and policies welcomed during the Laughlin period. Extending that principle, Douglas, Schultz, and Lange also epitomized the department's diversity in the 1930s and 1940s.

While Knight, Viner, and even Simons represented notable figures within the department during the interwar years, they clearly did not embody some dominant characteristic defining those passing through or residing in Chicago within that period. Even the future archconservative Aaron Director, the eminence grise of the Chicago School, originally came to the South Side as a PhD student after working for the Oregon State Federation of Labor. He initially served as a research assistant to Paul Douglas, with whom he published *The Problem of Unemployment* (1931). This stage of his academic progress was an interval immediately preceding his subsequent conservative conversion under the influence of the Mephisto-like entrancement of Frank Knight.[6] (Whether this moment should be classified as a Pauline-like event or simply as a reaffirmation of consistent tendencies and inclinations remains debatable.[7])

The Core of the Chicago School

> It's a sort of a "Marines" approach to Economics. Stigler was certainly one of the leaders of the Chicago School. I think that's what distinguished the Chicago approach. We take what we do very seriously. And we take it as far as you can. (Conversation with Sherwin Rosen, October 1997)

No inevitable progression can be distinctly specified that would inevitably lead from the previously defined Chicago tradition, even in its ultimate 1930s incarnation, to the postwar formulation that evolved into the recognizable Chicago School. For example, the Cowles Commission, which was located at Chicago, initially shared appointees including such eminent economists as Don Patinkin and Jacob Marshak.[8] The Chicago School was by no means a Keynesian-free zone, including within the department the Harvard-trained Lloyd Metzler, who provided intellectual and ideological ballast.

If we hunt retrospectively for unimpeachable landmarks, the hiring of Milton Friedman (who, despite the proffered low pay, accepted a position initially earmarked for George Stigler) marked the true beginning of the Chicago School.[9] Friedman, who managed to be Jewish, as well as being a truly abrasive renegade, fit the Laughlin outsider tradition all too nicely.[10] Ultimately, this passing of the Classical Liberal baton to the tender care of Milton Friedman, who didn't so much fumble it as engage in a creative refiguring, initiated the radical reformulation of the older Chicago tradition. Any passing resemblance to Classical Liberalism depended strongly on shared policy objectives. Though even here, the older version of cultivated liberalism never indulged in creating a totemic belief that flirted with market infallibility.

At the core of this new perspective was an almost compulsory production of theoretical justifications for the market, as well as the necessity that such models be firmly grounded within the compass of thoroughly tested empirical evidence. Such a discrete change did not occur instantaneously. Before being widely acknowledged as forming a distinguishable Chicago School, allies needed to be enlisted, and that took time. In the immediate aftermath of World War II, the formulation of such a well-defined approach was still in its infancy, existing at best as a notional aspiration. "There was no Chicago School of Economics when the Mont Pelerin Society first met at the end of World War II" (Stigler 1988b: 148).

> It was not until after I left Chicago in 1946 that I began to hear rumors about a "Chicago School" which was engaged in organized battle for laissez faire and "quantity theory of money" against "imperfect competition" theorizing and "Keynesianism." I remained sceptical about this until I attended a conference sponsored by University of Chicago professors in 1951. The invited participants were a varied lot of academics, bureaucrats, businessmen, etc. but the program for discussion, the selection of chairmen, and everything about the participants were so patently rigidly structured, so loaded, that I got more amusement from the conference than from any other I ever attended. Even the source of the financing of the Conference, as I found out later, was ideologically loaded. (Jacob Viner quoted in Patinkin 2003 [1969]: 112)

The Three Horsemen of the Apocalypse

As discussed in the previous chapter, prewar Chicago was eclectic. The rise of Keynesianism in the postwar era, along with a more activist state, left many pro-market economists feeling threatened.

> The Samuelson matter was again forced to a head—by Douglas—
> & thanks mainly to his efforts we lost badly. The dep't has voted
> to make Samuelson an offer. We don't yet know the end of the
> story. But whatever it is, I am very much afraid that it means
> we're lost. The Keynesians have the votes & mean to use them.
> Knight is bitter & says he will withdraw from active participa-
> tion in the dept. Mints, Gregg, & I are very low about it. (Letter
> from Milton Friedman to George Stigler, November 27, 1946, in
> Hammond and Hammond 2006: 46)

Thus, only in retrospect can we see the hiring of Milton Friedman
(coupled with Samuelson's decision not to come to Chicago) as the
germinating point from which flowed Chicago's subsequent counterrevolution. Friedman might represent an essential act of conception, but his appearance was not sufficient to denote the birth.
Two additional steps would bring this as yet ambiguous beginning
to fruition. Once accomplished, the essentially liberal characteristic of actively embracing dissent would fall by the wayside. However, through the late 1940s and mid-1950s, at least some of the
older Chicago tradition still residually persisted. Hiring continued
to focus on outsiders of different persuasions, who managed to
combine talent with ambition. There was a serious and concerted
push by Oscar Lange (before decamping for Poland) to lure Abba
Lerner to the University.

At this early stage, even as viewed by those within the department, any certainty that Chicago was on the verge, or even within
the neighborhood, of becoming a pro-market bastion would seem
to have been elusive at best. In fact, from the perspective of a
laissez-faire theorist like Friedman, the balance of the department
seemed to be irretrievably swinging relentlessly leftward. The offer
to Samuelson, though, would turn out to be the low ebb for those
sharing Friedman's beliefs and vision.[11]

The Chicago appointment that allowed the department to break
decisively from its distinctive Classical Liberal constraints, leading
to the final transformation of the Chicago tradition to the more narrowly defined Chicago School, came with the return and simulta-

neous elevation (or perhaps apotheosis) of George Stigler. His old classmate, Allen Wallis, successfully shaped that decision in 1958 by offering him the well-funded position of Charles R. Walgreen Professor of American Institutions.[12] Serious efforts to engineer some such triumphal return had been attempted earlier but had not succeeded. Although never articulated, Stigler, quite naturally, would have harbored some residual resentment at being dumped for what had seemed at the time to represent a fait accompli position. (In 1946, Stigler had been the preferred choice of the department for the position subsequently given to Milton Friedman. Stigler's appointment had not been expected to run into any foreseeable speed bumps. Exactly what the notoriously caustic Stigler said that doomed his candidacy during his mandatory interview with the University's president has never been reported in any precise detail.[13])

This addition of Stigler not only shored up the already unmistakable ideological bent of the Economics Department, but also allowed an unambiguous reflection of this reformed Liberal program to create a beachhead within the Business School as well. Under his nurturing eye, the faculty there would grow to rival that of its older counterpart. Like Friedman, George Stigler was an outsider in the sense that he remained the perennial provincial.[14] Like many of that remarkable postwar generation of economists, he possessed a finely honed, almost intuitive, sense of economics, remaining uncharacteristically well read, but above all, displaying an unwavering support for market capitalism.[15]

The growth of the Chicago School was augmented and even spurred by successfully sending offshoots to both the Law and the Business Schools. (Stigler, for instance, held a dual appointment in both the Economics Department and Business School. Yet he chose, perhaps significantly, to locate his office within the Business School.) In the same year of Friedman's arrival, the death of Henry Simons left his newly created position within the Law faculty vacant. Just as Simons had been saved from a precarious position within the Economics Department, another one of Knight's erstwhile protégées, Aaron Director, would have his academic career resurrected by means of a comfortable exile among the legal minds of the University. As we will discuss below, this appointment was made possible by Hayek's unexpectedly successful volume, *The Road to Serfdom*. The surprisingly influential book provided a foray into a plausible dystopia. It came equipped with a convenient touch of crystal ball gazing with which to rally those of a similarly political inclination. The widespread dissemination of a condensed version of Hayek's work subsequently attracted a series of sizeable grants from the Volker Fund.[16]

> In the end it was agreed to appoint Director for five years as research associate with the rank of professor to conduct what was called in the memorandum sent to the Volker Fund, "a study of a suitable legal and institutional framework of an effective competitive system." However, before the final arrangements were made, Simons died, and Katz asked that the terms of the Volker grant be modified to allow Director to do some teaching. (Coase 1993: 246)

Although Director would consistently shun publication during his long career, his subsequent influence seemed inversely related to the paucity of his articles. He was one of the few people who could clearly affect the thinking of George Stigler during Stigler's last thirty-three years at Chicago. Director operated as an almost hidden strategist, seeming to shape the counterrevolution mounted by his compatriots at Chicago. Though Director's hand could be discerned only by those insiders who presented the more public face of the project, often it was his hand that proved decisive. "Both in and out of the classroom, Director was extremely effective as a teacher, and he had a profound influence on the view of some of his students and also on those of some of his colleagues at the University of Chicago both in law and economics" (Coase 1993: 245–246).[17] These three future linchpins of the Chicago counterrevolution coalesced on the occasion of the first Mont Pelerin meeting, establishing a mutual self-reinforcement of ideas and an unshakable belief in their destiny. That collegial buttressing of ideas allowed them to sustain a belief in the market as a theoretical and fundamental principle that would come to define the Chicago School and contour the shape of subsequent policy formulations. Certainly, a more constrained directional focus, defining their published research, remains an identifying characteristic after this meeting of like-minded intellectuals.[18] Stigler's early work had been a rather mixed bag, not dissimilar to that of most recent graduates attempting to discover an identifiable voice and approach. His initial publications included some purely empirical pieces, an article that anticipated linear programming, a mainstream review of monopoly, and a rather provocative piece on cost curves. Friedman, in turn, when looking back on his early career, would puzzle over the degree to which he had succumbed to Keynesian thinking in his analysis. That ended with the Mont Pelerin meeting. Though the three were chaperoned at that meeting by Frank Knight, it would mark the beginning of a clear break from Knight's influence, and from the previous Chicago tradition. More than any other moment, this occasion can be identified with the birth of the Chicago School.[19]

Chicago Rising: The Logic of Conviction

> BILL BUCKLEY: Yes, some public regulation can be necessary. Suppose the democratic legislature made prostitution legal. Surely then requiring prostitutes to pass a monthly test for venereal disease is a worthy idea.
>
> MILTON FRIEDMAN: Not at all. If a woman on the street, professing to be disease-free does infect a customer, that will hurt her reputation. If, nevertheless, she does infect you, then that is a *tort* that you can sue her for in court.

As Paul Samuelson stated, "When Friedman's conservative Chicago colleagues chided him for such extremisms, he was unrepentant. Someone in each generation must go all the way with the truth, however much that dissipates his influence—that was his credo." (Samuelson, 2011: 864)

The older Chicago tradition had previously embraced renegades of all persuasions. The more customary perspective faded rapidly, becoming no more than a historical artifact. Its replacement would compose and evolve into the widely recognized Chicago School. With all the key players in place (circa 1958), the ruling triumvirate of Friedman, Stigler, and Director were now unhindered and able to deploy their not inconsiderable rhetorical skills in defending the market from those who dared to launch attacks, including policy-based initiatives. Barricades against such aggressive forays of the mainstream advocates of an economics of control approach were constructed. These designated speed bumps were scientifically based on what Chicago considered to be strictly theoretical foundations Policy debates were transformed into scientific theoretical debates, not debates about nuances of interpretation. Both sides (Chicago and MIT/Harvard alike) claimed science and empirical (statistical) evidence to be firmly on their side.[20] Classical applied policy methodology was abandoned by both sides.

This newly alchemized Chicago School of Economics continued to underwrite the idea of nurturing dissent, at least within a hypothetical context, but in practice, allowable dissent became a bit (if not at times decidedly) more of a one-sided and narrowly focused affair. When an argument is identified as being painstakingly scientific, one that is founded on theory carefully vetted by empirical evidence, any variance due to nuances in interpreting the results, which the previous Chicago tradition had emphasized, becomes far less important. Theoretical insights, cloaked in empirical validation, transform into a direct conduit for policy formation. Consequently, ensuing debates inevitably centered on issues surrounding formal theory and associated empirical results. For this "one size fits all" approach, specific factors encompassing economic and non-economic influences could be routinely dismissed. Provided with a self-defined scientific playbook, both contesting sides sought to interpret their "statistically verified" conclusions as supportive of their respective theories. Inevitably, disagreements over proposed policy approaches were transformed into issues concerning foundational theories.

Furthering what had become over time something of a unified objective at Chicago did not require an explicit or even conscious litmus test that served to screen and limit departmental applicants and subsequent hires.[21] But just as Stigler found that all good econometric work consistently tended to support his own cherished perspective, so he would tend to find that good economists, those with substantial promise, also managed to parallel, almost serendipitously, his line of thought to a large, though perhaps not to a total, extent.[22] Consequently, any serious attempt to conjure up a sizeable cohort of non-conservative economists who met his exacting scientific standards inevitably would rank as a forbidding task. Holding pro-market views didn't necessarily translate into being a competent economist, but in practice it tended to be a common characteristic of that positively identified group. What Stigler and his colleagues consistently demanded was an incisive mind, a thorough knowledge of economic analysis, and the ability to stand up to them in verbal arguments. From their standpoint, very few economists, especially those lacking a ferocious respect for the market economy, met these essential criteria.[23]

One economist who proved to be something of an exception to the rule was Robert Solow (though there is little evidence that this high degree of respect for Solow extended broadly throughout the department). Stigler attempted to woo him (somewhat ardently) to Chicago, even though his policy views differed sharply from those propounded at Chicago.[24] Stigler's powers of persuasion and intimidation within the department were legendary. Essentially, what George Stigler wanted, George Stigler got. Accordingly, had Robert Solow caved in and indicated his interest, he likely would have soon found a hard-to-refuse offer in the mail. The issue was, perhaps unfortunately, never put to the test.[25]

Solow was an exception to the usual adversarial rule dominating the department, a judgment consigning interlopers to a perpetually out of bounds existence. However, Solow seemed to embody a unique, rather than representative, case, an almost aberrant voice speaking to Stigler alone among the colloquy of Chicago academics. For the most part, Chicago tended to view the world, especially in the early years when positioned at the periphery of the profession, in the very definitive terms of "us versus them." In contrast, the idiosyncratic Solow-Stigler connection transformed the two into a classic odd couple, a relationship that struck both friends and colleagues as somewhat incongruous. Solow certainly wasn't widely accepted as "a good egg" within the confines of Chicago. But for the rest of the profession, especially during the height of the Stigler/ Friedman/Director regime in the 1960s and '70s, the Chicago renegades remained a band apart.

The Contours of South Side Policy: Seeking Theoretical Proof

> If a pure scientist—one believing only demonstrated things—is asked his opinion on policy, he must decline to answer—and listen to his intellectual inferiors give advice on policy. Hence the role of the pure scientist is terribly painful to assume in economics. (Letter from George Stigler to Milton Friedman, December 1948, in Hammond and Hammond, 2006: 96)

Chicago seemed to provide its adherents with a specific set of goggles from which to view and evaluate the world. Naturally, opposing schools and theorists were not without their own restrictive designer eyewear. But in contrast, the corrective aspect of the Chicago element at times appeared particularly severe, if not drifting into the astigmatic. It might be said that such luminaries as Friedman and Stigler unambiguously understood, in some, unwavering, deep sense, how the world worked. The resulting implication of such a perspective insisted that errant facts and observations needed to be cultivated, tamed and brought into concordance with a perceived vision of reality, one which either was, or perhaps should be. Such a decided viewpoint, buttressed by a professional discipline where modernism implied that theory would automatically meet the contours of scientific practice, channeled these stream-lined hypothetical constructs into unarguably distinct policy formations.[26]

> He [George Stigler] was absolutely sure the economy was on his side and if research was properly done it would show this. He

really believed that he understood how the world works. And the way the world works had been shown to him by the theory of price. (Conversation with James Kindahl, October 1997)

In the tumultuous postwar period, the older Chicago tradition, one with roots going back to the department's formation in 1892, mutated into a distinctive and formidable strategic approach, one nurtured under the critical eyes of Milton Friedman, George Stigler, and Aaron Director. The key players in what would come to be dubbed the "Chicago School" (and its other disparate satellites) naturally extended beyond those three, but this serendipitous triumvirate can best be understood to compose the effective architects who carefully constructed an impervious scaffolding. Their meticulously hewn fabrication would eventually engulf and define the department. In a series of ever more distinguishable departures, this postwar generation of Chicago nurtured economists found themselves breaking with the older tradition that had defined the department during its more formative years.

In one sense, this perceived break was merely business as usual. Protégées, especially those with the greatest promise, are ever wont to reject the ideas and methods of their teachers. Otherwise they flirt with being consigned to lasting mediocrity. They become in danger of turning into no more than a pale copy of the original. This potentially fruitful rejection can, in some ways at least, improve on the existing tradition while skirting a more dangerous path that allows core, and still vibrant, ideas to eventually wither and decay.[27] The Chicago School did continue the practice of cultivating a typically brash, *in your face* argumentation style. However, in this postwar transitional period, they tended to use it asymmetrically.[28]

This distinct deviation from the spirit of both the Chicago and the Classical traditions imbued the confrontational style of argument with a distinctively *pit bull* flair (deliberately leaping for the jugular and endeavoring to win debates whatever the associated costs).[29] A transformed methodology implied argumentation that refused to retreat when engaged in an academic battle.[30] They tended not to step back from entrenched and defined positions.[31]

Consequently, the "embrace dissent" approach that formed a central element of the original Chicago tradition was effectively sidelined, permanently shunted off to silently decay on a neglected bit of spur track. A focus on hunting out and destroying heretical viewpoints replaced the older, more ecumenical approach.[32] Opposing theories, especially those that favored multi- (or non-) equilibrium methods were viewed as provocatively dangerous to established price theory.[33] Such forays into the less than orthodox regions of price theory became demolition targets rather than occasions for analysis and examination.

> Evidence of Stigler's attachment to neoclassical price theory is also given by the part of his work mainly critical of the work of others. Price rigidity, administered price inflation, the theory of monopolistic competition, and X-efficiency were prominent targets, and each of them denied the efficacy of the neoclassical analytical framework. (Demsetz 1993: 800)[34]

This change in methodology distinctly set the Chicago School apart from the broader Chicago tradition which, despite using a similar grammar of confrontation, embraced a noticeably different gestalt. In the older approach, confrontation was designed to efficiently weed out faulty logic and ideas that were protected by social niceties and customs. The aim was to place everything equally under a blow torch of skeptical examination.[35] As reformulated by the Chicago School, the intention became one of protecting a particular market formulation and its confederated policy stance, while discrediting and indiscriminately destroying opposing approaches.[36] This difference is subtle and thus easily overlooked. Superficially the two can at times appear indistinguishable. Aaron Director can be portrayed simply as someone, who, like Knight, was unwilling to accept any generally accepted principle or idea at face value. While his objections are often well drawn, his sensitive antennae seem to quiver most strongly when confronted by a seeming challenge to the competitive market model. "Don't jump to conclusions. If you see something that is at odds with the competitive model, don't say immediately something like 'this is monopoly' but investigate it carefully and then draw your conclusions" (Peltzman quoted in Overtveldt 2007: 68). However, this perception that effectively separated the postwar Chicago School remains central to a correct understanding of its fundamental nature. What this bifurcation provides is a distinct categorization that, at times, underpins the foundation established by Director, Friedman, and Stigler with only a tenuous connection to the broader Chicago tradition. The lingering impression, at least, is that in postwar Chicago the conclusion came first, whereupon clever minds then were set to work to achieve the desired outcome.

> It seems to me that when you get to his [Stigler's] later work, say with Becker, you know what the conclusion is going to be before you start the argument. In a sense, you're assembling arguments to support a conclusion. I mean, that may be unkind and untrue but it's an impression. And, it's even more so in the work of Richard Posner. Have you read any of that? It seems to me that the plot is always the same, and the characters stay fixed. (Conversation with Ronald Coase, October 1997)[37]

Labeling Chicago's technique as reflecting an *in your face* aggressiveness might seem overly harsh and even unwarranted. Unfortunately, that precise propensity seems to have developed almost synchronously with its carefully cultivated (and more pronounced) maverick image. This postwar evolution entailed a potentially reflexive and entirely admirable unwillingness to bow down to the prevailing economic wisdom that dominated any given era. However, the long-standing Chicago tradition, stemming from the inception of the department, required participants to be as harsh when evaluating their own arguments as they were wont to be on the logic of their opponents. Obeying this older prescription meant following a course fastidiously set within the Classical Liberal tradition. Although, when filtered through the traditional Chicago approach, this perspective evoked a version that effortlessly employed a much more intense and industrial strength variant, rather than that depending on the gentle tones characteristic of a John Stuart Mill.

The Chicago School added a new twist to this recognizable formula. The argumentative aggressiveness remained in perfect conformity with the competitive style and personal characteristics of both Friedman and Stigler. But the pit bull style of not backing down, nor showing any convincing willingness to entertain a counterargument, projects a definitive shift away from the older, more liberal approach.[38] In this geography of debate, the opposition existed merely to be terminally mowed down, not to be afforded a conscientious hearing. Given such a narrowly focused perspective, the underlying belief embraces a mock Darwinian position that by operating within a fiercely competitive marketplace for ideas, the proposed theories, and their associated arguments, would soon prove their valor or would collapse under the weight of their own inadequacy. The Chicago School, to effectively market its focused program, required what can best be described as a one-sided form of skepticism, brooking acceptance of no other viable alternatives. Such deviant positions were there to be eradicated, rather than being awarded any serious consideration. Pro-market arguments, which Chicago School economists strongly supported, would accordingly face a much milder inquisition than would holders of any alternative or more heterodox theories.[39]

This seemingly incongruous result flowed directly from the two irreconcilable objectives that characterized the construction of the postwar Chicago counter-revolution. Restoring Classical Economic Liberalism had to be reconciled to the hard-edged reality defining that era, at least according to those domiciled on the more conservative or rightward side of the political spectrum.[40] The demands of economics as a scientific discipline were required to face and adjust to a genuine sense of urgency surrounding the perceived collectivist threat defining those years. Forces pushing for a more extensively planned economy seemed to be on the ascendant in that immediate Cold War period.

From the Chicago perch, such policies, no matter how well intended, would inevitably undermine the core liberal goal of individual freedom.[41] The first principle guiding this regime of thought was that individual freedom or liberty existed as the unarguable objective to which everyone irrefutably aspires. This common notion remained a fundamental and axiomatic value which implied that any perceived threat would need to be unquestionably demolished. As George Stigler succinctly noted, "I simply assume without argument that you and I wish to live in a free society" (1971a: 4). Given the ineluctable logic that anything short of the strictest vigilance would yield dire and lasting consequences, these counter-revolutionaries could justify the use of illiberal means to protect what they perceived as fundamental Liberal values.[42] Thus, the one-sided skepticism distinguishing them from their self-nominated predecessors becomes a compelling and incisive marketing stratagem. The convenient supposition that only a reconceptualized Liberalism provided a sane and reliable path capable of saving a just and humane society was sanctified to an almost totemic level as a fundamental objective which they now considered to be in peril.

6

Economic Policy Becomes a Science

THE RISE OF WELFARE ECONOMICS, AND THE CHICAGO ALTERNATIVE

Our focus in the preceding chapter was on how the Chicago School took shape. This chapter looks more carefully at Chicago's interaction with the mainstream of economics that conditioned its emergence. The catalyst to the postwar change was the mainstream adoption of welfare economics, which drew policy implications directly from economic theory. Composing a new approach, it directly specified what the "optimal" policy should be. This measure of decisiveness was in stark contrast to Classical Liberal methodology. For a Classical Liberal economist, policy did not follow directly from scientific economic theory. Instead, economic science and theory provided a useful tool that shed light on policy problems, but, on its own, had no immediate policy implications. These consequences could only be determined once one considered all the issues, not just a subset covered by economic theory. As a result, policy had to be deliberately separated from science.

The Classical Liberal view of the relation between economic theory and policy started to fade in the 1930s and did so increasingly by the 1940s. This decline coincided with a shift in public sentiment that was able to entertain a more favorable view of government planning and its aligned regulation of the marketplace. Consequently, in the 1930s and '40s, conceptions that claimed to define both Classical Liberal methodology and the ideology formulating Classical Liberal policy were changing. Particularly noticeable was a shift away from a more traditional judgment in favor of an essentially laissez-faire approach to policy matters.[1] For more traditional Classical Liberals, this altered sentiment, arguing for a more activist government policy, was a methodological question unrelated to the science of economics. This older perspective held that, to a large degree, policy arguments were based on relevant sensibilities and judgments. Such conclusions might be guided by the pertinent science, but they were not determined by that science. For a Classical Liberal, policy principles would, and should, change over time even if the underlying science did not.

The New Welfare Economics

In 1920, Arthur C. Pigou published his, at the time, seminal work, *The Economics of Welfare*. Pigou was Marshall's preferred replacement for the Chair of Political Economy at Cambridge.[2] The book consequently received serious attention upon publication. In it Pigou blended many of Alfred Marshall's ideas into a more general equilibrium framework, drawing constrained policy judgments guided by, but not determined by, the model. Faithful to the Marshallian tradition, the discussion was nuanced and highly qualified. Pigou carefully stated that he was not conducting pure science but was instead engaged in what he called *realistic* science—science applied to policy. He was introducing normative judgments and sensibilities into welfare analysis in order to draw policy conclusions. He concentrated on material welfare, but specifically recognized that welfare went far beyond these material limits. As a consequence,

Pigou presents his economic analysis as only an input into policy analysis. He did not claim it provided anything resembling a precise policy guide. Unfortunately, such limitations would soon be forgotten by his subsequent followers. Instead, a new, scientifically grounded policy methodology of applied economics would replace that constructed by Classical Liberal Economics.

Within this new mainstream approach, policy was based directly on theory and science. According to the emerging mainstream consensus, the science of economics indisputably informed economists that government intervention was needed to maximize social welfare, which was accepted as the goal of economic policy. Thus, this new welfare economics spliced the ideological component of Classical Liberalism with the rigor of scientific methodology, forcing opposed policy positions to be indicative of theoretical differences. Converts to this new methodology began to draw policy conclusions directly from theoretical economic models. As a result, the then-prevailing theoretical and policy mainstream of the day seemed to insist that the science of economics broadly supported direct state intervention (both at the micro and macro levels).

Pigou wasn't alone in attempting to rigorously blend Marshallian policy insights into a general equilibrium framework. The same procedure became a feature throughout the profession. In response, a new rash of journal articles indicated potential pitfalls when attempting to extend partial equilibrium arguments to general equilibrium policy contexts. This approach demonstrated the way in which such conclusions would change when extended to a general equilibrium context, providing credence to the general equilibrium model. Concurrent with this change was a parallel evolution in the way in which economists conceptualized policy. Focused formulations within this subject matter became their own field, now known as Welfare Economics. Welfare Economics changed the conception of policy work from a back-of-the-envelope analysis based on Marshallian supply and demand partial equilibrium models. These constructions, blended together with institutional and normative judgments, remained incapable of being formalized into scientific models. Marshallian policy analysis was at best loosely tied to theory. This approach explicitly did not see theory serving as a format for policy, as the alternative method of general equilibrium analysis certainly did.

Marshall had seriously questioned the appropriateness of extending policy analysis to encompass general equilibrium thinking. He had pointed out that his partial equilibrium models simply served as aids to judgment, not as a framework suitable for policy analysis. Conclusions drawn from this method would not necessarily carry over to longer chains of reasoning, which a general equilibrium perspective would require. Moreover, he questioned the use of any policy models based on long chains of reasoning, intrinsic to a general equilibrium approach. Those chains of reasoning lost sight of the large number of issues that partial equilibrium required a researcher to keep in the back of his mind. Marshall differentiated what he considered to be economics suitable for policy from scientific notions of pure theoretical economics.

> It seems strange to me to be asked my views as to the study of pure economic theory; as tho' that were a subject on which I were fit to speak. For indeed I was never a partisan of it; and for more than a quarter of a century I have set my face away from it. As early as 1873 (I think it was the year) Walras pressed me to write something about it; & I declined with emphasis. The fact is I am the dull mean man, who holds Economics to be an organic whole, & has as little respect for pure theory (otherwise than as a branch of mathematics or the science of numbers), as for that crude collection & interpretation of facts without the aid of high analysis which sometimes claims to be a part of economic history. (Letter from Alfred Marshall to W.A.S. Hewins, October 12, 1899, in Coase 1994: 172–173)

Lerner's Economics of Control

Marshall died in 1924, and with him were buried many of the qualifications that he associated with his perspective. His approach became increasingly displaced by a very different way of thinking.

Abba Lerner, a brilliantly provocative and outspoken young economist, who was not known for shying away from extending theoretical arguments to policy, was at the very forefront of this new methodology. He was one of the economists who did most to advance this transformed policy analysis during this period.[3] Lerner pointedly articulated this understanding of the role played by government within Pigovian welfare economics, first in a series of articles, and then in his book, *The Economics of Control* (1944). That book in particular spelled out the new scientific approach to policy that economists began to adopt in the 1930s. Lerner's work is important because it would serve as a fundamental text for many graduate programs in the 1940s. The volume would subsequently provide a template for Paul Samuelson's principles textbook (first published in 1948).[4]

Lerner's "economics of control' approach to policy consisted of two parts. The micro component extended Pigou's Welfare Economics framework (Pigou 1920 [2002]), transforming it into precise rules guiding policy interventions. He aimed to redefine policy justification away from relying on broadly philosophical and loose arguments in which economics had only a supporting role, to a precise, theoretically derived mathematical specification detailing optimal policies. Lerner's arguments had built into them a decided preference for government intervention. Government was considered to be a necessary driver of the economy. In stark contrast, Classical laissez-faire policy was equated to riding in a driverless car. (Such thoughts were formulated when self-driving cars were technically inconceivable.) Lerner (1951: 3–5) captured the view that government policy was needed by employing the following analogy:

> Our economic system is frequently put to shame in being displayed before an imaginary visitor from a strange planet. It is time to reverse the procedure. Imagine yourself instead in a Buck Rogers interplanetary adventure, looking at a highway in a City of Tomorrow. The highway is wide and straight, and its edges are turned up so that it is almost impossible for a car to run off

the road. What appears to be a runaway car is speeding along the road and veering off to one side. As it approaches the rising edge of the highway, its front wheels are turned so that it gets back onto the road and goes off at an angle, making for the other side, where the wheels are turned again. This happens many times, the car zigzagging but keeping on the highway until it is out of sight. You are wondering how long it will take for it to crash, when another car appears which behaves in the same fashion. When it comes near you it stops with a jerk. A door is opened, and an occupant asks whether you would like a lift. You look into the car and before you can control yourself you cry out, "Why! There's no steering wheel!"

For Lerner, the missing steering wheel could be effectively supplied by government fiscal policy. Such government direction, he argued, was scientifically needed. This particular insight irresistibly transformed itself to become Lerner's interpretation of Keynesian macroeconomics. In this recounting, government was installed as the driver of the aggregate economy. This framework then became the textbook version of Keynesian macroeconomics that was widely taught to students. Consequently, this version eventually became what people understood as composing Keynesian economics (Colander 1984). It made fun of the Classical Liberal concept of "sound finance," portraying it as an unsophisticated ideology rather than as a nuanced principle based on sensibilities and judgments formed by years of experience. Lerner contrasted "sound finance" with what he called Keynesian "functional finance" in which logic and science predominated over ideology and morality. From a scientific perspective, Lerner argued that concern about the deficit and debt should be focused on their functional effects on the economy as shown by Keynesian models. Concentrating instead on ideological beliefs that reflexively valued savings as inherently good and deficits and debt as inherently bad would only lead policy astray.

Consistent with this view, Lerner developed a set of marginal conditions at the microeconomic level that would lead to an optimal economic outcome—the best that could be done. Government intervention was needed to achieve that level of optimality. (These very same marginal conditions remain central to the teaching of microeconomics today.) Any economy achieving this state, not just capitalism, was, by definition, viewed as reaching the highest state of welfare achievable.[5] Consequently, an appropriately committed government, armed with an appropriate set of economic advisors, possessed the means of achieving the same results as did a capitalist economy. However, the guided alternative could capture this same objective in a much fairer manner. Therefore, no substantial (economic) obstacle prevented a system such as market socialism from replacing a regime defined by market capitalism.[6]

This change in policy justification established a theoretically mandated role for government action. Although the market was assumed to be good, government intervention could make it even better. Correcting the many externalities that existed in any economy soon became the springboard for future policy analysis. The same method held for the macro side of Lerner's economics of control approach. The market inevitably was flawed, and the problem could only be solved if government undertook an activist role, namely by providing a program of "functional finance" stabilization. Within this economics of control macro framework, full employment was an irrefutable goal that could be achieved only via the appropriate government policies. The economics of control approach employed the logic of externalities acting as a bulwark to underwrite its validity. Their existence provided the logical leverage for government intervention. This move toward a scientific foundation for policy differed markedly both in approach and in spirit from the policy perspective nurtured and preferred by John Maynard Keynes, perhaps most succinctly clarified in *The End to Laissez Faire* (1927).

> He envisioned a public sector that would engage in limited but forceful interventions to ameliorate the problems that were engendered when individuals were left to act alone. "The important thing for Government is not to do things which individuals are doing already, and to do them a little better or a little worse,"

he explained, "but to do those things which at present are not done at all." (Burgin 2012: 3)

In contrast, the welfare economics espoused by Lerner and others was based on Walrasian general equilibrium theory, which was believed to be providing the appropriate blueprint for policy formulation. Marshall had argued that economists should stick with partial equilibrium models, employed only as practical, heuristic tools. In contrast, the new welfare economics was based on general equilibrium theory where policy was formulated directly from formal models.

The New Welfare Economics:
The Social Welfare Function

The initial welfare economics was thought of as "scientific," operating independently of moral judgments. One moved from theory to policy recommendations directly. But it was quickly recognized that moral judgments played a necessary role in policy formulation and could not be avoided. Specifically, welfare economists evolved into what can be called the New Welfare Economics. This perspective differed from what was previously denominated as welfare economics in that it formally integrated a social welfare function directly into the analysis. According to this new approach, policy would not be designed simply to maximize an aggregate utility function consisting of a composite of individual utility functions. Instead, it would be designed to maximize a normatively grounded social welfare function (Bergson 1938).[7] This revision technically reintroduced moral judgments into welfare analysis.[8] But in terms of practical policy, this addition was merely cosmetic. It made almost no difference to the way applied economic policy was formulated.

The reason for this result was that in practice there was no way of determining what the social welfare function should include, or how a social welfare function would be determined. What this method offered was a philosophical cover cloaking the argument that policy involved normative judgments. Accepted was the principle that welfare could not be determined without a specification of those normative judgments. But there was a distinct failure to provide a workable method of adding those required judgments. This absence meant that adorning welfare economics with a social welfare function had only a negligible impact on the actual practice of applied economics. Economists had failed to develop an empirically grounded "social welfare function" that could be practically employed.[9]

From a determinately pragmatic stance, applied micro policy analysis degenerated into a type of loose cost-benefit evaluation. Many applied economists chose to interpret cost-benefit analysis as representing a move toward "scientific" policy analysis. This position held sway even though, to any observer who examines this approach carefully, the result is neither scientific nor normatively neutral.[10] What applied economists in effect used were rough and ready heuristic models devoid of any serious grounding in moral philosophy. Instead, these constructs included representative agent models that specified the costs and the benefits of various suggested policies. Accordingly, such formulations transformed into stubborn advocates for whatever policies offered benefits exceeding costs, at least as determined by those very self-same models. The problem with this from a Classical Liberal perspective is that without specifying the moral foundation underpinning the analysis, the costs and benefits remain ad hoc. Therefore, the results must be similarly ad hoc. Recommended courses were dubiously dependent on a set of unspecified moral judgments that were hidden and not part of the debate.

As economic policy became classified as a science, the inherent ambiguity attached to costs and benefits was downplayed, along with the failures of such models to capture the imprecisions attached to both of these aspects. Individuals on various sides of a policy issue used cost-benefit analysis as a strategic device that served to push forward their own preferred option. The approach devolved into something of a rhetorical tennis match in which each side would calculate costs and benefits in a way that revealed their favored outcome as being superior. Issues, such as the overall fairness of the process, the imperfection of government control mechanisms, and the value of freedom to individuals, were eliminated from formal, and eventually even from informal, analysis. All of these considerations were issues that Classical Liberals believed were central when deciding policy options. Correspondingly, on the aggregate macro level, the policy focus moved toward maximizing material output as measured by GDP, without any serious consideration given to the normative foundations of that goal.[11]

What Lerner's analysis lost was nuance and those sensibilities that could not be articulated and captured by equations or graphs. The Classical Liberal concerns about freedom, process, morality, and liberty, all of which went beyond material output (and beyond economics), were dutifully eliminated. Instead, economics arrived at policy conclusions, and proceeded to debate those conclusions, based solely on economic theory. The policy conclusions that the New Welfare Economics reached were that government was obliged to intervene in the market if society wanted to maximize social welfare. This position deviated significantly from the precept encapsulated by the more traditional laissez-faire policy. For a Classical Liberal, these differing policy conclusions might have been viewed as reflecting changes in the problems facing society. Differences therefore were not intrinsically inconsistent with Classical Liberalism. What was inconsistent was the way in which those policy conclusions were reached. These conclusions were now directly implied by economic theory. For Classical Liberals, any guiding policy principle had to be based on much more than theory alone, whereas for Classical Liberals, economists holding different policy views could both be using the same theory. The New Welfare Economics made that impossible since policy debates necessarily implied theoretical differences.

What Welfare Economics did was to transform the debate over laissez-faire policy from one focused on a wide range of issues into one focused solely on economic theory. Consequently, if you favored government managing discretionary fiscal policy to get an economy out of a recession, you were accepting Keynesian theory.

If you stood staunchly opposed to discretionary fiscal policy, you were accepting Classical theory. If you supported government intervening in the economy, you were accepting Pigovian theory. If you opposed it, you were accepting Classical theory. What was lost in this heightened, and overly simplified, ensuing debate was that only a single science could, in fact, exist. Science deals only with right or wrong as determined by scientific methodology. In contrast, policy by definition must deal with shades of grey, guided by argumentation for the sake of heaven.

For Classical Liberals, the actual policy that politicians adopted did not depend on the scientific theory economists held. The decision instead relied on how one interpreted that theory, as well as what aspects of that theory that were deemed to be most important. One could accept Keynesian theory, while arguing that governments should not run discretionary fiscal policy, because of government's basic inability to determine, and/or act, in what one considered the social interest. One could equally accept that the market did not ideally allocate resources and still not support government intervention. Doing so made perfect sense if one believed that intervention would make the apparent failure even worse. The fear engendered was that government intervention would undermine other aspects of the system—such as freedom of choice for individuals—that the standard model did not take into account. Classical Liberals, following their underlining methodology, could accept the same scientific theory, but still come to quite different positions on policy.

Welfare Economics discarded the Classical Liberal firewall, choosing instead to blend science with policy. The ensuing ideological policy battle relentlessly pitted market proponents against government planners. This conflict became almost totally entwined with the parallel methodological battle over the way in which economic policy analysis could best be conducted. In response, Classical Liberalism became exclusively identified with the struggle to defend individual liberty from the depredations of more totalitarian government tendencies, not with Classical Liberal methodology.[12]

The Chicago School Reaction: Extending the Boundaries

The economists that we have identified as composing part of the older Chicago tradition (and others who methodologically supported a Classical Liberal methodology) objected to the New Welfare Economics on methodological grounds. In drawing policy conclusions from theory, the new approach clearly violated the previously constructed firewall between theory and policy. These objections fell on deaf ears. The postwar generation of Chicago School economists deviated sharply from this older tradition. They joined with other mainstream economists in jettisoning Classical Liberal methodology. Consequently, their efforts were concentrated on saving what they saw as the core of Liberal ideology. Preserving liberty and individual choice were deemed to stand in direct opposition to the new emerging welfare economics that instead emphasized an ideology of state intervention.

In the eyes of Chicago School economists, the New Welfare Economics was fundamentally wrong. From their perspective, supporters were legitimizing this theoretical base in order to deploy a classic Trojan horse strategy. The implicit, and largely unacknowledged, purpose was judged to be an invidious attempt to gain support for what they deemed to be dangerous collectivist policies. Since policy, in this postwar view, followed directly from theory, the subsequent debate had to be shifted, even if forcibly. Within this framework, bad policy had to rest inherently on incorrect economic theory. It was at this juncture that Stigler, Friedman, and Director essentially discarded the older Knightian form of Liberalism.[13] They instead embraced a reformulated scientific foundation for economic policy, an approach consistent with that which largely defined their postwar generation of academics. This new approach was driven by the perceived, or at least the anticipated, improvements delivered by theoretical economics.[14]

An important catalyst for this scientific transformation was the Cold War.[15] This geopolitical tectonic shift appeared to threaten the deeply treasured liberal values of individual choice and personal liberty. No hypothesized coincidence could better account for the distinct break in the work of these economists after the war. Both Friedman and Stigler largely abandoned their purely empirical studies, and the more widely ranging pieces, that had cropped up in their earlier career. As late as 1943, George Stigler could write a stinging attack on the New Welfare Economics that clearly reflected the thinking of Frank Knight and the spirit of the older Chicago tradition. (Though even here it is possible to see Stigler diverting from the path carefully laid out by his teachers.)

> The new welfare economists claim that many policies can be shown (to other economists?) to be good or bad without entering a dangerous quagmire of value judgments. (Stigler 1943: 355)
>
> At the level of economic policy, then, it is totally misleading to talk of ends as individual and random; they are fundamentally collective and organized. If this conclusion be accepted, and accept it we must, the economist may properly exceed the narrow confines of economic analysis. He may cultivate a second discipline, the determination of the ends of his society particularly relevant to economic policy. This discipline might be called, following J. N. Keynes, applied ethics. (358)

As we discussed above, the New Welfare Economics, which Stigler had so gleefully attacked, could have composed an approximation of a workable framework for a science-based policy. Compatibility, however, depended on welfare economics being viewed as a loose heuristic guide, not as a blueprint for policy. This is how Classical Liberal methodology would have chosen to handle this issue, had its approach been followed. But this was not the path subsequently chosen. Theory was treated as an exact road map for applied policy. The Chicago School economists consequently felt themselves justified in appropriating, and to their minds vastly improving, the methodological underpinnings of the mainstream Harvard/MIT version of Welfare Economics. Consequently, the perceived need to put the discipline on a more scientific footing, allied with the exigencies of the Cold War, made the subsequent break with the older, Knight-based Chicago tradition, as well as the abandonment of Classical Liberal Economic methodology, nearly inevitable.

A continuation of ancestry worship in the face of their immediate objectives would have presented itself as being unproductive, if not downright perverse. They instead eschewed any restatement of the Mill-inspired Classical Liberal argument. Such an approach would have emphasized the inability of any formal framework to lead to any definitive policy conclusions. Accordingly, these proto-Chicagoans chose to adopt a contrary, but more strategic, form of argument. They insisted that their opponents supported non-valid policies since they clearly embraced the wrong scientific model. Friedman and Stigler, for instance, were then able to capture the scholastic high ground by demonstrating that compared to their opponents, they were productively cultivating a correct economic model. They were diligently constructing a framework that employed far more reliably scientific methods. More convincingly, at least as far as marketing their preferred alternative, they would insist on empirically testing any proposed theory, by employing the power of statistics to verify their arguments.[16] As a result, the Chicago School approach came to be defined by a strict regime which demanded that any proposed hypothesis be tested empirically. Stigler's longtime research associate (1958–1973), Claire Friedland, leaves no doubt as to the essential role this method played.

> George would never just write an article in which he said, "Yes anti-trust laws were mistaken, and a lot of the policies that they forbid were really efficient." This is only the result due to a good deal of work that has been done in Law and Economics over the last fifty years, since the time of Henry Simons and especially due to the analysis promoted by Aaron Director. George would never say a thing like that about anti-trust laws without attempting an empirical test, because anybody can have a theory. George said, in his 1964 Presidential Address, that you can find a theory to support any policy but the question is, "What is the evidence?" (Conversation with Claire Friedland, October 1997)

Gary Becker, on his return to his familiar South Side haunts, proceeded to subtly clarify this distinctive Chicago School approach, not only in his own research, but in his teaching as well.[17] As part of their boot camp–like training, Chicago graduate students were drilled incessantly in this one universal faith, the Chicago method. The idea of operating purely at a theoretical level never gained significant traction within this redoubt of conservative thought. During the crucial period of the 1950s and '60s, mathematical elegance failed to rule at Chicago in the same fashion that it came to dominate at other universities.

> But the Chicago tradition began to be that if you were a theorist, you had to do some empirical work. George certainly felt that. And that was what was conveyed to students. We had very few purely theoretical dissertations here. People had some theory and they went out and tested it. And a good theorist was an applied theorist who did some testing. (Conversation with Gary Becker, October 1997)

Differing Views on Empirical Work

This blending of theory with empirical testing was clearly a departure from the older Chicago tradition that remained skeptical of the conclusions provided by combining formal theory with formal empirical work. Economic science, as defined by this more circumscribed Classical perspective, was essentially deductive and clearly limited. Older economists consequently had believed that any policy counterpart was so multidimensional that even the best empirical work could not be entirely trusted.

As we mentioned in an earlier chapter, Gary Becker made this very clear in a conversation with one of us. In that conversation he highlighted Knight's skepticism about data and the fact that data would almost never sway his position. This approach to empirical evidence is very much in keeping with the Classical Liberal methodology. Stigler, Friedman and Becker all saw this as a serious failing of Knight—an unwillingness to accept that economics was an empirical science. But in our view there is an alternative interpretation that places Knight's approach in a much more favorable light. Specifically, it can also be seen as a recognition of the simplicity of the empirical tools available in the 1950s and 1960s, compared to the complexity of the empirical problems of pulling information from data, and also of the importance of philosophical and moral dimensions of policy. When empirical findings almost always match the policy positions held by advocates on one side of a policy issue or another, it is relatively easy to question the objectivity of the empirical science of the time.

The unbridgeable problem separating a Classical Liberal policy approach from its scientific successor was that, for a Classical Liberal, empirical work, even that using the latest cutting-edge tools, was almost never sufficiently conclusive for the broad policy questions that drove most debates. Different evaluations followed from an alternative framing of a given question, the proxies used, the way in which the evidence was collected and interpreted, the aspects of the question that were assumed away to make the model tractable, and many more such inevitable ambiguities. Occasionally, empirical results might provide a sufficiently strong "answer" to effectively underwrite a policy prescription accepted by all economists, but that remained the exception, rather than the rule. Inevitably, empirical results would allow for different policy interpretations. More often than not, empirical work, conducted by economists closely affiliated with a distinctive ideological policy position, would be deployed to fashion derived results into an effective rhetorical bludgeon. The subsequently promoted conclusion served to advance a distinctive objective rather than provide a beacon to shed light on the particular issue.[18]

> The interesting thing is he [George Stigler] was a great enthusiast for quantitative methods. So, it doesn't seem altogether consistent. But he certainly was. On the other hand, he knew what the answer was going to be. He just regarded it, as I say, as a way of persuading other people. (Conversation with Ronald Coase, October 1997)

Only a researcher who was consciously trying to follow the path of a Smithian impartial spectator approach could, according to this judgment, be even potentially trusted on his own to embrace anything approaching impartialness in any strict sense. Nor was there any systematic method for discovering and classifying such qualified individuals, should they actually exist. However, postwar economics had defined this issue away by subjecting policy to an assumed standard of scientific neutrality. Precisely this conundrum had encouraged Classical Liberals to create a virtual firewall between policy and theory. That adopted barrier would necessarily force any ensuing controversy to recognize the implicit sensibilities and judgments that play a central role in policy formation. In contrast, the subsequent adoption of the theoretical Harvard/MIT framework defining economic welfare policy eliminated that decisive firewall. Chicago, in a predictable response to this oppositional challenge, stitched together an alternative to this activist approach to policy. Scientifically formulated laissez-faire principles proved capable of generating Chicago's carefully enumerated, if only implicitly maintained, policy objectives.[19] In terms of these articulated views, the Chicago tradition and the Chicago School managed to sustain certain shared applied threads. Both favored a minimum of government involvement in the economy, but their methodology and argumentation supporting it differed significantly.

> It should be noted that Knight himself never accepted the kind of views that Friedman put forward in, for instance, *Capitalism and Freedom* which Knight regarded as an ultra-simplistic work that ignored many subtle problems. On the other hand, Knight was even more devastating in his analyses of social policies that differ from those advocated by Friedman. (Allen Wallis quoted in Overtveldt 2007: 61)

As the history of the 1960s unfolded, support by mainstream economists for activist government policy perceptively waned, especially as Jack Kennedy's New Frontier gave way to Lyndon Johnson's Great Society.[20] The growing experience of perceived government failure, combined with the increased strength and cultivation of

Chicago-style scientific arguments, succeeded in accelerating this transition. Viewed in terms of the approach championed by Becker and Stigler, these Chicago economists had taken accurate aim at the preferences embedded within most of the profession, namely telling consistent stories of market efficiency backed by formal statistical evidence.

As this transformation continued, driven in part by the persistence and skill with which this approach was marketed, what had been a Chicago dissent from mainstream policy views evolved into something that would blossom as a distinctly new pro-market policy mainstream. In many ways, the election of Ronald Reagan marked the fruition of this pro-market economic perspective, packaging it as a force capable of ordering (or perhaps rationalizing) US economic policy.[21] Chicago was no longer battling against, but rather helping to shape, the direction of mainstream economic thought.

Like any successful counterrevolution, this triumph carried with it an unfortunate dilemma for those at Chicago in sorting out their methodological and policy beliefs. A position once gained had to be maintained, with any attempt to re-shift the terms of debate suppressed. By choosing to embrace the consistently skeptical approach defining the Classical tradition, these triumphant counterrevolutionaries would be dangerously engaging in something akin to unilateral disarmament, at least according to the strategic vision constructed by George Stigler.[22] Resorting to this older tradition would have compelled these Chicagoans to strategically re-fashion their tactical offensive, based on rhetorical annihilation, so that the self-same strategy of contention would equally probe for the weak crevices and crevasses within their own strongly held pro-market formulations. Essentially, by agreeing to hold no unchallengeable positions, they would have had to confess to owning only the most tenuous of grasps on the way the world intrinsically worked. Doing so would encapsulate the core Classical Liberal notion of incorporating a consistent ethic that "embraced dissent." However, such a strategic deviation carried with it the obligation to willingly undercut the ideological certainty with which they operated and which had underwritten their success. Given this now embedded certainty, they declined to invite an unwelcome level of ambiguity into their tightly woven framework.

As we mentioned in Chapter 5 according to his colleague, James Kinkaid, Stigler was absolutely sure that the empirical evidence was on his side, and if it wasn't on his side, then it must have been done wrong. That belief allowed him to see economics as a science in which the theory was confirmed by the empirical evidence.

Consequently, adhering to what they maintained was no longer a relevant methodology would have obliged these battle-scarred cold warriors to quite willingly surrender the hard-won critical heights that they now commanded. Faced with this core requirement of the Liberal faith (inward skepticism), those at Chicago were not surprisingly inclined to demur. Such a decision, whether consciously made or not, would have generated no detectable qualms or measures of hesitation. Therefore, opting to disregard this traditional Classical Liberal methodological path would have failed to produce any noticeable struggle within the acolytes of the Chicago approach. There was no crisis of conscience that needed to be overcome given such conditions. Policy founded on a scientific basis was embraced just as fervently as it was by their Harvard or MIT counterparts. Though faced with an entrenched requirement if they were to compete on an equal basis within the marketplace for ideas, neither compulsion nor reluctance in its adoption played any evident role in their operational tactics.

The contrast between the Classical Liberal approach and that of the Chicago School is exemplified by George Stigler, who jumped effortlessly from the abstract world of the blackboard to that of everyday life. Like some sort of latter-day Hegelian, Stigler seemed to have as his fixed revelatory pole the assumption that "Das Denken ist das Sein." His abiding interest continued to be in the development of a general theory that could then be universally applied. Specifics and particulars consistently failed to catch his attention or sustain his interest. Delineated data, by his definition, could serve only as a springboard for further generalities.[23] Otherwise, such information acted more as a distraction than as a tool furthering useful and extended insight. It was similarities, rather than differences, that gained prominence in his work.[24]

In contrast, pragmatic concerns, rather than abstract theory, deliberately underlay the policy views of Classical economists.[25] The weight of past examples, and of available evidence, proved decisive for most Classical Liberals when relegating government intervention to the status of a policy of last resort.[26] But such beliefs, no matter how intensely they might be held, were not intended to shut down or hinder ongoing debate. In practice, these economists, for the most part, explicitly attempted to adhere to this prescribed level of conduct. They recognized that their policy principles reflected an inherent leaning against state action, but, given their interpretation concerning the intrinsic working of the state and of its policy, they felt that bias appropriate. There existed an undeniable obligation to counter the attempts of vested interests to employ the state to advance their own ends.

To counter this anti-government policy structure, given their laissez-faire foundations, the inherited Millian tradition not only tolerated but actively encouraged dissent and discussion.[27] That level of free-flowing discussion served almost as a requirement when attempting to reach anything resembling a widely held agreement.[28] It was that modest "handy rule of practice" approach to economic policy that was abandoned by the economics profession in the rush for scientific precision.

7

Roads Not Taken

THE STILLBORN VIRGINIA SCHOOL OF ECONOMICS

The map of the Chicago School story was unfolded in previous chapters with Chicago capturing the position of the Classical Liberal standard bearer. The narration need not have followed that given storyline. Austrian economics, Public Choice economics, Coasian institutionalist economics, and others competed for that same Classical Liberal mantle in the 1950s, '60s, and '70s. Had the stars aligned in a slightly different fashion, one, or perhaps a combination, of these groups could have become the Classical Liberal standard bearer.

One viable alternative to Chicago was what became known as the Virginia School. In the 1950s and early '60s many of these alternative Classical Liberal approaches were being simultaneously explored at the University of Virginia. For a few years in the 1960s, economists actually talked about a Virginia School in much the same way that they referred to a Chicago School. However, by the end of the 1960s the Virginia School was no more, and its two most likely leaders, Ronald Coase and Jim Buchanan, had both departed.[1]

In this chapter we discuss this stillbirth of the Virginia School by focusing on two of the approaches developed in Virginia at that time. We label one the Coasian institutionalist approach (named after Ronald Coase). We see this particular methodology as a clear attempt to maintain the sort of Classical Liberal thought fashioned in an earlier period by Frank Knight. The other, which we denote as the Buchanan political economy approach (named for James Buchanan), also had a stronger commitment to Classical Liberal methodology than did the Stigler/Friedman/Director version rapidly spreading within the Chicago campus.

Both Coase and Buchanan were at Virginia in 1960. Both of these insightful economists would later win Nobel Prizes for their work. However, neither one would become a recognized Classical Liberal standard bearer. Instead, their combined work was seldom considered to be part of any broader (emerging) mainstream approach that differed significantly in terms of methodology. Consequently, their work would create only limited enclaves of economists who carried on their tradition. Coase would manage to gain disciples (of varying fidelity) within the fields of Law and Economics, as well as Institutional Economics. Buchanan would have his greatest impact in the formation and growth of Public Choice theory. Their work would remain firmly on the periphery, and their research would never be entirely integrated within the mainstream of economics. While just about every well-educated layman would come to recognize the term "Chicago Economics," only a few would know of Coase, Buchanan, or their followers. Knowledge of the Virginia School would be relegated to the ranks of the historians of economic thought. Only a miniscule subset of today's economists would even know that there had ever been a distinct Virginia School.[2]

The Coase Dictum versus the Coase Theorem

What I showed in that article, as I thought, was that in a regime of zero transaction costs—an assumption of standard economic theory—negotiations between the parties would lead to those arrangements being made which would maximize wealth, and this irrespective of the initial assignment of rights. This is the infamous Coase Theorem, named and formulated by George

Stigler, although it is based on work of mine. Stigler argues that the Coase Theorem follows from the standard assumptions of economic theory. Its logic cannot be questioned, only its domain. I do not disagree with Stigler. However, I tend to regard the Coase Theorem as a stepping stone on the way to an analysis of an economy with positive transaction costs. The significance to me of the Coase Theorem is that it undermines the Pigouvian system. Since standard economic theory assumes transaction costs to be zero, the Coase Theorem demonstrates that the Pigouvian solutions are unnecessary in these circumstances. Of course, it does not imply, when transaction costs are positive, that government actions (such as government operation, regulation or taxation, including subsidies) could not produce a better result than relying on negotiations between individuals in the market. Whether this would be so could be discovered not by studying imaginary governments but what real governments actually do. My conclusion: Let us study the world of positive transaction costs. (Coase 1994: 10–11)

Ronald Coase's methodological approach to economics is in many ways a continuation of the Classical Liberal approach to designing policy. It relies on judgment, not models. Coase tried to construct an economics that was institutional and empirically based, but in a distinctly informal fashion. His framework does not make claims to reflecting scientific values that can be used to direct or formulate policy. The approach is designed to provide policy guidelines, not policy theorems. His structured system is not sufficiently known or comprehended, at least in any usable detail, to the great majority of the profession.[3] What is most widely known among economists is limited to the Stigler-authored Coase theorem. Many still believe that Coase's theoretical argument serves as a foundation for a laissez-faire approach to policy associated with that famous Theorem. This is exactly what it does not do.

How the Coase Theorem became Coase's legacy is the story we investigate here. In particular, there is an underlying conflict between the rational economic behavior model advanced by the Chicago School (particularly Stigler, Becker, and Director) and the older and more conditional approach championed by Classical Liberal stalwarts such as Frank Knight. Coase was a firm adherent of the latter, consciously drawing back from basing policy on models dependent on rational decision making.

> When you say it is un-Chicago, you mean that it is an unmodern Chicago View. Because Frank Knight was at Chicago, and I was brought up more on Knight than I was on any of the others. And my views were quite consistent with what he says. They're not consistent with what George Stigler, Gary Becker and Richard Posner say. Posner condemns me because I don't think people maximize utility. (Coase 1997: 3)

Coase's central insight is a simple one. Theorizing about the market using models that do not contain transaction costs fails to lead to any specific policy guidelines about whether the market is the best way to allocate goods. The reason is that market transaction costs, such as those of pricing, or setting up and enforcing property rights, play central roles in policy decisions. Consequently models, or any reasoning without explicit integration of transaction costs, provide no useful or direct policy guidance. What Coase (1937, 1960) pointed out in his two best-known works, "The Theory of the Firm" and "The Problem of Social Cost," was that economists were making inappropriate and unwarranted jumps from abstract models to policy recommendations, especially in regard to what coalesced, in the postwar era, as welfare economics.

> What is studied is a system which lives in the minds of economists but not on earth. I have called the result "blackboard economics." The firm and the market appear by name but they lack any substance. The firm in mainstream economic theory has often been described as a "black box." And so it is. This is very extraordinary given that most resources in a modern economic system are employed within firms, with how these resources are used dependent on administrative decisions and not directly on the operation of a market. (Coase 1994: 5–6)

The need to take transaction costs into account, when making policy decisions, formed the underpinnings of what might be labeled the "Coase Dictum." To point this out, his strategy was to conjure up a theoretical world lacking any remnant of a transaction cost.[4] In such a world, firms would not exist, and the market could solve all coordination problems costlessly. The goal was not to argue that such a model was relevant. Rather, the goal was to show the importance of transaction costs, and to undercut the use of models that did not include them. The intention was to direct a conceptual spotlight on the issue of inherent transaction costs. In this more practical approach, institutions providing the framework for exchange become a vital factor in analyzing specific cases. "If we move from a regime of zero transaction costs to one of positive transaction costs, what becomes immediately clear is the crucial importance of the legal system in this new world" (Coase 1994: 11). Policies, under this pragmatic imprimatur, only proceed from what, arguably, is the state of the world rather than from what any analyst insists that state should be. In emphasizing this, Coase lines up consistently with Knight's sense of Classical Liberalism.

> There are several reasons why the approximate character of theoretical economic laws and their inapplicability without empirical correction to real situations should be especially emphasized as compared, for instance, with those of mechanics.... The limitations of the results have not always been clear, and theorists themselves as well as writers in practical economics and statecraft have carelessly used them without regard for the corrections necessary to make them fit concrete facts. Policies must fail, and fail disastrously, which are based on perpetual motion reasoning without the recognition that it is such. (Knight 1972: 11)

These Coase-styled guidelines, if followed, clearly imply that economic theory has nothing directly to say about whether the government should or should not disrupt market mechanisms. Instead, Coase supported an approach essentially incorporating a fundamental aspect of Classical Liberal thinking, at least as filtered through such economists as Frank Knight. The approach carries theory to its logical conclusions, and carefully recognizes the assumptions that are necessary for the theory to hold. Theory is not applied directly to policy recommendations, unless the assumptions fit. Coase's argument, sustained by case studies, examples, and critical logic, contended that assuming away transaction costs excluded any "blackboard economics" model, no matter how intricately constructed, from being directly relevant to actual policy discussions. Blackboard economics remained incapable of resolving whether government intervention would make a positive difference given a specified set of circumstances. (Concrete market problems persistently fail to exist in the abstract or in a generalizable fashion.) Government administrators must face irritatingly time- and place-specific problems, not average or general ones. Decision making consequently had to be founded on available evidence, rather than be theoretically based. "I wrote that 'direct government regulation will not necessarily give better results than leaving the problem to be solved by the market or the firm. But equally there is no reason why, on occasion, such governmental administrative regulation should not lead to an improvement in economic efficiency'" (Coase 1994: 62). In principle, Coase's theoretical approach left room for too little, as well as too much, government. Both logic and relevant evidence insisted on such stipulations. This perspective closely followed the Classical tradition. Theory and models were used as aids to judgment, not definitive guides to policy. But, like many Classical Liberals, when applying theory (looking at actual case studies), Coase felt that in practice, government intervention had generally gone astray, creating more problems than it solved.[5] Thus his policy support tended to flow strongly toward supporting laissez-faire policy guidelines. He fully agreed that this judgment did not follow from scientific economic theory, but rather from carefully constructed case studies.[6]

What a policy analyst could not do was to use theory as a direct guide to policy, which is what the Pigovian and Lernerian policy framework suggested. Thus, in many ways, Coase was inspired, primarily negatively, by Pigou's work. His argument was that it could not be used in the way that it was being employed.[7] For example, he concluded that the standard policy framework was inappropriately generalized with regard to its analysis of public goods. A typical textbook approach would inevitably pinpoint the example of a lighthouse as representing an unarguable public good. The provision by default was left to government agencies since lighthouses by definition existed as both a non-exclusive and a non-rival good. This conclusion was based on purely deductive reasoning, extending back to John Stuart Mill and finding its place in the postwar textbooks devised by Samuelson and others.[8] Coase demonstrated that private suppliers historically had provided this service, detailing the precise conditions for their occurrence within the British Isles. Whether private or public provision of lighthouses made more sense followed not from public goods theory, but from careful institutional study.[9] An economist had to get his or her hands dirty and dig through actual records.

An analogous example of that violation was an economist's tendency to use a direct and unambiguous application of the marginal cost curve when discussing policies involving externalities.[10] The prevailing Pigouvian model, at least as then understood within the profession, not only failed to recognize transaction costs, but then implicitly analyzed the problem as if transaction costs were simply absent.[11] Coase argued that the application of such a model was simply misguided. He persistently maintained that if one assumed the total absence of transaction costs, then one should expect any externality to be effectively handled by inter-agent agreements. If that was indeed the brunt of the case, it followed that any discussion concerning government policy was moot. The problem could be resolved by the market, or by individual agreement, since contracting was essentially costless. Consequently, if there are no transaction costs, then there is no relevant need for government intervention, or for that matter most any aspect of government. Externality problems would be simply internalized by private negotiation.[12]

Of course, there are, undeniably, transaction costs. The point that Coase was trying to make with his argument was that in any policy discussion, transaction costs and how the policy would work in real-world institutions have to be a central part of the discussion. There is no a priori justification for assuming that transaction costs never dominate, or that a model of perfectly competitive markets approximates an actual economy. It might be that the best way to deal with such problems is through the market, by changes in property rights, or alternatively through changes in government intervention. It would all depend on the particular question as well as the specifics of each case. There could be no general answer. So what Coase's work was designed to show was what might be called the Coase Dictum: Economic models that do not include all relevant aspects of the problem do not directly lead to any applicable policy results. Instead, relevant models provide frameworks, which when combined with institutional knowledge, can deliver reasonable solutions to specific problems. This dictum embodies the Classical Liberal approach in which policy is removed from theoretical debate and placed in a pragmatic, real-world framework. In policy work, all aspects of the question must be taken into account when performing any fruitful analysis. No general answer can be achieved without a careful examination of how the model matches the real world.[13]

The "Discovery" of the Coase Theorem

The Coase Dictum has remained in many ways invisible to the profession. Instead, most economists associate Coase not with his own understanding of the problem, but with the formalistic Coase Theorem, which is George Stigler's ingenuous interpretation of Coase's work. In his intellectual autobiography (1988), Stigler described the "Eureka" moment when the Coase Theorem dawned on him.[14] It was in 1960 at a dinner at the home of Aaron Director.[15] Stigler weaves a nearly mythical story in which Coase single-handedly challenged and changed the minds of a cohort of Chicago's finest economists.

According to his own reports, following vigorous argumentation, the light went off for Stigler some time during that dinner, and he recognized the burnished truth of the Coase Theorem. Stigler interpreted this as proving simply that theoretically, once we have eliminated transaction costs, government intervention in the economy is unnecessary since the market is perfectly capable of solving the problem. Thus, Stigler could use Coase's argument to underpin his theoretical support for the market over government intervention by emasculating the Pigouvian-style externality problem.

The use of the Coase Theorem to support a narrow market approach serves as a useful demonstration of the argumentation style that formed an essential part of the Chicago School. The vision implemented is a policy-based agenda structurally anchored by an unimpeachable and universal system of markets and decision making. (Actors are defined as rational agents performing within a competitive market topography.) The emphasis is on the tactical advantage to be gained by framing the argument in this manner, rather than on any potential explanatory benefits afforded by such conceptualized responses.

The Coase Theorem, as stipulated by George Stigler, clearly deviates from Coase's intentions because it directly violates the Coase Dictum.[16] With the Coase Theorem, transaction costs have been removed from the central role of the argument. The intention instead is to facilitate Stigler's attempt to buttress his own particular, critical vision of the relevance of price theory to policy, his particular conception of how markets operate.[17] Consequently, the way in which the Coase Theorem subsequently evolved into a key building block in policy debates is instructive in reflecting the manner and extent to which the Chicago School managed to sharply deviate from and undermine Classical Liberalism. These competing objectives help explain why an alternative Coasian version of Classical Liberalism did not flourish.[18]

Stigler seized upon this Coasian argument, which persuasively undercuts the stark Pigouvian approach of moving directly from theory to policy. He summarized selected insights from a very extended article by transforming them into a slogan-length theorem. His newly hatched catechism of faith transformed a Classical Liberal methodological argument into one that followed the modernist instinct to move inevitably from theory to policy. The striking dif-

ference with the rejected Pigouvian stylized method was that Stigler's reformulation, which he neatly labeled the Coase Theorem,[19]
effectively buttressed a policy that commanded his a priori support.
Ideologically, he was insistent on leaving the market alone, since
the market left alone would achieve an efficient outcome.[20] Thus,
instead of interpreting the argument as Coase did, focusing on the
need to incorporate transaction costs when formulating policies,
Stigler chose to interpret the article's arguments as providing a
framework that would demolish the policy problem posed by externalities. He transformed Coase's intentions into a theoretical
support that buttressed free markets.[21] For Stigler, his reframing of
Coase demonstrated the preordained conclusion that markets were
capable of taking care of such troublesome issues. In Stigler's version of the Coase Theorem, the market mechanism was essentially
self-correcting.

Using his carefully tailored version of Coase's work, Stigler constructed an argument to serve as a bulwark against government intervention. Coase's insight, now reborn in the guise of the abstract
and indisputable Coase's Theorem, sported an implacable insistence
that in the absence of transaction costs, externalities should never
be considered as posing a problem. The Pigouvian externality, hith-
erto a thorn in the side of market fundamentalism, could now be
effectively extricated. Price theory would be able to provide both a
necessary and sufficient reason for supporting an unconstrained
laissez-faire policy. While technically (and nearly by definition) true,
the Coase Theorem was simultaneously irrelevant for any direct
policy application. The theorem unfortunately implied, though it
was often not noted, that in the absence of those same transaction
costs, there would be no need for markets and certainly not firms.
People would just freely negotiate all agreements.[22]

Advocates of Pigouvian welfare economics had a difficult time
challenging Stigler's creation and its tacit policies, because in order
to do so they would have to be willing to backtrack on the foundations of their own policy analysis.[23] Essentially, these academics
would need to confess the errors of their own proverbial transgressions. These critics would be obliged to admit that the Pigouvian

framework that they had embraced as a direct policy guide equally failed to propose any direct policy application. To effectively defeat the Chicago position, they had to be willing to surrender and discard their own.

Stigler's invention of a Coasian theorem inevitably became highly contentious, given its role as a rhetorical ploy. Stigler habitually courted such controversy.[24] However, when viewed from a more practical perspective, both market and government solutions inevitably involve a set of specific attributes and attached conditions. Unfortunately, in this case, theory triumphed over available evidence. Instead of promoting the reasonable Coasian position, that real-world decisions had to be made on a case-by-case basis, this "through the looking glass" transformation offered the seemingly more tantalizing gift of delivering policy absolutes. Under Stigler's skillful manipulation, Coase's Classical Liberal position transcended any imposed constraints, offering instead a rhetorical basis supporting an array of market mechanisms. Mainstream models could only hope to counter this torrent of logic by cannibalizing its own underpinnings. Would-be opponents proved reluctant to surrender the comfort of their own scientifically bolstered version of modernism.

James Buchanan, Political Economy, and Public Choice

There are subtle but important differences between the allocationist-maximization and the catallactic-coordination paradigm in terms of the implications for normative evaluation of institutions. In particular the evaluation of the market order may depend critically on which of these partially conflicting paradigms remains dominant in one's stylized vision. To the allocationist the market is efficient if it works. His test of the market becomes the comparison with the abstract ideal defined in is logic. To the catallactist the market coordinates the separate activities of self-seeking persons without the necessity of detailed political directions. The test of the market is the comparison with its institutional alternative, politicized decision making. (Buchanan in Breit and Spencer 1997: 169–170)

Another Virginia School economist whose work also could have served as a standard bearer for Classical Liberalism was James Buchanan. Like George Stigler, Buchanan was a star student of Frank Knight. He graduated from the University of Chicago at just about the time the Chicago School was forming.[25] Based on his agreement with Knight's policy views, he would have seemed to be a natural, practically founding, member. But he is usually not associated with the Chicago School. We suspect that an important reason why is that he did not share the theoretical vision of the economy that is delineated by the Chicago School's Coase Theorem. Nor was he entirely at ease with the mind-set that led to avowed support. He was much more comfortable with the Coase Dictum than he would ever be with the Coase Theorem, meaning, in effect, much more at home with Coase's methodology than with that of Stigler. We can hypothesize that, had he and Coase collaborated and blended their approaches into one, it is likely that they would have arrived at a methodological approach more closely resembling Classical Liberal methodology than Chicago managed to accomplish. But this never occurred. Coase soon left Virginia for Chicago, and it appears that he did not interact all that much with Buchanan in the ensuing years.

In 1984, however, Buchanan, in an article entitled "Rights, Efficiency and Exchange: The Irrelevance of Transaction Costs," made it clear that he found Stigler's interpretation of Coase's work unacceptable. In that article Buchanan argued that a social optimum, which Stigler's Coase Theorem implicitly accepted, could not be objectively defined. Thus, it was incorrect to frame the policy question as a situation in which externalities exist, since that starting point could not be discovered. It remains impossible to argue that such an efficient allocation exists. All decisions of this type were subjective, reflective of the parties to the transaction. Given the assumptions of the model, all the realized trades, whether under conditions of perfect competition or not, must be considered optimal, given the prevailing institutional framework. Assuming full rationality, no transactions costs, and perfect knowledge, that which is, is optimal, given the prevailing institutional structure. Of course, the actual institutional structure might not be optimal, but that raises different questions than arise when focusing on the transaction costs of exchange. Thus, as was the case with Coase, Buchanan recognized that Coase's policy analysis needed to be supplemented by an analysis of the relevant existing institutional structure and the costs of changing that structure.

Buchanan's Political Economy

> Buchanan was frankly skeptical of the capacity of majorities to develop policies that would redress their own moral, cultural, or economic failings. "A shift of activity from the market sector cannot in itself change the nature of man," he and Tullock concluded. "The man who spends his time at the television set or in his automobile in private life," they added drily, "is not the man who is likely to vote for more taxes to finance libraries, concerts, and schools." (Burgin 2012: 18)

Buchanan is best known for his work on Public Choice economics. Public Choice economics is an approach to economic policy that assumes government policy reflects the selfish goals of politicians and voters, not attempts to accomplish good through the instrumentality of government.[26] While this is consistent with the Chicago policy view or approach, it highlights different problems, providing a different reason to support markets.[27] Specifically, Buchanan's opposition to activist government policy was based less on the belief that the market would get it right and more on a belief that government would get it wrong. In Buchanan's view, government would inevitably be used by vested interests to further their narrow goals rather than achieve what most would consider society's desired objectives.[28] Put another way, Buchanan believed that government failure was more likely to occur than market failure. His

Public Choice School was meant to provide a theoretical proof for why government failure was inevitable.

This is quite different from the Chicago School attempt at underwriting market superiority as demonstrated by the Coase Theorem. The formal Coase Theorem support for the market was based on Stigler's interpretation of economic theory and empirical evidence. He accepted as an empirically determined fact the belief that the market would solve problems on its own better than would government instrumentalities.[29] In contrast, the Public Choice support for the market was based on a formal political choice model that held that politics would undermine government solutions to problems. Buchanan argued that markets might fail, but that, if people are rational, government policies will be even more likely to fail.

As we have seen in earlier chapters, this Public Choice concern about government failure has a long history in economics, going back to Adam Smith's argument that "the proposal of any new law or regulation of commerce which comes from this order ought always to be listened to with great precaution, and ought never to be adopted till after having been long and carefully examined, not only with the most scrupulous, but with the most suspicious attention" (Smith 1776/1961: 278). In that view, Buchanan was in sympathy with a key element of the reasoning underlying the Classical Liberal laissez-faire policy approach. Where Buchanan differed from other Classical Liberals is that he wanted to incorporate that general insight into formal economic theory, whereas Classical Liberal methodology would leave it differentiated. For Classical Liberals, since policy did not follow from theory, there was no need to have a fully developed theory to guide policy.[30]

From a Classical Liberal perspective, Buchanan's formal Public Choice justification for applying a strict rational choice model to politics is weak. It puts too much emphasis on strict rationality and selfishness. Yes, people may be somewhat rational (economically defined), but they are not fully rational. Moreover, they are not totally selfish, if this means entirely self-concerned. People have both social and private goals. One of the goals of policy could be to encourage individuals to focus on social rather than private goals. The very fact that people vote undermines the pure Public Choice model. Since the probabilities of influencing outcomes with one's vote are infinitesimally small, strictly self-concerned rational individuals would not vote. Thus, Buchanan's formal Public Choice theory of government failure was quite different from that of the more informal Classical Liberal argument. The Classical Liberal argument was a judgment based on case studies of how government intervention had worked in the past. The conclusion depended on a belief that people embodied complex blends of self-interest and social concerns, leading to different actions at different times. A key policy goal was therefore to design institutions to bring out the best in people for those aspects of policy that were most central. These incentive structures composed the constitutional rules under which society operated. Success required people to think about policy from an impartial spectator's position.

When government became more closely involved in the direct working of the economy, rather than in setting broad guidelines, there was little hope that people's more social nature would predominate. The unavoidable result would be policy guided by self-interest alone. In that case, the result of government intervention would be government failure.

The Classical Liberal argument forcefully directed economists to look at whether it was possible to design institutions to bring out the best in humans, an argument that individuals on all sides of the partisan debate could accept. In contrast, the Public Choice argument made the analysis into a partisan political issue. Consequently, Public Choice seemed to offer an ideological argument against government intervention. Expressed alternatively, the Classical Liberal argument was about the nature of government involvement, dependent on designing institutions so that people's social nature guided the resulting structure of those institutions. The checks and balances provided by democracy and competition together were fundamental to policy formation and implementation. Laissez-faire was meant to protect government from partisanship in its central rule-making role, not to undermine it. Unfortunately, the Public Choice argument was far less nuanced. The approach was commonly interpreted by economists as an argument that any government involvement would necessarily fail.

The Chicago School view and the Buchanan view are not necessarily inconsistent. Concerns focused on government failure were part of the Chicago School mantra. But they were not part of Chicago's formal theoretical concerns since the formal Chicago economic model did not necessarily include an analysis of the politics of policy implementation.[31] Buchanan differed from Chicago in that he attempted to formally expand rational choice analysis within this government context. The Chicago agenda did not need to do so since its theory held that government intervention was not necessary. An unfettered, free market was perfectly capable of solving problems on its own.[32]

The general insights of both Buchanan and Chicago were somewhat consistent with Classical Liberal insights. They emphasized issues that had to be considered when undertaking policy. They differed from the Classical Liberal approach in their attempts to develop formal models to prove those insights. Classical Liberalism had no need to develop such formal models since policy did not follow from theoretical models.[33] Had Buchanan stayed with an informal presentation focused on the problems with government intervention, he would have remained much more consistent with Classical Liberalism. But had he done it informally, Public Choice economic theory would likely never have thrived in the way that it did. The tenor of the times eschewed informally applied policy arguments. The modernist spirit forced those advocating any such concern to build that concern into a formal model from which direct policy conclusions could be drawn. That requirement is exactly what Public Choice analysis tackled.

Buchanan's formal development of Public Choice reflected his extensive collaboration with Gordon Tullock, a highly creative polymath lawyer, who took pride in pointing out that, although he worked successfully in economics, he had failed to take a single course in economics. Whereas Buchanan was philosophical and cautious about drawing policy implications from abstract models, Tullock was less so. Thus, while Buchanan was comfortable arguing within an *argumentation for the sake of heaven* framework, Tullock fit much more the Laughlin model of adopting a "win at all costs" approach to argumentation.[34] This meant that, like Stigler, Tullock was willing to make strong assumptions in models and extend those models to policy if it fit the point he was trying to achieve. Public Choice theory reflected Tullock's sensibilities and approach as much as or even more so than it did Buchanan's. Specifically, it claimed that, theoretically, Public Choice economics demonstrated that government policy would not work for society's benefit since rational individuals would vote their selfish interests, not that of society.

This Public Choice movement in economics has remained strong, even though it has never really captured the mainstream. Today it is seen as a small but distinct field within economics. Public Choice economics has had a larger impact on political science, helping to create a rational choice theory in that field. Formal Public Choice economics does not lie easily within a Classical Liberal tradition, but instead fits more easily within a more neoclassical tradition of modeling. The framework reflects the postwar preference for an approach that contains strong assumptions and a model empirically fitted to reality. As Peter Boettke (1987) notes, this in large part reflects Buchanan's coauthor, Gordon Tullock. Tullock's perspective was much more accepting of neoclassical simplifications than was the Classical Liberal tradition. Buchanan, then, wearing his Classical Liberal hat, wanted to model politics as exchanges in which individuals had varied goals, including both social and selfish objectives. Tullock, in contrast, wanted to model politics strictly in terms of self-interest. Buchanan (1986) notes that this created a tension in Public Choice theory that went unresolved, and that remains so today.

Could It Have Been Different?

A blending of Coase's and Buchanan's approaches to economic policy would have been much closer to the Classical Liberal methodological tradition than that offered by the Chicago School. But the approach proposed by Coase or Buchanan did not catch on. A likely reason for this lack of professional enthusiasm was their insistence on maintaining aspects of a Classical Liberal methodological approach. Coase's work became well known only when it was reformulated by Stigler into the Coase Theorem, and in this fashion integrated into economic theory. However, this bit of packaging essentially stripped Coase's work of its institutional and contextual methodological approach.[35] Buchanan's work only became well known when it was translated into a formal Public Choice framework that could be integrated into formal theory. Doing so, however, forced it to deviate from Classical Liberal methodology.[36]

The tenor of the modernist times of that era was not conducive to a Classical Liberal methodological approach. The postwar period was a time when the economics profession implicitly dictated that policy answers were to be found in formal scientific theory. Any group that did not agree with that conviction was ejected from mainstream economics. Within such an institutional ecostructure, one that encouraged drawing policy from economic theory, the evolution of the Chicago tradition, which previously had been tied to Classical Liberalism, became obsolete. Only those approaches that would willingly jettison Classical Liberal methodology remained viable.

8

The Classical Liberal "Argumentation for the Sake of Heaven" Alternative

What significance does the history described in the previous chapters hold for economics today? In our view, it means that there was a more desirable, alternative path that the economics profession could have followed. Instead of seeing economics as having evolved from Smith to Ricardo, Walras, Samuelson, and Friedman, it could have chosen a path with a much different emphasis, namely one meandering from Smith, through to Mill, Marshall, Viner, Keynes, Coase, Buchanan, and Amartya Sen (whose work we will discuss in the next chapter). Modern policy analysis of welfare economics, as embodied in the thinking defined by Samuelson and Friedman, would be seen as an important side path that, while clearing up some issues in our understanding of allocative efficiency, led the economics profession astray in how normative issues are best integrated into policy analysis.[1] This misdirection was due to a flawed methodology that attempted to draw policy conclusions directly from economic theory, rather than maintaining the Classical economic firewall between them. Only in the twenty-first century, with the development of complexity theory and behavioral economics, did a viable alternative implying something of a return to its Classical roots present itself to the economics profession.

The Arts and Crafts Path versus the Science Path

The key difference between these specified paths lies in the underlying methodology employed by economists. The path that mainstream economics (the MIT–Samuelson variety), as well as that prevailing in Chicago (the Friedman variant), followed can best be defined as a "science" path. Most of what economists do is characterized as economic science. The alternative approach provided by Classical Liberal methodology emphasized an "art and craft" path. In fact, this alternative interprets most of what economists do as an art and craft that is informed, but not determined, by science.

Both paths see economics as involving both art and science, but the relevant emphasis is quite different, especially when it relates to how economic theory is treated. In the science path, theory is highly important, with formal empirical work providing an accurate judgment of which theory is correct. Policy follows from theory, so theory is treated with the greatest respect because of its scientific empirical foundations. In the art and craft path, theory receives far less respect. The limitations of scientific empirical work are accordingly given more focus, which means that the limitations facing scientific solutions to policy problems attract additional attention. The necessity that policy analyses include non-scientifically based judgments on normative values is explicitly recognized. These in turn are intertwined with relevant sensibilities and non-scientific factors. Such aspects of policy analysis are unlikely to be usefully debated by employing the exacting methodological rules of science.

The difference between the two views is usefully revealed by two alternative interpretations of a joke that economists sometimes tell as a way of explaining why theory is so important. In it, a physicist, an engineer, and an economist are given a stopwatch, a string, and a ball. They are then told that the person who can most accurately measure the height of a building will get into a Scientific Hall of Fame. The physicist ties the ball to the string, hangs it down from the roof and (using the stopwatch) proceeds to calculate the length of time it takes the pendulum to swing from side to side. From that information, he estimates the height of the building. Next, the engineer takes the ball and drops it off the top of the building. He then uses the stopwatch to determine how long the ball takes to fall, in this way estimating the height of the building. The punchline of the joke is that the economist then comes in and chooses to ignore both options. Instead, he takes the stopwatch, string, and ball to the guard in the building and trades them for the blueprints of the building. He then reads the height of the building from the blueprints, and by doing so wins his place in the Scientific Hall of Fame. Conclusion: theory trumps practice.

The joke captures the way in which the "scientific" path values economic theory as occupying the central role in determining policy.[2] Theory acts as an economist's blueprint. This framework forms an absolute requirement for guiding policy. Thus, a thorough knowledge of theory, in all its intricacies, is an indisputable necessity for any economist focused on policy formation and evaluation. That specific vision guides economic training, one that stresses the need to provide students with technical training in reading theoretical blueprints and in empirically testing theories. Students receive little formal training in the practical craft of economic policy.

There is, however, an alternative punchline to this joke. In this version, when the building was constructed, the builders hit numerous unforeseen problems and were forced to make adjustments. They consistently deviated from the blueprints. They did whatever worked instead. When they did so, they failed to specify those adjustments in the blueprints on file. Consequently, the economist doesn't end up winning a place in the Hall of Fame, because the blueprints fail to match the actual building. The previously treasured scientific artifact turns out to be a poor guide to the building's actual state. This alternative punchline captures the essence of the Classical Liberal and the modern complexity view of economic theory (Colander and Kupers 2014).

The described alternative perspective sees the economy as having evolved from the bottom up, without a blueprint, in a highly complex evolutionary way.[3] Therefore, the hope of finding a definitive set of blueprints to guide policy is essentially impossible, if not foolhardy. For a Classical Liberal economist, theoretical blueprints might sometimes be helpful, but they do not serve as a plausible substitute for having direct knowledge of the institutional structure of an economy and a set of tools that can plausibly guide and help interpret that knowledge. Policy is a craft that goes far beyond simple blueprint reading.

To show the difference between the two paths, consider the way in which economists talk about general equilibrium. Captured by the science path, general equilibrium proofs of existence, stability, uniqueness, and optimality are extremely important when thinking about the economy and economic policy.[4] As Franklin Fisher put it, "It is not an understatement to say that they (the results of GE theory) are the underpinning of Western capitalism" (Fisher 2011: 35). The current mainstream methodological view of economics agrees completely with that sentiment. Consequently, the training of economists is necessarily focused on providing graduate students with the ability to manipulate science—to develop and empirically test theories.

The Classical art and craft view employs a quite different attitude to the role of theory. It understands theory to be a useful organizing tool, but not one capable of delivering a set of precise blueprints. This approach holds that Western capitalism would exist regardless of any results provided by general equilibrium theory.[5] Whether general equilibrium theorists can or cannot prove existence (they can do so under certain conditions) or stability (they cannot prove stability in a wide range of conditions) is irrelevant to the functioning of Western capitalism. The economy would continue to exist and exhibit any requisite levels of stability or corresponding lack of stability regardless of any pertinent general equilibrium proofs. To understand the economy in a way that might prove productive for policy formulation, one must have close interaction with the economy itself. This understanding goes far beyond an abstract theoretical level; it is an understanding that can only be gained by experience.[6] Hence, the appropriate training of economists versed in the art and craft approach requires much more than just instruction and experience in developing and testing relevant theories.[7]

How Classical Methodology Was Lost by Friedman

Since the two paths differ in terms of methodology, in the remainder of this chapter we look specifically at Milton Friedman's "The Methodology of Positive Economics" (1953/1966). This article encouraged the profession to ultimately jettison and disregard Classical Liberal methodology. Friedman's tract subsequently became the best known discussion of economic methodology by any economist (whether deserved or not).[8] It still guides the thinking, at least implicitly, of most economists on methodological matters, despite the severe criticisms leveled against it by philosophers and methodologists alike.[9] Our goal in examining this work is to display the way in which, almost unwittingly, Friedman abandoned the Classical Liberal art and craft methodology and substituted his own brand of positivist "science" methodology in its place.[10]

The abandonment occurs when Friedman specifically states that advances in positive economics can resolve numerous policy debates, such as whether there should be a minimum wage, or whether regulation makes sense (a list of policy debates that Friedman (1953/1966) says can be "extended infinitely"). He further argues that if his "judgment is valid, it means that a consensus on 'correct' economic policy depends much less on the progress of normative economics proper than on the progress of a positive economics in yielding conclusions that are, and deserve to be, widely accepted" (6).

Friedman then admits that his "judgment that the major differences about economic policy in the Western world are of this kind is itself a 'positive' statement to be accepted or rejected on the basis of empirical evidence" (Friedman 1953/1966). It has now been more than sixty years since Friedman wrote his still influential article. In our estimation (and, we believe, in that of most fair-minded observers), it is clear that advances in positive economics have not resolved the major policy issues facing society. The same debates about regulation, minimum wage, and tariffs exist now as existed much earlier. This status continues despite much extended study, as well as the advancement in both empirical methods and analytic tools. Contrary to Friedman's hypothesis, that advancement has not led to any lasting agreement about policy. At different times, different policy positions have gained favor, but there has been no overall scientific finding, either in theory or in scientific empirical studies, that has definitively answered such policy questions. There likely never will be; there are just too many dimensions to the problems to conclusively answer most policy questions. The theory and empirical evidence may be suggestive, but suggestive is quite different than definitive. Consequently, the empirical hypothesis upon which Friedman claimed his argument should be judged (whether advances in positive economics will resolve policy differences) has shown that Friedman was wrong. Advances in positive economics have failed to resolve most policy differences.

Resolving Policy Debates through Argumentation for the Sake of Heaven

If advances in positive economics fail to resolve such policy differences, how are policy differences to be resolved? Our answer is that those debates are fundamentally irresolvable by science alone. Resolutions, when they come, will be based on a better understanding of differences in interpretation, sensibilities, and normative judgments. These are differences best resolved through a method we have previously labeled "argumentation for the sake of heaven." This method entails an honest exploration by economists (of varying policy persuasions) focused on advancing understanding, not on winning debates. It is a quite different type of argumentation style than the Chicago School pit bull style.

Argumentation for the sake of heaven can only occur if one recognizes that it is needed. Friedman's methodological prescription does not acknowledge such a need.[11] Our claim then is that in his methodological essay, Friedman, and hence the Chicago School, followed in the wake of the mainstream MIT/Harvard branch of economics by making the same fundamental methodological mistake that caused them to abandon Classical Liberalism. In that essay, Friedman formally jettisoned a central element of Classical Liberal methodology, namely the proposition that the scientific branch of economics, devoted to searching for the truth, *should not be* extended to policy issues.[12] Instead, according to Classical Liberal dictates, positive economics should focus its analysis on finding truths that all economists could agree upon based on the empirical evidence. Policy issues were not to be included among such truths. Any attempted consensus on policy issues could only be achieved through argumentation for the sake of heaven. So, while eliminating pluralism is conceivable in science, since there are assumed to be workable, albeit imperfect, empirical methods to distinguish scientific truths, pluralism in policy debates cannot be eliminated. Instead, it must be embraced.[13] Consequently, institutions should be designed to provide checks and balances to whatever the conventional wisdom is thought to be. Internal critics are critical to successful applied policy work.

Implementing an argumentation for the sake of heaven methodology would require economists ascribing to opposing views on policy to willingly personally discuss the nuances of their policy differences. The mutually held goal of these debaters arguing for the sake of heaven would be to reduce differences. To the degree possible, the overriding objective would be to reach a consensus, or at least a specification of what type of evidence might persuade economists on both sides of the policy issue, to change their mind.[14] Institutions to do that would need to be developed. These structures would encourage researchers with differing policy sensibilities to work together to discuss those differences. The aspired goal would encompass the oversight of jointly conducted research developing evidence that both might find convincing.[15] Such conscious joint exploration by researchers with different sensibilities would go beyond scientific research. Their efforts would also evaluate various moral philosophical arguments that might help to resolve any seemingly intransigent differences.

We recognize that this methodological approach provides no simple panacea, nor does it offer a convenient mechanical algorithm to follow. But this method, while deliberately complex, was the best that Classical economists could develop, and we have nothing better to offer. Since the profession's postwar dismissal of this perspective has led to the proliferation of sterile debates, it would seem to be a perspective worth exploring once again.

The Separation of Theory from Policy

As we have emphasized throughout this book, a key pillar of Classical Liberal methodology is the firewall lodged between theory and policy. This approach attempted to separate the positive science of economics from the policy branch. It did so not because it held that a purely positive economics science was possible, but because it believed that even such an imperfect separation might prove useful. Doing so would allow economists to better concentrate on the goal of finding truth in the scientific branch of economics, while concentrating on finding reasonable policy solutions in the applied policy branch. Classical economists did not believe that positive science was irrelevant to policy, nor did they believe that a perfectly value-free, positive economics was possible. They recognized that values permeated all aspects of analysis, and that scientific exploration might, and likely would, have important policy implications. But, choosing a more pragmatic way of advancing understanding, they argued that it was useful to differentiate economics into these two branches according to the degree to which values and sensibilities were necessarily intertwined with analysis. Adopting this strategy allowed them to use different methodologies specifically tailored to the relevant analysis.

In Classical Liberal methodology, economics ceases to be a unified field of research endowed with a single method. Instead, the discipline splits into a variety of related fields of inquiry, each sporting a different specific methodology which represents the state of the art and craft. It will likely involve micro methodologies, each with their own appropriate niche. For example, the methodology chosen to investigate a question with good empirical data will differ sharply from the methodology that may prove relevant in the case of a policy issue for which a distinct lack of empirical data prevails. Labor economics will likely have a different methodology than public finance, which in turn will be differentiated from that of macroeconomics. For Classical Liberal economists, the applied policy branch of economics remains essentially a craft. That craft consists of multiple subcrafts embracing only a very loosely applied governing methodology.

For early Classical Liberals, scientific methodology, as applied to economics, involved mainly logical deductions, with little empirical testing. The reason for this emphasis was that formal statistical techniques meeting the requisite high scientific standards acceptable to most economists failed to exist at that time. Consequently, economists had to carefully avoid claiming scientific validity for their untestable theories. Such theories that prevailed served primarily as organizing structures. One could still theorize, but one could not base policy conclusions on such theories. Nonetheless, some economists of that era, such as David Ricardo, did exactly that.[16] However, within the Classical Liberal methodology, which we see as the dominant strain of that era, that movement from models to policy implications was widely considered to be inappropriate, with Ricardo representing an exception rather than the rule. Making such a connection became known as the Ricardian vice (Schumpeter 1987/1954), notable for being essentially an invalid and misleading method.[17] During this period, John Stuart Mill stands out as something of an exemplar of the type of Classical methodology that we advocate. He emphasized that theories and models provided at best half-truths. To relate theory to policy, one had to add moral, humanitarian, and interpretative considerations that went far beyond science alone. These considerations required a method that could incorporate argumentation for the sake of heaven.

That disposition dramatically changed in the postwar era, especially dominating the current thinking within economics. With the development of new statistical tools, the proliferation of data, and the startling advance in computational power, a scientifically configured branch of empirical economics that can reasonably guide some aspects of policy is becoming more of a possibility. Still, such an approach has a long way to go before gaining a sufficient level of reliability. At this point, deep learning computational solutions can assist, but not substitute for, the reasoned judgment that Classical Liberals relied upon.

Separating out a branch of economics that restricted a wide range of value-laden analysis from entering into the scientific realm served to protect (and provide legitimacy to) the science of economics. Classical Liberal economists were wary of scientists holding strong policy views, or those who fashioned theories in relation to desired policy conclusions. Policy sensibilities would inevitably taint scientific judgments as well as erode a neutral observer's perception of his or her objectivity. A pronounced tendency in this direction would muddle the validity of any scientific work.[18] So paradoxically, the value of positive science to policy construction was enhanced by the extent to which a scientific researcher could be deemed uninterested in matters of policy. That lack of policy focus allowed more objective science to occur, ultimately making such investigations intrinsically more useful for subsequent policy formation.

Putting Economists in Their Place

Classical economists recognized that much of what economists did was related to policy matters. They felt that their concern about policy was justified. The desire was for economists to feel encouraged to do policy work. But these Classical economists viewed putting a firewall between scientific and policy conclusions as a necessary step in making positive economics unassailable, and hence as useful as possible. They urged economists to clarify their conclusions. Consequently, any analysis conducted with policy applications in mind *should not* be considered as positive economic science. Instead, it should be considered to belong to a distinctly different branch of economics, one that explicitly integrated all relevant factors into policy analysis. They labeled this alternative branch the *art of economics.*

Since most of what economists do is related to policy, proposing that economic scientists remain unconcerned with policy issues would contradictorily seem to drastically reduce, if not eliminate, the scope of economic practice. But such a conclusion is erroneous. This position simply states that when economists are doing applied policy work, or even doing background work designed to shed light on a policy on which they are not neutral, they should not consider themselves scientists seeking some unvarying truth. Rather, they should consider themselves as acting in a more humble capacity.[19] They should envision themselves as being engineers, gardeners, technicians, (Keynes suggested dentists), or perhaps specialists providing information that can inform policy makers. Economists, in their role as economic engineers, need to accept more of a backstage role, rather than seeking to absorb the limelight, unless they are willing to go beyond economics and consider all aspects of the policy analysis. In that instance, they would be tentatively stepping into the role of statesman rather than remaining in the more comfortable confines of economics.

Not seeing oneself as a scientist does not mean that when one is working on a policy issue, one should not try to be objective. Nor does it mean that economists should fail to provide the best possible answer to the proposed policy questions in a fashion that is independent of one's individualistic values or beliefs. Classical Liberals assumed that in policy analysis, an economist should incorporate his or her best estimates of society's normative judgments, not his or her own normative judgments. These would manage to incorporate objective interpretations of institutional realities as far as possible. True, these judgments involve a greater degree of uncertainty than do judgments that can be subject to generally accepted scientific methods based on empirical verification. That's why Classical Liberals felt that, as a practical matter, it was useful to separate out the science of economics from its application to policy. Doing so was particularly essential when, as was generally the case, the economist harbored an a priori view about what the appropriate policy might be. Even if they succeeded in that regard, the remaining part, which Classical Liberals called economic science, could not be entirely value free. But they hoped the careful separation would make that part accepted as science more value free than it otherwise would be.

Value-Transparent Theory and Analysis

The goal of Classical Liberal policy analysis was not to be value free, but instead to be *value transparent*. Researchers should clearly state the value judgments underlying the policy prescriptions and recognize that their understanding of the policy would reflect their individual sensibilities. Thus, they should submit all policies to argumentation for the sake of heaven and be modest in their claims so that outsiders could decide whether they were in agreement with them.

Since values play a key role in the Classical Liberal approach, determining how to arrive at those values was a key part of that methodology as applied to policy formation. We will not explore that here since it is a complicated issue and one in which we are not specialists. We should however mention that to arrive at a normative compass, Classical economists often used some variant of Adam Smith's impartial spectator. As they integrated values into their analysis, the appropriate Classical Liberal methodology evolved into the necessity to make an argument that (the economist believed) would convince an impartial spectator.[20]

Adam Smith was vague about what that moral policy foundation might be. Subsequent Classical writers blended a moral philosophy based on an impartial spectator approach together with a more general moral philosophy of utilitarianism.[21] They argued, based on this impartial spectator analytic, that it was reasonable to arrive at a loose, normative goal for economic policy that could be summarized as "the greatest good for the greatest number." These Classical Liberals recognized that such a goal was both ambiguous and at times even contradictory. That ambiguity would doubtless have posed a problem had the goal of utilitarian philosophy been one of arriving at some specified policy. However, that was not the goal.[22] Classical utilitarianism can be better understood as a starting point for a policy discussion conducted as an argument for the sake of heaven approach.[23] The strength of this perspective rested on the broad reach of its goal. Utilitarianism could help rule out a set of policies that were so far removed from achieving the greatest good for the greatest number that any ambiguity and inherent contradictions within them did not matter for that rejected subset. The goal was a partial, not a complete, ordering of policies.

Classical liberals recognized that in espousing certain policies, economists would find it difficult, if not impossible, to avoid letting such value-laden considerations affect their judgment. Consequently, the pragmatic goal was not to entirely avoid these prior beliefs, as one explicitly attempted to do for the positive science of economics. Biases were instead an accepted fact that was simply unavoidable. However, such ideological leanings could be balanced, to some extent, by attempting to reach as high a level of transparency as possible. Therefore, developing institutions that had embedded checks and balances was vital to objective policy analysis. Economists needed to be honest, to others as well as to themselves, about their pre-ordained sensibilities and judgments.

Lionel Robbins, who with Milton Friedman is seen as having developed modern economic methodology, differed fundamentally from Friedman in that Robbins continued to espouse a Classical Liberal approach. Robbins set himself apart from Friedman by contesting those who saw his arguments as providing support for a brand of positive economics that led directly to policy conclusions. He considered such an interpretation of his work to be seriously misguided. Robbins was very clear about the need to separate positive economic analysis from policy analysis. In his 1980 Ely Lecture (Robbins 1981), he explicitly stated that he had been misinterpreted in this manner. He argued that the economics profession had incorrectly interpreted his argument to imply that economists should avoid value judgments. That was not what he was arguing. Robbins insisted that while the *science of economics should avoid value judgments*, the entire field of economics should not. Instead, the discipline necessarily included a policy branch that embraced values. As he pointed out: "My suggestion here, as in the *Introduction to my Political Economy: Past and Present*, is that its use should be revived as now covering that part of our sphere of interest which essentially involves judgments of value. Political Economy, thus conceived, is quite unashamedly concerned with the assumptions of policy and the results flowing from them" (7–8). By making this particular argument, he was doing no more than reiterating Classical liberal methodology.

Where Friedman Broke with Classical Liberalism

There is little indication in his writings or presentations that Friedman saw himself as deviating from Classical Liberal methodology. In fact, in claiming that policy results would follow from the positive science of economics, Friedman specifically stated that he was basing his approach on that of John Neville Keynes (1891), whose book on the *Scope and Method of Political Economy* was a summary of Classical Liberal methodology. In it Keynes was very clear that economics should be separated into three distinct branches. While Keynes's book focused on the appropriate method required for the positive science of economics, he argued that the science of economics had a quite different methodology than did applied policy economics.[24]

The likely reason why Keynes did not devote much space to the methodology appropriate to the applied policy methodology is that an applied exploration did not have strong methodological rules. It was a craft, not a science, more a matter of judgment. As a craft, it was defined by a very loose methodology, one that was learned by doing. What Friedman missed (whether deliberately or by oversight) was that, while Keynes did not focus on the methodology of the art of economics, he saw it as the appropriate methodology for applied economics and made it clear that its methodology had to go far beyond economic science.[25] Keynes writes:

> [F]ew practical problems admit of complete solution on economic grounds alone ... [W]hen we pass, for instance, to problems of taxation, or to problems that concern the relations of the State with trade and industry, or to the general discussion of communistic and socialistic schemes—it is far from being the case that economic considerations hold the field exclusively. Account must also be taken of ethical, social, and political considerations that lie outside the sphere of political economy regarded as a science. (1891: 34)
>
> We are, accordingly, led to the conclusion ... that a definitive art of political economy, which attempts to lay down absolute rules for the regulation of human conduct, will have vaguely defined limits, and be largely non-economic in character. (83)

Friedman initially presented himself as being in accord with this thinking by beginning his essay with a quotation from Keynes that makes exactly this point. Friedman writes:

> In his admirable book on *The Scope and Method of Political Economy*, John Neville Keynes distinguishes among "a *positive science* ... a body of systematized knowledge concerning what is; a *normative* or *regulative science* ... a body of systematized knowledge discussing criteria of what ought to be ... ; an *art* ... a system of rules for the attainment of a given end"; comments that "confusion between them is common and has been the source of many mischievous errors"; and urges the importance of "recognizing a distinct positive science of political economy. (1953/1966: 3)

Friedman then continues by explaining:

> This paper is concerned primarily with certain methodological problems that arise in constructing the "distinct positive science" Keynes called for—in particular, the problem of how to decide whether a suggested hypothesis or theory should be tentatively

accepted as part of the "body of systematized knowledge concerning what is." But the confusion Keynes laments is still so rife and so much of a hindrance to the recognition that economics can be, and in part is, a positive science that it seems well to preface the main body of the paper with a few remarks about the relation between positive and normative economics. (1953/1966: 3)

In making that statement, Friedman seems to be saying that he is continuing in Keynes's footsteps by attempting to spell out the methodology of positive economics. Where Friedman fumbles in this effort is by placing policy analysis within the grasp of positive economics and not in a third applied policy branch of economics—the branch Keynes called the art of economics. So here is the irony. Even though Friedman specifically cited Keynes's three-part division, he proceeded to discuss only a two-part division between normative and positive economics. Keynes's third branch (the branch that was central to Classical liberal policy analysis) vanishes without a trace. By doing so, Friedman eliminates the Classical Liberal methodology.[26]

Friedman explains his view with regard to the minimum wage policy:

I venture the judgment, however, that currently in the Western world, and especially in the United States, differences about economic policy among disinterested citizens derive predominantly from different predictions about the economic consequences of taking action—differences that in principle can be eliminated by the progress of positive economics—rather than from fundamental differences in basic values, differences about which men can ultimately only fight. An obvious and not unimportant example is minimum-wage legislation. Underneath the welter of arguments offered for and against such legislation there is an underlying consensus on the objective of achieving a "living wage" for all, to use the ambiguous phrase so common in such discussions. The difference of opinion is largely grounded on an implicit or explicit difference in predictions about the efficacy of this particular means in furthering the agreed-on end. Proponents believe (predict) that legal minimum wages diminish poverty by raising the wages of those receiving less than the minimum wage as well as of some receiving more than the minimum wage without any counterbalancing increase in the number of people entirely unemployed or employed less advantageously than they otherwise would be. Opponents believe (predict) that legal minimum wages increase poverty by increasing the number of people who are unemployed or employed less advantageously and that this more than offsets any favorable effect on the wages of those who remain employed. Agreement about the economic consequences of the legislation might not produce complete agreement about its desirability, for differences might still remain about its political or social consequences but, given agreement on objectives, it would certainly go a long way toward producing consensus. (1953/1966: 5)

Classical economists held a quite different view about how policy agreement would be reached. They did not see scientific empirical work as being able to resolve policy differences. As Lionel Robbins put it: "What precision economists can claim at this stage is largely a sham precision. In the present state of knowledge, the man who can claim for economic science much exactitude is a quack" (Robbins 1927: 176). These Classical Liberals believed that economists could come to quite different policy conclusions even though they agreed on both some broad theoretical and empirical scientific results, as well as concurring on normative goals. The reason for coming to different positions lay in how someone might interpret scientific results and how they might interpret normative goals. That interpretation inevitably involved numerous judgments, informal analysis, and sensibilities that differed among people. Good economists, sharing the same values, using the same theories, and accepting the same empirical work, could arrive at quite different policy results because of subtle differences in interpretations and sensibilities. For Classical economists, movement toward agreement about policy *would not* come about primarily from any advancement in positive economics. Progress would derive from a better understanding of, and coming to agreement on, subtle differences in interpretation and judgments.

To allow for that disagreement, and to make it possible to think of positive economics as relatively value free, Classical Liberal economists defined the positive science of economics quite narrowly. They placed policy analysis into a separate branch labeled the art of economics. Creating this separate branch was central to the Classical Liberal methodology. This bifurcation allowed the relevant methodology to be tailored for resolving debates concerning values and issues. Such disputes could not be answered with scientific precision simply by employing economic science. By not acknowledging the need for a third branch—an art of economics—Friedman helped, whether intentionally or not, to undermine classical methodology.

By suggesting that developments in the positive science of economics would answer questions about the minimum wage and other contentious policy issues, Friedman's essay dismissed Classical Liberal methodology. As we stated earlier, the same debates continue today, and are just as contentious as they were when Friedman first conjured up his distinctive strategy. Despite advances in examining the positive economic analysis of the minimum wage debate, these have failed to resolve existing differences. When one group of researchers finds evidence seeming to support the usefulness of a minimum wage law, another group of researchers almost simultaneously finds contrary evidence, or finds reasons to disregard the evidence of that other group. For example, when Card and Krueger (1994, 1995) found evidence that the minimum wage did not create a significant degree of unemployment, another group of economists[27] challenged their study and suggested that other side effects of the minimum wage were sufficiently important to negate any pretentions of representing good policy.[28] Given the continued debate that inevitably flairs up over such policy, even after some sixty years of ongoing investigation, it seems pretty clear that Friedman was wrong about the ability of positive economics to resolve such disputes.[29]

Some Summary Comments

In summary, by eliminating the art of economics as the branch within which policy disputes could be debated and resolved, Friedman removed the method devised by Classical economists for keeping positive economics relatively value free. Doing so, despite protestations to the contrary, effectively reduced the possibility of arriving at a consensus about both scientific economic theory and about applied economic policy. In removing policy from the art of economics, without a discussion of why, Friedman and the Chicago School joined the rest of the profession in abandoning a central element of Classical Liberal methodology.

The consequences of this seemingly small change in methodology have had an enormous effect on the economics profession.[30] As economists tried to force answers on policy issues onto the territory defined by positive economics, they retreated to abstraction. Economic theory became a set of formalisms (marginal social benefit should equal marginal social cost) that represented reasonable generalities, but failed to be operational, lacking any practical way of being implemented. The discussion of how they could be made implementable never occurred. As J. de V. Graaff concluded in his famous consideration of welfare economics, *Theoretical Welfare Economics*, "the possibility of building a useful and interesting theory of welfare economics—i.e. one which consists of something more than the barren formalisms typified by the marginal equivalences of conventional theory—is exceedingly small" (Graaff 1957: 169).

9

The Art and Craft of Economics

THE CLASSICAL LIBERAL ATTITUDE

We began this book by arguing that economic policy does not follow from economic theory. Policy contains too many dimensions to be drawn directly from theory.[1] We argued that, instead, policy had to be drawn from a complicated blend of judgments based on ambiguous empirical evidence, normative issues, and sensibilities, which when artfully combined might be framed in a manner consistent with scientific theory. However, differences in these judgments were not resolvable simply by applying scientific theory. J. M. Keynes, in his reflection on Marshall, expressed this view clearly:

> The Theory of Economics does not furnish a body of settled conclusions immediately applicable to a policy. It is a method rather than a doctrine, an apparatus of the mind, a technique of thinking, which helps its possessor to draw correct conclusions. (Keynes quoted in Guillebaud and Friedman 1958: vii)

The scientific method is a methodology that is useful for certain types of policy issues, but not for all types. Specifically, it is *not* a methodology that is especially useful in guiding those aspects of economic policy analysis concerned with the broad design of policy where values are in play.[2] The scientific method limits both the scope of policy questions addressed and the methods used to answer those questions. The scientific methodology may be very important for a subset of technical problems, but those are often not the ones that cause disagreements among policy makers. This means that rigid adherence to scientific methodology in applied economic policy analysis is highly problematic. Trying to use the scientific method to reach conclusions about policy: (1) tends to undermine any achievable consensus on the relevant science; good science does not lead to policy conclusions without the addition of normative judgments; (2) hardens, rather than resolves, sensibilities and nuanced judgments where there is natural disagreement about policy; and (3) discourages the exploration of creative and imaginative approaches to policy.

If a scientific method is not the approach economists should use in applied policy, what is? In this final chapter we provide our answer to that question as best we can.[3] More precisely, we attempt to provide guidance in constructing an applied policy by employing a Classical Liberal methodology. Our intention is to offer a measure of useful guidance, but we want to warn the reader. We will not (indeed cannot) provide a set of fixed rules based on Classical Liberal methodology. There will be no step-by-step instructions, no precise algorithm, no ultimate guide that cracks the mystery of doing applied economics in some cookbook fashion.[4] That would demand employing the very opposite to what we understand to be Classical Liberal methodology.

The methodology for constructing applied policy that we support takes a fire hydrant approach to any highly specified set of rules. Such dictums are best used as a watering post. A central theme of our analysis has been the scarcity (if not near non-existence) of usefully analyzed, non-contextual, methodological rules that support Classical Liberal policy analysis. A reason why a formal set of these instructions fails to exist is that the appropriate rules are hardly worth discussing. They are obvious rules of thumb on which most would agree.[5] The difficulty arises when attempting to implement these rules, which boil down to the following: do good work; continually reflect on what good work is; recognize the limitations of good work; and recognize the tendency of individuals (including oneself) to harbor a built-in bias favoring one's own viewpoint and thus the need to enforce impartiality on oneself as well as on others.[6] (These principles could equally appear at a Google workplace. They verge on the innocuous.) Further: Do so by constantly subjecting one's work to an impartial spectator test; operate in an institutional environment where partial spectators on the opposite side provide checks on one's impartiality.

As should be clear from the discussion so far, we are not above providing mundane methodological rules. But we don't seriously believe that these rules are anything more than a beginning. For us, methodology is more attitude than rules. So, if, by guidance, one refers to a specified set of methodological rules, by definition that is not achievable. But what can be provided is a sketch of how we believe applied economics policy analysis should be done, or at least a rough version of that approach. In this chapter we provide that guidance by sketching out the work of six economists whom we see as exemplifying the Classical Liberal method. Our methodological suggestion to economists is to emulate them; consider their writings carefully and decide what aspect might apply legitimately to a variety of contexts.

The economists we have chosen are, by design, diverse. The common thread among them is a shared attitude toward existing economics that is respectful, but not reverent. Their perspective consistently emphasizes an implicit firewall that effectively separates science from policy analysis.[7] All of them are mainstream economists (or at least they are comfortable operating within that landscape). But they are simultaneously often critical of that same mainstream.[8]

While we believe that holding a Classical Liberal attitude is not actually a rarity, expressing that attitude is often difficult since it involves criticizing a power base that remains firmly wedged within the discipline itself. There are always strong forces in any profession primed to defend a status quo that allows the profession to hold a high opinion of itself and protects it from criticism.[9] The ecostructure within which economists work often pushes Classical Liberal methodological concerns aside and encourages would-be members to go along with the directive flow of mainstream thought. Such a gravitational pull exists even if one consciously disagrees with it. This state of affairs has only been reinforced by the ruling ecostructure that reinforces a polar orthodox/heterodox structure which undermines argumentation for the sake of heaven.

The prevailing methodology pays conspicuous lip service to the general rules, despite work being actually guided by a set of built-in (and usually unstated) methodological structures. What we are arguing is that, within economics, not only is there a standard received methodology, there is also what might be called a largely unacknowledged nano-methodology, operating almost invisibly, that plays a central role in how economics (and other social sciences) is practiced. It is a nano-methodology that includes such rules as: don't criticize colleagues with whom you share policy views; don't disparage economics because non-economists will use your comments to inappropriately malign economics; don't consider ideas unless they conform to the prevailing modeling structure ... and many similar guidance rules.

Put another way, what we are calling Classical Liberal methodology is determined more by an attitude than by some irreducible formal method. It involves recognition that any useful methodology is embedded in practice. Consequently, the way research is actually done, and must be done, involves a series of judgments by the researcher. For example, when one lacks a perfect measure to quantify a concept, what proxy does one use? When tractability requires simplification, what precise route should be taken? The list of nano-decisions one must make as a researcher is almost endless. How one makes those decisions plays an important role in what one ultimately concludes. The actual methodology is defined by the nano-decisions that researchers use while conducting research. Classical Liberal methodology then is distinguished by deliberately focusing on the way research is actually done. It spends less time on generalizing abstract rules that are no more than educated common sense or on attempting to make them more precise. Classical Liberals are also specifically conscious of the institutional incentives that researchers face, as well as the power those inherent incentives have to distort their work.[10]

What we continue to argue is that economists need to take such nano-methodology seriously. They can do so by accepting that an educated commonsense approach, not an approach based on abstract methodology pronouncements, can best guide policy analysis. The applied policy methodology we are advocating eschews any one-size-fits-all generalization. Instead, it is more of a bespoke variety—custom tailored to speak to the particular problem at hand and the issue in question. Put another way, the appropriate methodology is not left to some outside classifier to determine. It is best accomplished by those doing actual applied policy research, those aiming to discover what works and what doesn't. At the heart of this method then is "what works," or at least what has worked in the past. What actually works continues to depend on the context of the research project and what engineers call the state of the art.[11]

Classical Liberal Methodology Is Defined By an Attitude, Not By a Set of Rules

Summarizing our arguments, Classical Liberal methodology is defined more by an attitude than it is by a particular methodological approach. That attitude blends a deep-seated skepticism of mainstream theory, often manifested by heterodox economists, with an appreciation of the gains that have been made by mainstream theory, an appreciation generally lacking among heterodox critics. A Classical Liberal attitude would also display a mutual respect for the methods that have evolved in mainstream and non-mainstream traditions to handle theoretical problems. Thus, for example, the smug disdain for humanist approaches that one often senses in elite mainstream corridors fails to find even a tacit concurrence within Classical Liberalism.

The best way of conveying our conception of what is at least suggestive of a Classical Liberal stance is to present a handful of economists who, in our view, reflect this attitude.[12] We have chosen six economists: Edward Leamer, Ariel Rubinstein, Alvin Roth, Paul Romer, Amartya Sen, and Dani Rodrik. Each have, in our view, displayed a Classical Liberal attitude to methodology in important aspects of their work.[13] We consider the way in which they have attempted to relate scientific theory to practical policy concerns, arguing that each has adopted an identifiable Classical Liberal approach. We are not singling out any one of their specific practices as a model that should be followed assiduously. Instead, we are suggesting that they provide role models that might fruitfully be emulated by any cohort of young economists.[14]

All six belong within the mainstream. However, if one characterizes the mainstream as following a standard approach of neoclassical positivism, as applied to policy matters, they are far from mainstream in their policy approach. All six have proved willing to challenge policy positions that standard economists have commonly maintained.[15] Moreover, the inferences they make from theories differ from those of many mainstream economists. All refuse to see models as clearly drawn, scientific blueprints. Instead they treat them as rough, ad hoc heuristic guides, whose applicability varies with the problem considered. Consequently, they look to modify them whenever their educated common sense suggests that doing so would be useful.

The Con in Econometrics

An economist who acerbically pointed out the importance of nano-methodology back in the 1980s is Edward Leamer, a UCLA economist who serves as our first example of an economist exhibiting a Classical Liberal attitude. Back in 1983, he wrote a well-known paper entitled "Let's Take the Con Out of Econometrics." In doing so, he encouraged the profession to reflect on the way it routinely conducted econometric applications (Leamer 1983).[16] He pointed out that the way applied econometrics is taught to students, and is employed in policy formation, makes it appear to be a highly scientific procedure—what Leamer described as "econometrics of the top floor." He then pointed out that the way applied econometric research is actually done is the way it is done in the basement. This locale functions as the site where many of the top floor rules are broken, not because the researcher doesn't care about them, but because following the rules is impossible. The data inevitably don't fit the rarefied problems that top floor methodology is designed to resolve. Standard methodological rules inevitably must be broken when conducting real-world research.

This insight implies that there is a secondary set of operative rules—what we are calling nano-methodology. A clear need exists to shape less formal (more implicit) dictates that can usefully guide the necessary breaking of the official (and less flexible) rules. These unacknowledged norms form a central part of practical economic methodology—what actually works. These are skills learned through practice rather than instilled within the confines of the classroom or lecture hall. In this realm, standard scientific methodology provides little guidance that productively assists research. Instead, the models used on the top floor provide scientific cover for the work-a-day heuristics employed in the basement.[17] Leamer points out that this need to break these rules makes the field of applied econometrics a craft, not a science (Leamer 2012). The Classical Liberal methodology explicitly recognizes that this practice puts much more focus on nano-methodology than on the official, canonical methodology generally acknowledged by the profession. In much the same fashion, the field of applied economics is a craft. Our argument is that the methodology of the art and craft of economics lies in concentrating on the actual practices favored by economists, especially the practices adopted by the leaders in the field. How they approach their craft is central to understanding an economist's working methodology. More focus needs to be given to what they do, not to what they say.[18] Leamer's work led to a reconsideration of econometric practice, as well as an even broader consideration of economic rhetoric (McCloskey 1985).[19]

Economic Theory as Fable

Let's turn next to an economist who, we suspect, few would tend to include as a Classical Liberal, but who, in our view, fits perfectly into this mold. He exemplifies many of the top mainstream economic theorists who in practice exhibit Classical Liberal tendencies, but who don't explicitly acknowledge (or are acknowledged as having) a flirtation with this embrace.[20] Most economists, even if so inclined, are seldom tempted to discuss methodological issues.[21] One exception to this tendency is Ariel Rubinstein, a theoretical economist at NYU and Tel Aviv University, who has written the standard graduate text in game theory. He continues to do path-breaking work in that field. What marks him as leaning toward a more Classical Liberal attitude is his view of how game theory relates to policy applications. Rubinstein (2012) captured this view precisely in his book, *Economic Fables*, where he summarized the manner in which he thought economists should begin many of their policy discussions.

> I would like to start with what I believe every academic should do when appearing in public, especially when speaking about political and controversial issues—to clarify the extent to which he is incorporating his professional knowledge in his remarks, when he is expressing views with the authority supported by academic findings, and what part of his comments are nothing more than his personal thoughts and opinions.... to the best of my understanding, economic theory has nothing to say about the heart of the issue under discussion here ... Because as an economic theorist, I would like to state that economic theory is exploited in discussion about current economic issues, and I don't like it ... , to put it mildly.
>
> Everything that I say here, even in an academic context (and I intentionally use the word "academic" since I do not think that the word "scientific" is appropriate for economics) is completely subjective, controversial and therefore perhaps describes me no less than it describes economic theory. (2012: 13–14)

He further explained his view in an interview that expanded on his underlying methodological approach:

> In general, my view about formal models is that a model is a fable. Game theory is about a collection of fables. Are fables useful or not? In some sense, you can say that they are useful, because good fables can give you some new insight into the world and allow you to think about a situation differently. But fables are not useful in the sense of giving you advice about what to do tomorrow, or how to reach an agreement between the West and Iran. The same is true about game theory. A main difference between game theory and literature is that game theory is written in formal, mathematical language. That has advantages and disadvantages. The advantages are that the formal language allows us to be more precise, it allows us to get rid of associations that are not relevant and it allows us to better examine some arguments. The disadvantage of formal language is the level of abstraction, which has two main downsides. First of all, it makes the theory very far away from one minus epsilon of the population. Even among the academic community, most people who claim to use game theory hardly understand it. Secondly, abstraction has the negative side that once you abstract things, you miss a lot of the information and most of the details, which in real life are very relevant.
>
> In general, I would say there were too many claims made by game theoreticians about its relevance. Every book of game theory starts with "Game theory is very relevant to everything that you can imagine, and probably many things that you can't imagine." In my opinion that's just a marketing device.[22]

The attitude Rubinstein displays here, and in much of his other work, both theoretical and policy oriented, can essentially be characterized as falling within the Classical Liberal basket. Were all economists to abide by a similar view as they move from theory to policy, we believe that the structure of economic science, as well as the nature of policy debate, would be much improved. The key is the continuing maintenance of a productive separation between the two spheres.[23]

The Economist as Engineer

Whereas Ariel Rubinstein demonstrates the Classical Liberal approach to the abstract game theory, Alvin Roth demonstrates the Classical Liberal applied policy approach to the use of game theory. Roth, using insights from game theory, has developed matching systems for physician residencies, for school systems, and for kidney transplants (Roth and Peranson, 1999; Roth, Sönmez, and Ünver 2004). These systems are not controversial; most observers agree that they are systemic improvements. (He received a Nobel Prize for his work in 2012.) Roth uses insights from theoretical game theory, but applies those insights to real-world problems, accepting the normative views of society about what is fair as a necessary part of the analysis and system design. He makes no attempt to remain formally scientific. His method is to use whatever tools provide relevant insight. Thus, for example, rather than call for a market in kidneys in which people could buy and sell kidneys, he developed a system of transplant chains that did not require any explicit monetary pricing, but that allowed direct exchanges and also allowed for altruistic donors to generate multilevel donor chains.

What leads us to classify him as Classical Liberal is that he explicitly describes himself as an engineer, not a scientist (Roth 2002). He integrates computational and experimental tools into his design work and explicitly defends his engineering approach. He writes: "Engineering is often less elegant than the simple underlying physics, but it allows bridges designed on the same basic model to be built longer and stronger over time, as the complexities and how to deal with them become better understood (1342).[24]

An important reason why his, and similar, matching systems work is that, instead of using existing wealth relationships to underpin the system, as would be the case in a standard "market" solution, he develops an alternative property right structure that is more in tune with how an impartial spectator would judge fairness in the system. Concerns about efficiency and fairness are blended into the design of the system. Developing systems that are seen by impartial spectators as fair is a central aspect of system design for

Roth. Blending considerations of fairness into the initial design of the system is crucially missing in much applied work that sees itself as scientific.

The Trouble with Macro

Leamer is an econometrician, Rubinstein is a microeconomic theorist, and Roth is an applied microtheorist. Our next example is a macroeconomist; macroeconomics is an area in which the mainstream profession has most deviated from a Classical Liberal perspective. As discussed in previous chapters, in the 1960s and '70s macro theory and policy became closely wedded—Keynesians used an IS/LM model to demonstrate the necessity for an activist monetary and fiscal policy.[25] To counter this imperative, Chicago economists used a reduced form monetarist model, to insist upon a laissez-faire policy. Both sides implacably claimed to have cultivated an implacably scientific basis for their divergent policy arguments.[26] These ongoing debates were never adequately resolved (they were basically unresolvable), but by the late 1970s they started to fade away.

That vanishing act occurred while macroeconomics almost simultaneously underwent a radical transformation. IS/LM models were abandoned by macrotheorists and were replaced with more formal scientific models that focused on "micro foundations" and rational expectations. This work was initially labeled New Classical theory. Eventually it would evolve into DSGE (Dynamic Stochastic General Equilibrium) macroeconomics. By the year 2000, DSGE macro had conquered the entire field.[27] Any reputable economist working in macro was expected to use DSGE models. They had become de rigueur. If you were sufficiently foolhardy to use an alternative approach, you would find yourself essentially barred from publishing in any top economic journal. Economists who questioned the usefulness or ability of using DSGE models to solve applied policy problems were ostracized (and effectively dismissed) as holding heterodox views. These unfortunates were condemned to dwell on the periphery of the mainstream macroeconomic research community.

This practice established the dominance of DSGE modeling even when the economic focus was on macro policy work. Any policy advocated by a macroeconomist was expected to follow from a DSGE model. The problem was that to make the model tractable, one had to accept assumptions that so deviated from the real world that it was hard to see what relevance the resulting model might hold. Specifically, to be operable, the analyzed economy had to contain only one representative agent, a supposition that essentially assumes away any coordination problem by any subset of heterogeneous agents. Agents in the DSGE model were designated as blessed with super rationality, while any expected frictions (or transaction costs) were assumed to be conveniently non-existent. But somehow, despite these narrowly defined constraints, the model was still touted as providing the user with reliable policy guidance. As opposed to treating the model as a fable, sometimes useful, sometimes not, the DSGE model became transmuted into an accurate blueprint of the truth. Taking such an absolutist approach clearly violates both the essence and spirit of the Classical Liberal attitude.

Within the profession, few economists objected openly. If you did, you were essentially shunned. DSGE was the only allowable methodological approach, the proverbial only game in town. From a Classical Liberal perspective, using such an abstract model for applied policy analysis made little, if any, sense. The DSGE model might have been the best available scientific model (because being logically consistent it was in many ways scientifically preferable to the logically inconsistent IS/LM model). But for a Classical Liberal, the best science has to offer does not necessarily produce the best policy model. That alternative position was not allotted serious consideration because of the insistence that policy must necessarily follow from scientific models. Consequently, given this presumed nexus, policy as dictated by a DSGE model possessed a certain persuasive logic. As with many such models, by adding sufficient "adjustments" and modifications to the DSGE version, clever economists were able to make it fit just about any situation that might arise. DSGE models were claimed to be the only appropriate way of doing macroeconomic policy.[28]

Modern Macroeconomics in Practice:
How Theory Shaped Policy

Given that background on DSGE modeling, we now turn to Paul Romer. What makes Romer worthy of mention as an example of a Classical Liberal attitude is his 2017 essay, "The Trouble with Macro." It is a no-holds-barred attack on modern DSGE theory.[29] So even though Romer has long been considered as an insider in the field, he was not reluctant to seriously discuss the problems associated with the DSGE model.[30] In this article he argues that "for more than three decades, macroeconomics has gone backwards," and he places the blame on a failure of the leading figures within the macro profession to criticize one another. Because of this reluctance, these economists developed a type of group think, one that effectively allowed educated common sense to be overlooked. We fully agree with that assessment. It accurately pinpoints another aspect of violating the preferred policy/theory firewall.

Romer argues that "macroeconomic theorists dismissed facts by feigning an obtuse ignorance about simple assertions, such as 'tight monetary policy can cause a recession.'" Instead, he argues that their models are based on imaginary causal forces. He specifically points out that economists use Friedman's methodological argument as a convenient escape hatch that allows them to dismiss informed critics' reasoned complaints. By taking this stance, he underscores the fact that the theory these economists offer fails to match the world they imagine they are discussing. He writes:

In response to the observation that the shocks are imaginary, a standard defense invokes Milton Friedman's (1953) methodological assertion from unnamed authority that "the more significant the theory, the more unrealistic the assumptions" (p. 14). More recently, "all models are false" seems to have become the universal hand-wave for dismissing any fact that does not conform to the model that is the current favorite. The noncommittal relationship with the truth revealed by these methodological evasions and the "less than totally convinced ..." dismissal of fact goes so far beyond post-modern irony that it deserves its own label. I suggest "post-real."

Romer gives two examples of how the sociology of the profession tends to reinforce prevailing beliefs. Specifically, he argues that modern macro DSGE modelers have tended to limit their attacks on colleagues who share their policy views. This claim implies that top researchers hold those who agree with them to much looser standards than those willing to oppose their positions. These different standards follow naturally from an "us" versus "them" sensibility, reflecting precisely the type of approach to policy that we are arguing against.[31]

Restricted to the scientific portion of the economic discipline, that opposition pitting scientist against non-scientist makes some limited sense. All scientists should be committed to a search for the truth, and the appropriate methodology to do so includes an acceptance of scientific methodology. Scientists are assumed able to legitimately separate themselves from non-scientists who are not obliged to follow the same rigorous and precise methodology.[32] If policy is part of science, then that same opposition can carry over to policy matters. In that case, anyone who dared to disagree with the standard policy view would be labeled as being beyond the pale, creating within the profession a strong herd-like tendency to reach common policy conclusions. In contrast, by strictly separating out policy analysis from science, that tendency is significantly reduced. A more open discussion of the limitations of models is accordingly encouraged, creating a wider range of policy views consistent with the same scientific base.

Amartya Sen and Income Distribution Policy

Amartya Sen captures another, quite different, research approach that fits within the Classical Liberal mold. Sen is well known as a major contributor to theoretical economic science (in the field of social choice and welfare economics), as well as applied policy work. He is probably the best known of the six economists presented here, partially because of the Nobel Prize he received in 1998. Sen's theoretical work has shaped social choice and welfare theory, demonstrating, among other things, the way in which Arrow's Impossibility Theorem is so structured that it must necessarily lead to its unsettling result. However, still starting from Arrow's premise, Sen managed to find a way to navigate around the restrictive Impossibility Theorem, provided that one is willing to accept partial rankings (Sen 1977). He also has demonstrated that the Pareto Efficiency criterion commonly adopted in economics can be inconsistent with Liberal values (Sen 1970a), thereby undermining much of the standard practice of drawing scientific policy conclusions from economic models.

Our interest here lies not so much in Sen's scientific and theoretical work, but in his applied policy efforts that focus on development issues and related income distribution conflicts.[33] That applied analysis is not entirely unconnected to his theoretical work, but it is largely separable from that narrower context. Instead of approaching the issue of income distribution as theoretical by nature, he handles the problem from more of a policy perspective. Income distribution problems become especially important in times of famine. Sen investigated the causes of famines and potential efforts to ameliorate and even resolve such horrors. In that work we see a major difference between how Sen approaches the issue of income distribution compared to the way in which standard economists approach the same issue. Specifically, rather than thinking of development and income distribution as issues that are separable from broader social considerations, Sen treats them both as deep-seated problems that go far beyond economics. His proposed policy solutions reflect those complex interconnections.[34]

Setting income distribution within the context of economic development enables Sen to propose the existence of a set of linked freedoms. Sen argues that development has to be thought of, and dealt with, as linked to a philosophical sense of freedom. It should not, therefore, be demoted to merely a technical economic problem. Specifically, Sen argues that development consists of the removal of various types of what he calls "unfreedoms" that leave people with little choice or opportunity of exercising their reasoned agencies. This focus on freedom was central to Classical Liberalism,[35] and in many ways Sen can be seen as a faithful successor to Mill in his concerted attempt to advance the system of Classical Liberal moral and philosophic thought.[36] For Sen, human freedom, not material welfare, is the preeminent objective of development. According to Sen, real development cannot be trivialized to a simple increase in GDP or income. Rather, true advancement requires a set of overlapping mechanisms that progressively enable individuals to exercise a growing range of freedoms.

This focus on freedom makes it impossible to discuss development without examining political freedoms and transparency in personal relationships. Such a discussion involves freedom of opportunity, including freedom to access credit and effective economic protection from abject poverty. Any workable solution to income distribution issues is to be found by testing alternative assignments of rights and freedoms, not in the operation of the economy with a given assignment of rights. Within mainstream theory, that connection has not been explored. Rights are accepted as given, and policy designed to change those rights is not normally discussed. Sen's analysis of distribution changes that way of thinking.

Sen's approach to the problem of distribution is thus similar to John Stuart Mill's. Income distribution is not an economic problem to be solved by narrow economic thinking. Instead, it is a problem that blends moral philosophical, economic, and political elements. It is not a problem to be approached by standard economic analysis. Mill argued that distribution was a societal decision built into the legal structure, norms, and laws of the land, not a technical outcome reflecting the workings of an economy.[37] For this reason, Mill, like Sen, argued that any workable distribution policy needed to concentrate on the assignment of property rights, rather than focus on a study of supply and demand. Mill writes:

> The laws of property have never yet conformed to the principles on which the justification of private property rests. They have made property of things which never ought to be property, and absolute property where only a qualified property ought to

exist. They have not held the balance fairly between human be-
ings, but have heaped impediments upon some, to give advantage to others; they have purposely fostered inequalities, and
prevented all from starting fair in the race. That all should indeed start on perfectly equal terms is inconsistent with any law
of private property: but if as much pains as has been taken to
aggravate the inequality of chances arising from the natural
working of the principle, had been taken to temper that inequality by every means not subversive of the principle itself; if the
tendency of legislation had been to favour the diffusion, instead
of the concentration of wealth—to encourage the subdivision of
the large masses, instead of striving to keep them together; the
principle of individual property would have been found to have
no necessary connexion with the physical and social evils which
almost all Socialist writers assume to be inseparable from it.
(Mill 1848: 209).

This focus on the underlying norms and legal structures of society
as the key to fostering policy debate presents an important aspect
of distribution policy as analyzed by a Classical Liberal approach.
This method contrasts sharply with that of standard economics,
which displays a marked propensity to disregard property rights
and norms. Instead, the focus remains frozen on measuring technical relationships such as marginal productivities.

The difference in policy prescription that follows from these
alternative approaches can be seen in Sen's analysis of famine and
in his proposed policies to deal with them. Sen argues that famines
aren't created by food shortages. Standard economics implicitly assumes these shortages to be the root cause. Sen argues that absolute scarcity—where there is not enough food to feed everyone—is
extraordinarily rare. In Sen's view, most famines are created by the
social and legal systems that determine how a society's food is distributed. Famines are caused by changes in distribution mechanisms
in which some individuals fail to have sufficient entitlements to the
available supply of existing food. This alternative analysis leads
to distinctly different policy proposals. Sen argues for the need to
shift our attention from questions of food availability to questions

of distribution, or to the social systems that guide this distribution. He writes: "If one person in eight starves regularly in the world, this is . . . the result of his inability to establish entitlement to enough food; the question of the physical availability of the food is not directly involved" (Sen 1981: 8). He concludes his work, *Poverty and Famines*, with this famous observation: "The law stands between food availability and food entitlement"[38] (166).

As we stated above, Amartya Sen is unquestionably a famous economist. His work is well known and respected throughout the profession. But despite his fame, the reality remains that few graduate schools today include a careful study of any of his vast output. Students are not told that his approach to policy should be seen as a good role model for how applied policy should be done. Introducing students to Sen's applied policy methodology is not considered to be central to training students in practical applied economics. This reality reflects the nearly universal "science" approach to applied policy that has successfully preempted the art and craft that categorized Classical Liberalism. Sen's methodology is considered tangential to standard economics precisely because he works outside the normal scientific framework. Students are implicitly taught to shy away from the dangerous chasm of heterodoxy. Instead, the career advantages of conformity are absorbed during their training without the need for any conscious reminders. Students are taught to approach economic policy problems scientifically, which means that the many non-economic dimensions of the problems, which Sen's work highlights, do not get integrated into economic policy analysis. Were the profession to adopt a Classical Liberal methodology, both teaching and practice would radically change.[39]

Dani Rodrik and International Trade

Our final example of an economist who demonstrates a Classical Liberal methodological attitude is Dani Rodrik, an international trade theorist at Harvard. Although he is highly respected within the economics profession, Rodrik has managed to carve out an approach to trade policy that clearly differs from the discipline's accepted standard. He has also written extensively about the economics profession itself.

Back in 1997, Rodrik authored a book, *Has Globalization Gone Too Far?* In it he argued that economists' arguments for free trade and globalization were far too strong. There were numerous additional dimensions to trade policy that should persuade economists to be more circumspect when discussing it. In a blog posting entitled "Straight Talk on Trade," he reflected on that previous volume, as well as on economists' continued tendency to advocate free trade without the nuances that all good economists know accompany such advocacy. (He expanded upon the ideas in Rodrik 2015.) He writes:

> As my book *Has Globalization Gone Too Far?* went to press nearly two decades ago, I approached a well-known economist to ask him if he would provide an endorsement for the back cover. I claimed in the book that, in the absence of a more concerted government response, too much globalization would deepen societal cleavages, exacerbate distributional problems, and undermine domestic social bargains—arguments that have become conventional wisdom since.
>
> The economist demurred. He said he didn't really disagree with any of the analysis, but worried that my book would provide "ammunition for the barbarians." Protectionists would latch on to the book's arguments about the downsides of globalization to provide cover for their narrow, selfish agenda.
>
> It's a reaction I still get from my fellow economists. One of them will hesitantly raise his hand following a talk and ask: Don't you worry that your arguments will be abused and serve the demagogues and populists you are decrying?
>
> It has long been an unspoken rule of public engagement for economists that they should champion trade and not dwell too much on the fine print. This has produced a curious situation. The standard models of trade with which economists work typically yield sharp distributional effects: income losses by certain groups of producers or worker categories are the flip

side of the "gains from trade." And economists have long known that market failures—including poorly functioning labor markets, credit market imperfections, knowledge or environmental externalities, and monopolies—can interfere with reaping those gains.

Nonetheless, economists can be counted on to parrot the wonders of comparative advantage and free trade whenever trade agreements come up. They have consistently minimized distributional concerns, even though it is now clear that the distributional impact of, say, the North American Free Trade Agreement or China's entry into the World Trade Organization were significant for the most directly affected communities in the United States. They have overstated the magnitude of aggregate gains from trade deals, though such gains have been relatively small since at least the 1990s. They have endorsed the propaganda portraying today's trade deals as "free trade agreements," even though Adam Smith and David Ricardo would turn over in their graves if they read the Trans-Pacific Partnership.

This reluctance to be honest about trade has cost economists their credibility with the public. Worse still, it has fed their opponents' narrative. Economists' failure to provide the full picture on trade, with all of the necessary distinctions and caveats, has made it easier to tar trade, often wrongly, with all sorts of ill effects.

In short, had economists gone public with the caveats, uncertainties, and skepticism of the seminar room, they might have become better defenders of the world economy. Unfortunately, their zeal to defend trade from its enemies has backfired. If the demagogues making nonsensical claims about trade are now getting a hearing—and, in the US and elsewhere, actually winning power—it is trade's academic boosters who deserve at least part of the blame.[40]

This posting, and the attitude and sensibility behind it, are very much within a Classical Liberal methodological tradition. This tradition emphasizes nuance. Doing so creates an effective barrier discouraging the tendency to jump from abstract models to policy prescription without carefully specifying the caveats attendant on such a heedless leap. Rodrik knows international trade models inside out. But he does not base policy directly on them without being fully cognizant of the parts of the model that refuse to quite fit the world to which he is applying them. What he emphasizes are precisely the type of caveats and nuances that are automatically thrown out by a form of standard economics that persistently nestles applied policy issues within the context of positive economics.[41]

Rodrik's post also captures the cost to public policy of the continuing penchant for drawing definitive policy conclusions from abstract models. He argues that this method has largely undermined the intrinsic credibility of economists. Rodrik's posting displays a number of different elements that are central to a Classical Liberal approach to policy formulation. The problem lies not with the models per se, but with a tendency of economists to focus strictly on the results of such models without providing a sufficient emphasis on their limitations. Policy implications of models depend upon highly constrained conditions to render them strictly applicable. Consequently, Rodrik recognizes that differences concerning trade policy among trained economists are not due to theoretical differences. For the most part, they are all using the same models. The differences stem more from sensibilities, caveats, the very assumptions buttressing the trade model, as well as conflicting interpretations of ambiguous empirical evidence. Those differences will not be resolved by remaining firmly within the realm of scientific thinking, narrowly defined. Rodrik further recognizes that having a policy view as one develops a theoretical model taints the subsequent interpretation of scientific facts. This feedback of policy work to the theoretical model creates a distinct danger of having the policy tail wag the theoretical dog. Thus, there are strong arguments for separating the science of economics from the economics attached to policy formation.[42]

A Return, Not a Departure:
Reinstating Classical Liberalism

We could have chosen many more examples of economists exhibiting a Classical Liberal attitude. That attitude can be found in economists throughout the profession, and we are happy to say that there are many economists who display Classical Liberal tendencies. Unfortunately, the institutional structure of the economics profession discourages economists from emphasizing that attitude. Starting with the first principles course, students are taught primarily formal models that are then related to policy with a lot of hand waving. This teaching approach is justified by pedagogical expediency. In graduate school, the models become much more complicated, but their connection to policy is still accompanied by furious, even faster hand waving, once again justified by pedagogical expediency.

The implicit lesson students learn: forget the nuance—it makes the analysis too messy. The practiced imperative is to get the students up to speed analytically. Afterward, they can figure out the way in which theory and empirical evidence fits to policy on their own time. Moreover, it doesn't matter if they don't, because their advancement will depend on academic publications, which discourage discussions of nuance (expect a statement at the end of the research paper that more research is necessary). Given the institutional structure of the academic profession, the fine granular consideration of the connection between models and their policy use receives little focus. Students turn to writing their dissertation and to writing papers in a manner that meets scientific methodological standards (meaning—in a fashion that conforms to publication requirements in academic journals). Considerations of method (especially if they challenge the existing standard) are vigorously discouraged. Such considerations will reduce your publication output and doom your chance of advancement.

Adopting a Classical Liberal attitude will change that. Doing so will encourage the teaching of economics to focus a bit more on how their models and tools relate to policy. Adding a bell or whistle to an existing model will be discouraged, at least somewhat. Theory and applied policy might then be usefully separated. Applied policy economists could be honored even if they lack any consummate skill at developing theoretical models or even fail to excel at doing formal empirical work. Where applied policy economists need to excel is in knowing what good theoretical work is, recognizing good empirical work, and possessing the ability to relate that good work to policy questions, even when doing so involves criticizing the current standard approach. The six economists we discussed in this chapter provide role models for that approach.

It's All Heuristics

Internal criticism—inside the mainstream heterodoxy—is encouraged by the Classical Liberal attitude because that attitude sees all theory and all methodology as heuristics. Criticizing standard practice does not make one heterodox; it is simply being honest. If a Classical Liberal policy methodology is successfully adopted, the current tendency of economists to regard criticism of their favored model as a personal disparagement, or an attack on their science, would be significantly reduced. When everything is considered ad hoc, the criticism that one's own work is ad hoc is easier to stomach. A world where everything is heuristics leaves no one left to defend capital T Truths, or capital M Methodology. What remains is simply small t truths, and small m methodology; after all, it's all heuristics. There is always another turtle.

That also goes for the argument we are making in this book. We do not claim that we have unraveled deep issues in the methodological thicket. We are simply arguing that encouraging a Classical Liberal methodology for applied policy is a better heuristic than encouraging the current positive scientific methodology. The change is not radical. We will still have the same models, and the same empirical methods to apply those models. But the way we interpret the results of that technical work for policy will be more nuanced.

Accepting the art and craft methodology implies that all economic models should be treated as heuristics, not as rigid guides for policy. If that happens, the Classical Liberal attitude will reframe many of the current technical theoretical and policy debates. They could then transition to debates concerning whether the model or methodology one is employing is useful for the question at hand.[43]

Chapter 1. Sweet Science

1. The term "sensibilities" is used to reflect essential policy considerations and factors that are not easily measured or quantifiable.

2. This blending characteristic of art and craft defined by the term "art and craft" requires both a formal component that is consistent with math, science, philosophy, and engineering, and a creative humanities–based component that deals with and integrates ill-defined concepts into the analysis.

3. Put simply, facts never speak for themselves. They require interpretation.

4. Much depends here on how science is defined. But to worry about whether any part of economics is scientific is to lose track of the methodological issue at stake. Classical Liberal Economics separated out economic theory from policy applications, or at least believed such a separation should be maintained, dividing economic theory from policy applications. Whether or not economic theory qualifies as science, in some sense of that term, is largely beside the point.

5. To reiterate, the question as to whether economics should be classified as a science is entirely outside the scope of our concern. Our view is that it is difficult to deny the existence of economic theories and models that economists treat as scientific, even if one denies that such constructs are genuinely scientific.

6. To argue that there should be a separate scientific branch of economics is not to argue that that branch can fully avoid the fact/value entanglement. It is only to argue that, as a pragmatic matter, some questions can be treated as less entangled than others. The science branch of economics has focused on questions—such as whether the conclusions of a model follow from the assumptions, or whether empirically we can develop standards for considering something a fact—where there was broad agreement on how to do so. Policy questions that involved values were far less likely to attract such broad agreement. One such survey underlining the lower level agreement on these matters can be found in Fuchs, Krueger, and Poterba (1998). These issues are also discussed in more depth in Colander and Su (2015) and Su and Colander (2013).

7. Like the Chicago School itself, many of its opponents identified Classical Liberalism with a set of ideological principles rather than a specific methodological approach.

8. As we will discuss in later chapters, Classical Liberals used the term "precept" to describe a generally held belief about policy. A precept described a rule of action and was based on scientific economic principles and moral judgments. They distinguished such precepts from theorems, which were logical deductions from theory and from principles, which were generalizations about theorems. "When price goes up quantity demanded will fall" is an economic principle. It involves no moral judgments. "Government should not impose price controls" is a precept based on value judgments and non-scientifically grounded insights. You could have principles of economics within the science of economics. You could not have precepts of economics within the science of economics since moral judgments have no scientific basis.

9. This drive was spearheaded by Milton Friedman. Economists such as Stigler or Director took focused aim at the regulatory aspect of government intervention, leaving the macroeconomic aspects to Friedman and his disciples.

10. We first heard the term "argumentation for the sake of heaven" phrase in an unpublished speech by the President of Middlebury College, Lauri Patton.

11. Though, like Marshall, hardly a mathematical innocent, Keynes possessed a knack of offhandedly dismissing mathematical models. In his discussion of the employment function (*The General Theory*) he could preface that analysis by stating: "Those who (rightly) dislike algebra will lose little by omitting the first section of this chapter" (Keynes 1936/1964: 280 n.1).

12. The level of deliberation and consciousness that lay behind the rejection of this traditional methodology by such rising young economists as Samuelson or Friedman is more muddle than clarity. The problem of cognitive dissonance often lurks in the background. It is possible to argue that the rejection was deliberate, because they found the former approach dated and no longer functional. Or perhaps, more accurately, in their need to engage in the pressing exigencies of being a working economist, they only gave at best a passing thought to what had preceded them and any similar philosophical quandaries. In that case, conceding too much importance to such stray quotes might only succeed in overstating the consequences that such issues held for them.

13. When it strategically suited him, John Maynard Keynes also crossed this designated and acknowledged line. This was even more prominent among his students and close cadre of disciples, who weren't as immersed in the Classical Liberal tradition. See Colander and Rothschild (2010).

14. One reviewer of the manuscript argues that crossing the firewall is inevitable as long as some part of economics is considered a science. As stated above, we do not see crossing the firewall as inevitable, and the issues quickly morph into debates about what demarcates science from non-science. As long as one holds that the part of economics that is considered science has no direct policy implications, whether or not some part of economics is a science becomes close to irrelevant. Similarly with the issue of whether the firewall is consistently maintained or not: Recognizing the need to sustain such a barrier to prevent science from being used to support policy arguments is what distinguishes Classical Lib-

eral methodology. We agree that it is difficult and practitioners often do not practice what they preach.

15. In essence this meant rejecting the zero-sum adversarial environment of the courtroom for the more congenial and mutually advantageous surroundings of the seminar room.

16. Economists across the board have a decided capability of knowing how they should act while failing to perform in a manner consistent with such avowals. Friedman also professed to be cognizant of the need to quarantine ideology from shaping economic policy, let alone economic science. But there seems to be a certain lack of awareness on his part of the difficulty involved in maintaining a firewall if one takes strong, as opposed to equivocal, policy positions.

> During my whole career, I have considered myself somewhat of a schizophrenic, which might be a universal characteristic. On the one hand, I was interested in science, *qua science*, and I have tried—successfully I hope—not to let my ideological viewpoints contaminate my scientific work. On the other, I felt deeply concerned with the course of events and I wanted to influence them so as to enhance human freedom. Luckily, these two aspects of my interests appeared to me as perfectly compatible. (Friedman quoted in Cherrier 2011: 335)

Others, including some of Friedman's Chicago compatriots, took a more pragmatic approach to the research that defines academic endeavors.

> I doubt there is a truly unbiased academic ... If you think the [Chicago] GSB is an unbiased environment, think again. They are recruited for their views. I wonder how many free marketers would get jobs in anthropology or sociology ... It's true of any institute. You state a mission, attract funders. They expect the mission to be fulfilled. Very rarely do people fund pure knowledge. (Heckman quoted by Nik-Khah 2011: 380)

On the other side of the ideological divide, some notable economists assumed that since in terms of their policy framework, government actions could be either good or bad, they had managed somehow to clearly finesse the underlying problem.

> Value judgements ended up playing a role in your assessment of parameters and of the evidence we consider ... and there is no question that Milton and I, looking at the same evidence, may reach different conclusions as to what it means, because to him, it is so clear that government intervention is bad that there cannot be an occasion where it was good! Whereas, to me government discretion can be good or bad. (Modigliani quoted in Cherrier 2011: 354)

What they failed to recognize, or perhaps admit, was that their theory-tinged framework, constructed to resolve policy issues, ruled out considerations that could seriously undermine their "good" or "bad" conclusions. Instead, the contagion spreading from their ideological and normative views heavily constrained those policy conclusions.

17. The Progressive Era is a case in point. Those years marked a period during which scientific management and the concentrated professionalization of trades, such as law and medicine, aggressively gained traction. Within that same period, the American Economic Association was born, responding to a perceived need to professionalize the discipline and to firmly exclude amateurs and other enthusiastic outsiders. This yearning for the precision and accuracy usually accorded to scientific frameworks could be identified in the time-motion studies of this period (Taylorism), as well as in the rise of city managers. The latter represented an attempt to break free of the political machines and attendant corruption found in US cities during the turn of the century. Science offered a sheltering wall against the floods of emotion, ideology, and ingrained self-interest that all too often seemed to threaten societal well-being.

18. This mind-set reached something of a peak during the Kennedy administration when he sought the advice of outside experts and hired management professionals (like McNamara) to run government departments. The inherent flaw at the heart of this one-size-fits-all mentality was carefully explored in Halberstam's (1972) *The Best and the Brightest*. (Note the irony the title itself conveys.)

19. We are reminded of the quote attributed to Max Planck, namely, that science progresses one funeral at a time.

20. The embryonic beginnings of this shift occurred in the 1930s, as a select core of young graduate students and tyro economists focused on using mathematical models, statistics, and other empirical evidence to analyze the economy. A mix of these British and American upstarts, including Lerner, Sweezy, Hicks, Kaldor, Allen, and others, joined forces to establish the *Review of Economic Studies*, a journal in which their pioneering work could find a home, one that was otherwise denied. This mathematically inclined analysis sought to replace the purely discursive pieces found in the more established publications. "Journals in the pre-war period were nothing but a bundle of assertions and undocumented claims. Some of it was just pure crap" (Conversation with Armen Alchian, October 1997). This scientific position contrasts sharply with that of John Maynard Keynes writing in the previous decade about his teacher, Alfred Marshall. In describing the skills necessary to perform as a successful economist, Keynes reflects Marshall's conception as well.

> The study of economics does not seem to require any specialized gifts of an unusually high order. Is it not, intellectually regarded, a very easy subject compared with the higher branches of philosophy and pure science? Yet good, or even competent, economists are the rarest of birds. An easy subject, at which very few excel! The paradox finds its explanation, perhaps, in that the master-economist must possess a rare combination of gifts. He must reach a high standard in several different directions and must combine talents not often found together. He must be mathemati-

cian, historian, statesman, philosopher—in some degree. He must understand symbols and speak in words. He must contemplate the particular in terms of the general, and touch abstract and concrete in the same flight of thought. He must study the present in the light of the past for the purposes of the future. No part of man's nature or his institutions must lie entirely outside his regard. He must be purposeful and disinterested in a simultaneous mood; as aloof and incorruptible as an artist, yet sometimes as near the earth as a politician. Much, but not all, of this many-sidedness Marshall possessed. But chiefly his mixed training and divided nature furnished him with the most essential and fundamental of the economist's necessary gifts—he was conspicuously historian and mathematician, a dealer in the particular and the general, the temporal and the eternal, at the same time. (Keynes 1924: 321)

21. The difference, curiously enough, is clearly enunciated in the first *Pirates of the Caribbean* film (in 2003). There the young heroine dismisses convoluted discussions about possible violations of the pirate's code by pointing out the obvious. They are pirates acting outside the law and as such any code should be considered mere guidelines rather than hard and fast rules.

22. This temptation is one reason some observers argue that economics should not consider any part of its analysis as being scientific. Inevitably scientists will use their science to win arguments. We recognize that tendency and see the firewall as an imperfect way to deal with it. Yes, there is science, but that science has no direct policy implications. Seeing economics as including different branches, and creating a firewall between the branches, is, in our view, more likely to alert people to the inappropriate appeal to scientific rigor as a means to support policy than is the assumption than no part of economics is scientific.

23. The term neo-Keynesian signified an acceptance of the mathematical, neo-classical synthesis model of classical and Keynesian thought, which economists such as Paul Samuelson advanced.

24. The concept of the impartial spectator has a long history in moral philosophy, and there is considerable debate about its precise meaning, including what Smith meant by it. Our use of it is general and does not attempt to touch on these philosophical debates. We are simply arguing that Smith believed that, in order to discuss elements of policy, one needed some normative reference point, and the impartial spectator concept served that purpose. See, for instance, Raphael (2007).

25. These qualifications were so strong that unwavering, pro-market advocates (not in any sense impartial spectators) such as Murray Rothbard consider Smith to be a socialist.

26. This "vice" involved generalizing from a set of time and place specifics. Namely, the perspective seemed to insist that what might work in England at a given time formed some type of universal precept. However, that particular danger had not in fact been first identified by Schumpeter. English economists, as

represented by Mill and Marshall, warned against such lazy thinking years before Schumpeter was a recognizable force in the discipline.

> Political Economy, therefore, reasons from assumed premises—premises which might be totally without foundation in fact, and which are not pretended to be universally in accordance with it. The conclusions of Political Economy consequently, like those of geometry, are only true, as the common phrase is, in the abstract, that is, they are only true under certain suppositions, in which none but general causes common to the whole class of cases under consideration—are taken into account. (Mill 1968: 144–145)

Essentially, Classical Liberals recognized the work of Ricardo, and the continued efforts of his followers, as being employed largely for rhetorical purposes. It had been commandeered to support given policies. Scientific authority provided a false certainty, shifting the argument back to the purview of the theoretic models from which such policies flowed. The same sort of methodology was adopted in the postwar period, strangely enough a reversion to the approach previously championed by Ricardo and Marx.

> So they (advocates of free-trade) based sweeping general propositions on English facts and English conditions. This gave to their argument much apparent lucidity and simplicity, which hastened their victory and their victory was two-fold. For it was followed by so great an increase of England's prosperity, that other nations began to open their ports in imitation of her and this doubled the benefits which free trade conferred on England ... other nations would have been warned beforehand that the removal of Protective duties could not be expected to confer the same unmixed benefits on their best industries as it had done on those of England. As things were, they had to learn it in the hard school of experience. (Marshall 1923: 84–85)

27. While Classical Liberal economists generally accepted a utilitarian moral philosophy, their methodology did not demand such allegiance. It offered merely one possible heuristic that could be developed when looking at normative judgments from an impartial spectator position.

28. Although the central ideas of utilitarianism have a long history and can be found in the writings of David Hume (1742) and Francis Hutcheson (1755), those ideas were only formalized into precise guidance for policy in the writings of Jeremy Bentham. Thus, while it is possible to see Smith as a utilitarian, it is also possible to see him as someone who blended a rights-based moral foundation with one founded on utilitarian principles. These are issues that go beyond the focus of this book. Our argument is only that Smith believed that moral philosophy was an important input into policy analysis. We leave it to specialists to decide what that precise moral philosophy might have been.

29. See Colander (2007b).

30. For instance, Vilfredo Pareto took a decidedly different approach to welfare policy. In contrast to the Kaldor-Hicks notion focusing on potential compensation as a sufficient foundation to justify trade agreements, Pareto required actual payments, not merely some notional accounting adjustments, to underwrite specific policy proposals. Kemp and Pezanis-Christou (1999) sketch out convincing evidence of Pareto's viewpoint on this matter.

31. The difference is between theory-based policy and rules of thumb flowing from experience. Thus, it would be stretching the notion of theory to say that Smith's preference for a laissez-faire approach was theory-based. George Stigler (1971c), a great admirer of Adam Smith, would take him to task for his failure to use narrow self-interest as the basis for explaining government objectives and policy. Such chastisement seems to stem from core methodological differences. Stigler, while professing to be saving Classical Liberalism, abandoned the methodological perspective strongly favored by his teacher, Frank Knight, who viewed the ambit of economic science to be highly limited. Knight (1940, 1946) was not shy about making this limitation distinctively clear. Stigler, a convert to postwar scientific modernism, rejected Knight's methodology. Support for laissez-faire under his tutelage was no longer considered a useful rule-of-thumb approach to policy.

32. Thus, for early economists, a strict policy of laissez-faire didn't enter into any emphatic economic equation. They were constitutionally leery of government intervention, given the British Crown's tendency to reward favorites and overlook corruption, but the extent of government involvement was always more situational than proscribed by hard and fast dictates.

> The phrase laissez-faire is not to be found in the works of Adam Smith, of Ricardo, or of Malthus. Even the idea is not present in a dogmatic form in any of these authors. Adam Smith, of course, was a Free Trader and an opponent of many eighteenth-century restrictions on trade. But his attitude towards the Navigation Acts and the usury laws shows that he was not dogmatic. Even his famous passage about "the invisible hand" reflects the philosophy which we associate with Paley rather than the economic dogma of *laissez-faire*. (Keynes 1926)

33. Perhaps it may be of some use to remember that the writings of Paine and Rousseau were considered to be quite radical in the highly class-structured British society of their time. The French Revolution was looked upon with horror, not only by such politicians as Burke but by writers, poets, and essayists such as Carlyle and Wordsworth (or at least by Wordsworth in his later incarnation).

34. John Maynard Keynes similarly points out the attachment of Smith to liberty, a matter enshrined in the Chicago School credo but not arising from Smith's economic framework. "As Sidgwick and Cliff Leslie have pointed out, Adam Smith's advocacy of the 'obvious and simple system of natural liberty' is derived from his theistic and optimistic view of the order of the world as set forth in his *Theory of Moral Sentiments*, rather than any proposition of political economy proper" (Keynes 1926).

Chapter 2. A Classical Garden of Liberal Economics

1. All economists from this period should not be included within the confines of what we define as Classical Liberal methodology. As will become quite clear, David Ricardo would certainly rest uneasily within the tradition we are describing. He proved determined to barrel down a spur line set orthogonally to the spirit with which many of his compatriots approached economics. Ricardo at the very least marketed a noticeably different brand of wares than others peddled. Fortunately, economists are not required, either at that time or in the present, to move together in consistent lockstep. As mentioned, John Stuart Mill welcomed dissent and opposing views.

2. Empirical science composed of quantifiable and empirically measurable phenomena could get you further, but economics and social science at the time did not have the tools to be a formal, empirically based science. For policy analysis, an economist's empirical tools remained weak, as we will discuss in later chapters.

3. In a historical and military sense, the arrayed Neoclassical/Classical Liberal economists presented a formidable shield held together by an interlocking common purpose. They all attempted to keep a sufficient, though not absolute, separation between theory and policy.

4. Marshall was the master of qualified analysis, what his detractors might with less goodwill describe as a compulsive need to fudge. As Keynes noted, "Jevons chiselled in stone while Marshall knitted in wool" (Keynes 1933/1951: 241).

5. Notice the degree to which such an encouragement of diversity accords with Mill's dictum of characterizing openness to alternative views as being one of the principle virtues of Classical Liberalism.

6. Pointing out the inevitable transgressions to these principles in the work of nineteenth-century economists does little to undercut the validity of these such insights. Transgressions are necessarily measured by the precepts from which they stray.

7. John Stuart Mill took a complex view toward laissez-faire, refusing to accept it as a principle, but instead seeing it only as a precept applicable in certain instances: "a doctrine (laissez-faire) generated by the manifest selfishness and incompetence of modern European governments, but of which, as a general theory, we may now be permitted to say that one-half of it is true and the other half false" (Mill 1965: x).

In much the same way, Marshall also rejected the sort of bedtime stories for well-behaved infants, which posited some type of simple-minded, invisible hand assiduously tasked to guard against individual folly. "There is no general economic principle which supports the notion that industry will necessarily flourish best or that life will be the happiest and healthiest when each man is allowed to manage his own concerns as he thinks best" (Marshall 1923: 736).

8. The same argument has often been used to justify democracy. For example, Winston Churchill writes: "No one pretends that democracy is perfect or all-wise.

Indeed, it has been said that democracy is the worst form of Government except all those other forms that have been tried from time to time" (Churchill 1947).

9. Classical economists did not extend their economic theory to include state action, as later economists such as Tullock and Buchanan would attempt to do. Using a model featuring a fictitious rational economic man was questionable enough when discussing material welfare. Extending it to politics was pushing it far beyond the point where it even had a hope of being useful. In politics, these economists preferred that an individual's social self would guide policy, not their selfish self.

10. Classical economists recognized that fully separating the science branch of economics from values was impossible. But as a heuristic, it proved useful to separate out a part of economics, namely that part which attempted to be as value-free as possible. This was the selection that they labeled science. Science was that part of economics where value judgments were to be consciously left at the door.

11. Frank Knight, who continued to operate within this tradition, made the distinction sufficiently clear and precise. Theoretical economics was inherently limited since by definition, a science of history was indisputably not within the realm of possibility (putting him, and the Classical tradition, at odds with thinkers like Hegel and Marx).

> Statics: "Reasoning" about "economic change" in the only possible method: varying one thing while holding others constant/ Dynamics: Cannot exist as "economic science" ... though perhaps as "evolutionary or historical economics." (Knight quoted in Machlup 1959: 95)

12. As Myrdal points out, "Cairnes, the last of the great classical writers, put the point even more vigorously." The end of political economy, Cairnes said, is "not to attain tangible results, not to prove any definite thesis, not to advocate any practical plan, but simply to give light, to reveal laws of nature, to tell us what phenomena are found together, what effects will follow from what causes" (Myrdal 1954 [1930]: 3).

13. It is important to note here that these Classical economists would not have accepted the Friedman/Stigler construct of positivism. Rather, they were concerned with the soundness of the assumptions made.

> John Stuart Mill and subsequently Cairnes, both of whom were better versed in philosophy than Senior, were eager to stress that economic theory is a "hypothetical science." The truth of any deduction was supposed to depend upon the adequacy of the assumptions. Senior, on the other hand, stressed that the assumptions need not be arbitrarily chosen. Instead, valid generalizations ought to be formulated on the basis of empirical reality. (Myrdal 1954 [1930]: 7)

14. We will discuss this separation of theory and policy in much more detail below. It was a key element in John Neville Keynes's summary of economic

methodology at the turn of the nineteenth century (Keynes 1891). Like Senior, John Neville Keynes also separated what he labeled as the applied policy branch from what he deemed to be positive economics, a relatively narrow aspect of the discipline. Senior saw this applied study as comprising the more complex art of economics. He argued that the two branches needed to be separated because they had quite different methodologies. "A definitive art of political economy, which attempts to lay down absolute rules for the regulation of human conduct, will have vaguely defined limits, and be largely non-economic in character" (Keynes 1891: 83). Keynes argued that in science, economists developed theorems. In policy analysis they developed precepts, which were based on judgments that went far beyond science.

15. Mill stated this view succinctly in *On Liberty* (1859). He writes; "the only purpose for which power can be rightfully exercised over any member of a civilized community, against his will, is to prevent harm to others. His own good, either physical or moral, is not a sufficient warrant. He cannot rightfully be compelled to do or forbear because it will be better for him to do so, because it will make him happier, because, in the opinion of others, to do so would be wise, or even right."

16. As with most policy matters, economists could only be said to roughly hew to any strict boundaries on issues like paternalism. Marshall, perhaps based on his religious underpinnings, failed to entirely smother his propensity for wanting mankind to be so uplifted. In distinct contrast, Friedman felt impelled to raise a red flag to his old friend, George Stigler, about following Marshall down this deceptive path.

> You cite Marshall. In him, "the improvement of man" equals the remaking of other peoples into the image of the Englishman, which is warning enough that this slogan has danger of leading to the narrowest kind of presumptuous provincialism.... I can't help but feel you're right in saying Marshall's chief touchstone was what he regarded as improving the human race. But I have always shuddered at Marshall's ethical judgments, at what for him was improvement. (Letter from Milton Friedman to George Stigler, February 7, 1948, in Hammond and Hammond 2006: 78)

Friedman however would not accept the importance played by methodology in defining Classical Liberalism. Thus, from Friedman's perspective, at some point in his career, John Stuart Mill was drummed out of that respected classification seemingly from the time when he came under the supposed malevolent influence of Harriet Taylor. "Didn't [John Stuart] Mill end up a socialist?" (Letter from Milton Friedman to George Stigler, February 7, 1948, in Hammond and Hammond 2006: 78).

17. Hayek strongly rejected conservatism, as well as collectivism, for its inherent distrust of individual choice.

> This timidity and fear to trust to the uncontrolled working of social forces is closely connected with two other characteristic attributes of conserva-

tism: Its authoritarian or paternalistic leanings and its dislike and consequent lack of understanding of the operation of economic forces. As it distrusts both abstract theories and general principles it neither understands the spontaneous forces on which a policy of freedom relies, nor has it a basis for formulating principles for policy. (Hayek 1957: 4)

18. For Knight, additionally, the ethical considerations infused within any individual decision could not simply be dismissed as tiresome complications. Individual choice was not entirely sacrosanct despite being honored for its positive qualities. "An examination of the ethics of the economic system must consider the question of the kind of wants which it tends to generate or nourish" (Knight quoted in Burgin 2012: 113).

19. Compare this to the acknowledged touchstone of the Chicago School, Stigler and Becker's (1977) attempt to reinvest the sanctity of consumer sovereignty, "Degustibus, Non Est Disputandum."

Can we say this is illegitimate if the public wants it? Is that consistent with our extreme position on consumer sovereignty which is that no matter what horrible things the public wants, as free market economists we can never question it. That's certainly one of the basic principles of neoclassical economics. Consumer sovereignty is both the end of the story and the beginning. And we don't argue with the consumer, no matter how self-destructive these demands are or how inappropriate. (Conversation with Claire Friedland, October 1997)

20. Of course, any study would be remiss if it failed to note that many mainstay figures of Classical thought, economists on the order of Mill and Marshall, pursued the study and formulation of economics with a view and a desire to improve social welfare.

21. Experience demonstrates the skill willingly employed in the rationalization of narrow self-interest. Few practicing opportunists will publicly and very brazenly dismiss the supposed general welfare benefits of any given proposal.

22. As we discuss in chapter 7, this argument would later be picked up by Public Choice economists such as James Buchanan. He argued that government intervention created an opportunity for the more unscrupulous to manipulate a general lack of policy knowledge into a personal rent-seeking opportunity.

23. As we will discuss in detail in a later chapter, they differed markedly from the later Chicago School, whose leaders almost casually assumed that freedom and liberty were what individuals wanted and should want, whatever the circumstances. For these distantly removed Liberal descendants, resident in Chicago, it remained an unarguable position, an indisputable first principle.

24. Though a firm believer in narrow self-interest as a fundamental and even testable hypothesis, George Stigler drew the line at endorsing a broad-based, all-enveloping, interpretation. Otherwise, the sole conclusion that could be reached upon observing a man swallowing battery acid was that this individual certainly liked battery acid. In essence, in trying to explain everything, nothing could be

explained. Stigler's approach would be to demonstrate that despite appearances, a given action was actually driven by recognizably narrow self-interest.

25. Marshall also perceived an urgent need for the professionalization of economics on terms that he considered to be imperative. His campaign would help transform universities into the ultimate gatekeepers. Popular writers, such as Henry George or John Hobson, would be stripped of any mantle of respectability and thus much more easily dismissed by authoritative academics.

26. This description would cover a period roughly from the Chicago department's establishment in 1892 till perhaps 1946, when Jacob Viner departed and Henry Simons died. Though there were notable economists who flourished in the department during this period despite failing to fit nicely into the Classical Liberal cupboard.

27. Core Chicago figures, such as Friedman, Stigler, and Director, all claimed to be devoted followers and propagators of Alfred Marshall's economic thought.

> *I know he [George Stigler] saw himself in the tradition of Marshall. Do you think he was actually a Marshallian in approach?*
>
> He certainly was always very respectful of Marshall. (Conversation with Ronald Coase, October 1997)

Certainly, the commonly held belief in postwar Chicago was that only they were the true keepers of the Marshallian sacred flame.

> Or for that matter in England, where the conventional kind of Marshallian price theory went to hell. I mean Marshall invented a lot of that stuff. [laughs] Yet it was gone by World War II. You couldn't learn it there. You had to come to the US to learn about it. That was shocking. (Conversation with Sherwin Rosen, October 1997)

28. In this respect, Pigou never entirely broke with Marshall and particularly with his methodology. For Pigou, his departure from Marshall was more of a shift away from central themes rather than a clean break from the ideas of his mentor.

29. Stigler is being his usual sardonic self in this statement. In this succinct lecture, one of five interrelated talks presented at the London School of Economics in 1948, Stigler intends to demonstrate that the Classical economists were skilled and able professionals in terms of practical application and problem solving, no matter what they may have lacked in theoretical finesse. Given this context, our current sense of superiority should be recognized as being widely misplaced and misjudged. "I just don't dare send you an article on how smart the classical economists were, or you'll give up completely" (Letter from George Stigler to Milton Friedman, November 1947, in Hammond and Hammond 2006: 67). Examining the existing technical apparatus used in their investigations could under such circumstances only mislead by encouraging an overly earnest or a naïve evaluation. Here we need to remember that Stigler served a rigorous tutelage under Viner and Knight, both in their own ways faithful to the Classical Liberal tradition. [Stigler's dissertation written under the jaundiced eye of Frank

Knight (subsequently published in 1941) was an archetypical history of thought effort.] His distinct break with his teachers, at this stage in 1948, existed only at an incipient, but clearly discernible, stage. Stigler thoroughly understood this older, and in many ways admirable, methodology. Nevertheless, he would come to reject, though not explicitly renounce, this older approach to economics.

> The discrepancies between pronouncements and practice are notorious in the field of methodology; can it not be so also in the theory of value? In writing their treatises, may not the classical economists have employed apparatus which is different and in modern eyes inferior to that which they employed to analyse concrete problems? (Stigler 1949c: 25–26)

30. John Maynard Keynes, taking on the mantle of his father (John Neville Keynes) or his teacher (Alfred Marshall), could continue to claim allegiance to Liberalism. However, in keeping with the older methodology that characterized that tradition, he could also maintain at times a skeptical perspective on the efficacy, let alone morality, of the marketplace.

> It is *not* a correct deduction from the Principles of Economics that enlightened self-interest always operates in the public interest … We cannot, therefore, settle on abstract grounds, but must handle on its merits in detail, what Burke termed "one of the finest problems in legislation, namely, to determine what the State ought to take upon itself to direct by the public wisdom, and what it ought to leave, with as little interference as possible, to individual exertion." (Keynes 1963a [1926]: 312–313)

Chapter 3. Planting the Seeds of a Chicago Tradition

1. The University of Chicago, opening on October 1, 1892, was essentially a collaboration between John D. Rockefeller (financial wherewithal) and William Rainey Harper (theologian and first president of the University).

2. Laughlin was chosen by the first president of the University of Chicago, William Rainey Harper. Harper had planned to hire Richard Ely, an economist with policy views (and an approach to economics) at odds with that of Laughlin's. Had Harper been willing to meet Richard T. Ely's financial demands, the subsequent course of the department might have evolved in a significantly different fashion.

> While his relations with Ely were turning sour, Harper accidentally met James Laughlin, a fierce critic of Ely's economics and a staunch defender of orthodox classical economics. In December 1891, Harper became convinced that Laughlin was the right choice after Laughlin impressed him during a debate on monetary issues in New York. Legend has it that following the debate, Laughlin and Harper spent the whole night walking the streets of New York City, and at five o'clock in the morning Laughlin

agreed to start up the department of political economy at the University of Chicago. (Overtveldt 2007: 46)

3. This sort of inveterate skepticism can often skate a fine line that easily slips into a habit of being cantankerous almost for its own sake, a form that flirts with self-indulgence. Aaron Director, one of the major, if less recognized, founders of the Chicago School could easily be classified as residing on either side of that treacherous divide.

> Aaron Director was extremely conservative. Why, I don't know. By the time I knew him he was already like that. And he was an iconoclast. But he didn't develop new data with respect to industrial organisation. He didn't develop and articulate new theories. He just said that the conventional belief wasn't so. (Conversation with Paul Samuelson, October 1997)

4. There is probably some psychological syndrome that attempts to explain this obsessive behavior. The goal in part certainly appears to be a desire to provoke a rise out of opponents (and perhaps random individuals), to leave these targets spluttering with rage. Those who dabble in these darker realms tend to deny or rationalize away the actual pleasure they derive by inflaming the passion of others. However, such guilty pleasures tend to lurk at some subterraneous level, even if largely unacknowledged.

5. Temporarily doesn't refer in any sense to being told to leave or to being summarily booted out. Instead it indicates that Chicago was employed as something of a way station during their careers.

6. This particular impression could only be magnified by Laughlin's rigid opposition to the progressive political ideology and policies favored by Richard T. Ely, one of the founders (1885) of the *American Economic Association*. This competition and antagonism was by no means mollified when Laughlin came to Chicago once William Rainey Harper (the University's first president) refused to meet Ely's compensation demands.

7. This bit of contention deftly paralleled a similar competitive friction between Chicago and such East Coast cities as New York. The impetus behind the 1893 World's Fair could be understood as an attempt to establish the importance and legitimacy of this Midwest outpost. In fact, some commentators view the Chicago nickname of the "windy city" to refer to its turn-of-the-century habit of civic boasting, rather than describing the blustery winds roaring in from Lake Michigan.

8. This sense of a "band of brothers" is reminiscent of the famous St. Crispin's Day speech in Shakespeare's *Henry V*. The anchoring sentiment here is one of an outnumbered group of brothers staving off and defeating the mainstream hordes of economists. Such thinking remained as an active principle defining Chicago throughout the years to come. This definitive mind-set was very self-evident during the heyday of the Friedman-Stigler-Director era.

9. Not coincidentally, upon arriving at Chicago, Laughlin established the *Journal of Political Economy*, not just to market his newly established department,

but as an act of defiance against the only other existing competitor, the *Quarterly Journal of Economics*, the flagship of Harvard University, the very embodiment of establishment economics. The tension between the two departments (to which one could later add MIT) would continue and thrive through the reign of the postwar Chicago School as well.

> It is utterly amazing how, in MIT for a period of years, particularly in Samuelson's classes, but also in Solow's classes, hardly a lecture went by without some sort of a quip aimed either at Milton, or at Chicago, or at the Midway or something like that, you know. (Conversation with Arnold Harberger, October 1997)

10. This contrary spirit is in many ways reflected in the types of students the graduate department attracted. George Stigler still maintained a whiff of the provincial Northwest about him even after many decades as a renowned academic. Milton Friedman was the eldest son of working-class Jewish immigrants genetically imbued with a combative streak that was nurtured by and later flourished at Chicago. This very Chicago idea of a band of brothers staunchly allied against the formidable forces of received wisdom, and especially in opposition to entrenched theory, would to a large degree underwrite the ensuing Chicago School. Encouraging such a romantic sense of destiny would serve to buttress what initially seemed to be a quixotic campaign against economic orthodoxy.

11. According to former students as diverse as Samuelson and Stigler, Knight was not, at first glance, an initially prepossessing figure. Though almost idealized by some of the brightest graduate students of the time, others found his course to be incomprehensible and obscure at best.

> Who could forget Frank Knight, a little dumpy figure in a workman's cap when he first gave a guest lecture to us University of Chicago sophomores? His squeaky voice emitted a mixture of Will Rogers' profundities and Ludwig Wittgenstein one-liners. Anyone so un-understandable you knew had to be a deep thinker. (Samuelson 2011 925)

12. The extended quote by Mill precisely lays out the other major characteristic of Classical Liberal methodology. Although most of the focus here is on the postwar shift that muddled theory with policy in the name of scientific progress, equally important to liberal thought is a willingness to understand and take alternative and even oppositional theories with all the due seriousness they deserve. As the need to market one's theories, allied with an urge to push ideological stances, became evident, academic debate took on a more combative and unproductive shading, turning any argument into a zero-sum game of winners and losers.

13. Those familiar with George Stigler's attacks on heterodox theories during his postwar reign at Chicago, will recognize a similar strategy, razor sharp remarks and tactics aimed at demolishing, rather than grappling with, opposing views. "It [the classroom] was the perfect place for Stigler to conduct a Demolition Derby. Nor was he hesitant about the task. Theories like 'monopolistic competition' and

'countervailing power,' which were treated reverently at Harvard (where they originated), were eviscerated by Stigler" (Sowell 1993: 787).

14. Cutting the umbilical cord that tends to link these two eras in the topography of Chicago economics means that we are able to forego confusing designations like the old and new Chicago or the first and second Chicago School. What immediately, and justifiably, should come to mind in employing the term the "Chicago School" is its postwar eruption. To try to corral the admittedly diverse department during the interwar years into a simplified designation seems at best counterproductive, if not emphatically misleading. Geography in this instance is not destiny.

15. Knight in some ways epitomized Mark Twain's statement, at least when it came to empirical knowledge. "It's not what you don't know that kills you, it's what you know for sure that ain't true." He at times seemed impervious to formal empirical evidence.

16. Unlike his students Stigler and Friedman, Viner was never a worshiper at the shrine of the empirical. We can see this classic skepticism in Viner's take on Kelvin's famous quote, "when you cannot measure it, when you cannot express it in numbers, your knowledge is of a meagre and unsatisfactory kind."

> Viner asked him why he had not given the full version which ended "And even when we can measure a thing, our knowledge will be meager and unsatisfactory." After an extensive search, Ogburn returned to Viner and said that he could find no record of the additional phrase in Kelvin's work. Viner calmly said, "He should have said it." (Letter from Donald McCloskey [as then was] to George Stigler, September 23, 1985)

17. The Knight and Viner examples both reflect the extent to which there remained a strong Classical Liberal methodology during those interwar years in Chicago. Moreover, it displays the broad reach characteristic of such an approach, nurturing economists that were far from carbon copies of one another. Viner tended to be perhaps more pragmatic than some of his other colleagues. Ideology did not blind him to either talent or worth, as Samuelson pointed out.

> Although Jacob Viner had the reputation of a conservative economist who defended the orthodoxies of neoclassical and classical economics, he played a role of modest importance in Franklin Roosevelt's New Deal. Henry Morgenthau, Jr., Secretary of the Treasury, was no great intellect but he came to have respect for Jacob Viner. Through Viner, Harry Dexter White was called from Lawrence College in Wisconsin to begin his Napoleonic rise in the Treasury. Indeed not a few Chicago students of Viner, who were identified in the McCarthy hunts as communists or fellow travelers, were recommended by Viner. This occasioned some snickers among Chicagoans who were critical of Viner on fine points of doctrine, but who should have had reason and experience to know that Jacob Viner was a center to right-of-center thinker and actor. (Samuelson 2011: 591)

18. A useful introduction to this less than overworked topic of anti-Semitism within the economics profession might start with Reder (2000).

19. The discipline at that time was in something of a ferment. The problems generated by the Great Depression loomed large. Internal debates featuring perceived theoretical deficiencies had become increasingly common. "Beginning with the 1930s, there was a period of very active work on economic theory, macro and micro, in both areas. What became prestigious was work in a kind of economic theory, namely pure and largely mathematical oriented. And it did not really have any considerable history" (Conversation with Milton Friedman, Rose Friedman, and Aaron Director, August 1997).

20. Desperate times were eliciting desperate proposals and remedies. Radical solutions from the sort of self-selected amateurs that Marshall abhorred were increasingly coming to the fore.

21. It is hardly surprising that George Stigler presented his series of lectures at the LSE in 1948. Perhaps even more than Chicago at that time, his thoughts would be communicated to a more receptive audience in the heart of London. Chicago in particular, immediately after the war, was the site of a pitched battle between the new wave Keynesians and those who at least professed a faith (however superficial) in Classical Liberal positions.

22. Simons was dead by 1946, Viner left for Princeton in that same year, and Knight was rapidly losing interest in Economics. He estimated the discipline to be too narrow to convey anything of significant value.

23. Lester Telser remarked how during the 1960s there was a definite inner circle in the Chicago Department centering on Friedman and Stigler (Conversation with Lester Telser, October 1997). For Friedman, as noted in his letters, there were individuals who could be characterized as "our kind" and "one of us" versus all the others. A unified vision, extending through many aspects of their outlook (though of course not to all), would come to define those at Chicago.

> They defended each other. Now, Aaron Director, for example, would never have written a good letter of recommendation for somebody who wasn't a staunch conservative but neither would Milton. And I remember for years after I left the University of Chicago, when they were contemplating influential appointments they would ask me about the person, "Is he really sound?" In fact, Milton once showed his naïveté to me, but it wasn't about appointments. He said, "Tell me the truth, is Galbraith a Commie?" You know the amount of naïveté that's in that. (Conversation with Paul Samuelson, October 1997)

24. Aaron Director was the exception here, serving as a staff lecturer in the 1930s (Paul Samuelson's first instructor into the mysteries of economics). He had initially arrived at Chicago to study under Paul Douglas, jointly publishing a book with Douglas in 1931. For an interesting investigation into Director's early years, time wouldn't be wasted by having a look at Van Horn (2010a, 2010b).

25. The very best of the Chicago graduate students of the 1930s (Stigler, Wallis, Friedman, Jones, Hart, and a young undergraduate student named Paul Samuelson) all seemed to come under the spell of this physically unprepossessing academic, Frank Knight. The magic did not last.

> By the last part of his life, whether in the last half or the last third, it was my impression that George was of the opinion that *laissez-faire* itself pretty much approximated to tolerably effective competition. And I think Aaron Director was the prime source of this view. George also gave signs, I don't know whether it's in his biography of Frank Knight in *Palgrave*, of real disaffection with Frank Knight. The besottedness faded away. And I think that may have also been Aaron Director, although Aaron Director and Frank Knight were close and intimate. (Conversation with Paul Samuelson, October 1997)

26. Even these two notably market-oriented economists, Knight and Viner, could hardly be conceived as in any way united in their methods or economic thinking. Each was generally conservative in their politics and in their economic analysis, but in a complex and distinctly different fashion. Viner was certainly more empirical in his work than someone like Knight.

> I think the way he worked was more similar to Jacob Viner than to Frank Knight. The sort of economics he did was more like Viner's custom theories and so on, which were empirically based. Knight would not look at any data. So, I guess, he differed with Knight in this regard but that was not unusual. He began to differ with Knight in a lot of respects. I'm saying he becomes more like Viner. Look at Viner, early on in Viner's own dissertation on international trade, he is already testing the Canadian and American data. George became a big, empirical testing guy. As with Friedman, Viner was the greater influence. Not Knight. (Conversation with Gary Becker, November 1997)

27. The use of the term "Chicago School" was more often adopted by its opponents to initially refer to the Knight/Viner/Simons group that held sway until 1946. Later, Edward Chamberlin used it as a term of opprobrium to include in broad sweeping terms the department from the time of publication of his milestone work up to and including 1957. This was not, although Stigler claims it to be the case, the first written example of using the label the "Chicago School" to denote a particular approach to economics. As Stigler mistakenly tries to explain:

> Edward H. Chamberlin had written a chapter on the Chicago School in his *Toward a More General Theory of Value* in 1957, the earliest such explicit essay I have found. He found the school to be distinguished "by the zeal with which the theory of monopolistic competition has been attacked." And called it the Chicago School of Anti-Monopolistic Competition. What was a minor recreational activity for us was the raison d'être to him! (Stigler 1988a: 150)

But, as Chamberlin points out in that same quoted article, Stigler's erstwhile classmate Martin Bronfenbrenner had used the same terminology earlier. (Ironically the school is characterized by Bronfenbrenner (1950: 487) as being concerned with income redistribution via progressive taxation policies. Stigler would soon come to entirely reject this Henry Simons–inspired objective.)

> The so-called Chicago School of economic policy, whose intellectual parent is Frank H. Knight, but whose best-known publicist is Henry C. Simons, author of *Economic Policy for a Free Society*, believes these optimum conditions would, in fact be realized quickly and painlessly in a free economy despite the complications raised by economic progress and the possible multiplicity or instability of equilibrium conditions, if these conditions were satisfied. (Bronfenbrenner 1950: 487)

In contrast, Milton Friedman, who had shown no antagonism toward the Miller piece, saw more value in the notion of branding than his colleague George Stigler did initially. See Medema (2014) for a useful discussion concerning the Chicago brand.

> To economists the world over, "Chicago" designates not a city, not even a University, but a "school." The term is sometimes used as an epithet, sometimes as an accolade, but always with a fairly definite—though by no means single valued—meaning. In discussions of economic policy, "Chicago" stands for belief in the free market as a means of organizing resources, for skepticism about government intervention into economic affairs, and for emphasis on the quantity of money as a key factor in producing inflation. In discussions of economic science, "Chicago" stands for an approach that takes seriously the use of economic theory as a tool for analyzing a startlingly wide range of concrete problems, rather than as an abstract mathematical structure of great beauty but little power; for an approach that insists on the empirical testing of theoretical generalizations and that rejects alike facts without theory and theory without facts. (Friedman 1974: 3)

28. Early disputes with the Cowles Commission, spearheaded by Milton Friedman, attempted to push back against these two particular aspects of the postwar tide in economics. Despite some common membership existing between the two institutions, the resulting tension led the Cowles Commission to pack up and shift their base to Yale University in 1955.

29. Starting with its first edition in 1948, the textbook is still an ongoing proposition, with the nineteenth edition coming out in 2016, some six years after Samuelson's death.

30. Neither Milton Friedman nor George Stigler found any advantage to dropping what they understood as Marshall's use of partial equilibrium for the Walrasian alternative, no matter how tone deaf they often appeared to be when evaluating Marshall's application methods. There is little doubt that, having learned

economics from reading (and rereading) Marshall, both Friedman and Stigler saw themselves as operating within that tradition. In a 1941 review, Friedman points out that Marshall was "concerned with the kind of competition that prevails in the real world" (Friedman 1941: 390). But less certain is the grasp either one of them had mastered of understanding how Marshall employed his theoretical apparatus to analyze that real competition.

31. As students, and one-time admirers of Knight, it would be difficult to conceive that this trio of counterrevolutionaries were unaware of the Classical Liberal methodology espoused by economists like Knight, Simons, or Viner for that matter. A look at their early work shows every sign of the influence their teachers exerted. (Given the personalities of these young apprentices, it would come as something of a surprise if such a focused influence did not manage to dissipate quickly.) Moreover, one of the five lectures presented by George Stigler (1949) focused on the fashion in which Classical Liberal economists constructed policy despite having at their disposal only a primitive form of economic theory, or perhaps more likely by largely ignoring that same framework. But, as young economists operating in unsettled times, they would feel no reluctance in departing from a methodology that had, in their view, outworn its usefulness, ceasing to be relevant in a more modern age. Though conservative by inclination, this did not translate into any recognizable variety of ancestor worship. The need to place economics on a scientific footing, while pushing back the tide of collectivism, would demand a much greater priority.

32. Aaron Director, while at the London School of Economics in the late 1930s, formed a close relationship with Friedrich von Hayek. The friendship forged at that time would prove instrumental in persuading the University of Chicago Press to publish *The Road to Serfdom* (1944).

33. Neil Hart (2013) provides some useful insights into Marshall's objectives as well as his methods.

34. In the world of Chicago, government intervention in the form of regulation could now be refuted universally through empirical testing. Thus, in their pioneering work, Stigler and Friedland (1962) would demonstrate empirically that regulation failed to accomplish its objectives. This breakthrough opened the floodgates for others to equally indicate that regulation was in fact a counterproductive policy.

> There were two things, two things coming out of that. One was the methodology. (This was the early 60s, it's old hat by now.) There is a systematic way of testing a hypothesis that should be applied to this area. That would have had an impact. It is clear it would have had an impact. But then, there was of course the result of applying it, which was shocking. People then believed that it was shocking. (Conversation with Sam Peltzman, October 1997)

35. Though professing devotion to their personal version of Marshall, a more accurate evaluation might dispassionately lump them together with the battalion

of "loyal but faithless" Marshallians, a deft turn of phrase by Dennis Robertson. Whether he himself adhered to the spirit of Marshall remains an open question.

36. To be more precise, this form of Classical Liberalism defined a segment of the department, most notably dominated by the trio of Knight, Viner, and Simons, with other such as Harry Gideonse also in this camp. However, also resident at Chicago were Paul Douglas and Henry Schultz, as well as such institutionalists as John Nef, Chester Wright, and Simeon Leland. As will be emphasized later, nominating Chicago during these interwar years as an example of a unified "school" is fanciful at best.

37. Reder makes this point sufficiently unequivocal.

> In essence the Chicago View, or what I term "Tight Prior Equilibrium" theory (TP), is rooted in the hypothesis that decision makers so allocate the resources under their control that there is no alternative allocation such that any one decision maker could have his expected utility increased without a reduction occurring in the expected utility of at least one other decision maker. (Reder 1982: 11)

However, for Chicago, unlike the Classical economists, what is never a matter for debate is the strict assertion that individual rational choice is the irreducible method for understanding and modeling all human decisions. Any apparent deviation from this singular result is seen, in Chicago terms, as a challenge that requires unflagging remediation.

> Any apparent inconsistency of empirical findings with implications of the theory, or report of behavior not implied by the theory, is interpreted as anomalous and requiring one of the following actions: (i) re-examination of the data to reverse the anomalous finding; (ii) redefinition and/or augmentation of the variables in the model, particularly the permissible objects of choice and the resource constraints; (iii) alteration of the theory to accommodate behavior inconsistent with the postulates of rationality (constrained optimization) by one or more decision makers (resource owners); (iv) placing the finding on the research agenda as a researchable anomaly. (Reder 1982: 13)

38. One reviewer posed the question of whether the postwar movement of Chicago suggests that there should be two firewalls rather than one—one firewall separating science and policy and another separating science from ideology. He suggests that both firewalls were breached in the interwar period. We believe this approach may overly complicate the issue. In our view, science had then and still has a firewall requiring a separation of science from ideology—science should be the same regardless of one's ideology. While that might not reflect practice, and there are numerous postmodern critiques of science generally and economic science specifically, letting science reflect ideology does not reflect the idea of science. So, in our view, to discuss a separate Classical Liberal firewall on ideology would be superfluous and would not differentiate the Classical Liberal economic

view of methodology from the current methodological view. That said, we agree, science often fails to meet its goal of separating science and ideology, but exploration of that issue, even when limited to economic science, goes far beyond the "applied policy" focus of this book. It is in applied economic policy methodology where we are making a contribution, and we specifically avoid the much more thoroughly explored issues involving the methodology of science.

39. Stigler saw no place, or any possible role, for psychology to play in analyzing economics. "this tradition of independence of economics from psychology has persisted" (Stigler 1960: 44).

> Well, I know he thought, I mean I don't think he thought that much of *The Moral Sentiments*. He thought *Wealth of Nations* was the greatest book ever written in economics. There was no question about Smith as the greatest economist. I can't recall exactly what he said, I mean about Smith, except he would sometime speak about the literature on the so-called Smithian problem. How could somebody who wrote the *Wealth of Nations* write a *Theory of Moral Sentiments*? (Conversation with Gary Becker, October 1997)

40. Steeped in the Classical tradition, Frank Knight could not help but be aware of Smith's (and later Mill's) diffidence in pushing individual self-interest as encompassing the sole basis for human action, or as a singular entry point for the entirety of the economics discipline.

> The deeper aspect of this theory, that capitalists make the division between themselves and their laborers by arbitrary fiat, is strongly confirmed by the tone of the discussion in Smith (Book II, chap. iii) and Mill (Book I, Chap. V, sec. 9), which is one of downright fear lest they may not choose to "destine" to the support of productive labor enough of the product to maintain the social capital. Smith is obviously preaching (if not scolding), as well as analysing motives, in his emphasis on the "uniform, constant, and uninterrupted effort of every man to better his condition." (Knight 1956: 81–82)

41. The implicit assumption is that the paths taken matter even if the end destination is identical. Journeys conducted using the guidance provided by Classical Liberalism are open to continued debate and re-evaluation, while scientific modernism yields hermetically sealed, foregone conclusions.

Chapter 4. Ashes and Diamonds

1. Evolution here is not used to denote the usual Darwinian sense of gradualness, something resembling a smooth and continual stream of incremental changes. Instead, the shift from the previous Chicago departments of economics to the postwar Chicago School can best be described as something of a saltation type of evolutionary change, one marking a disruptive, and markedly different species.

2. Chicago of course, under the leadership of Friedman, Stigler, and Director, never embraced mathematics in quite the same way as its professional competitors at MIT or the Cowles Commission.

> Mathematics, which I [Samuelson] was beginning to get interested in, was laughed at by the Knight wing. Chicago was happy when the Cowles Commission left Chicago after the war, and they left because they felt that it was a hostile environment. (Samuelson 2011: 158)

During the early postwar years, George Stigler went so far as to dismiss Samuelson as a mathematician manqué. "On Samuelson's definition, I suppose, one writes an essay on mathematics, on the conventional definition, one writes an essay on economics" (Stigler 1949a: 100). However, Stigler's remarks at this time are also widely applicable to the older, Classical view on policy formation. However, a younger, more impatient, postwar generation came to dominate the methodological thinking in this area, whether leaning politically to the right or left. As their teachers inevitably died off, so did the older approach, being still maintained only at the margins of the profession. The use of mathematics in economics was hardly a new phenomenon. Edgeworth certainly did not stint in respect to this technique. During his time as a graduate student at Columbia University, Milton Friedman would certainly have run into Harold Hotelling, who pioneered aspects of this approach. (Hotelling is given credit for steering a young Kenneth Arrow toward shifting from mathematics and actuarial studies into applying his penchant to the field of economics.) Consequently, the surge of interest in applying mathematics, beginning in the 1930s and surging in the 1940s, did not mark an event without precedent. The wrinkle distinguishing this new breed of mathematical economists was that, this time, the far from novel technique achieved a position of dominance within the discipline.

3. Samuelson's Walrasian mathematical approach would quickly become a matter of derision to an always critical Chicago cohort, both in public and private. Their dismissive attempt was to write Samuelson off as being just a little too precious, a dilettante compelled to compulsively show off. In a letter to Milton Friedman, George Stigler condemned Samuelson's efforts: "It may merely be prejudice, but I'm inclined to write him off as an economist. Two of his recent jobs ... were pure mathematical exposition, as is also his current *Economica* item" (Hammond and Hammond 2006: 97).

4. While initially Samuelson did not want to leave Chicago, reflecting back he felt it was a providential move. (Harvard was not his only option, but clearly Harvard was then, as now, a leading department with a world-renowned faculty.)

> If you'd asked me five years after I went to Harvard, in 1940 when I left Harvard for MIT and after being a Junior Fellow for three years, I would have said, "Thank God I left Chicago. Because the three biggest things in economics have been the Keynesian revolution, the monopolistic competition revolution, and the mathematicization of economics," and Chicago was against all of these things during that period of time. (Samuelson 2011: 982)

5. It should come as no surprise that Marshall was best able to sum up this attitude somewhat dismissively:

> (1)Use mathematics as a shorthand language, rather than as an engine of enquiry. (2). Keep to them till you have done. (3) Transfer into English. (4) Then illustrate by examples that are important in real life. (5) Burn the mathematics. (6) if you can't succeed in 4, burn 3. (Marshall 1996 [1906]: 130)

6. While Chicago eschewed Samuelson's strong focus on mathematics, it would be a mistake to think of the most notable Chicago graduate students of the 1930s as sharing Knight's aversion to statistics or mathematics. Certainly, neither Friedman, Wallis, nor Stigler received much in the way of a foundation in either area at Chicago. However, Milton Friedman worked as a research student for Schultz at Chicago and finished his PhD under Kuznets at Columbia University. Allen Wallis, at least academically, was better known as a statistician than as an economist. The third of the three musketeers, George Stigler (1945), in one of his earliest published pieces, would attempt, with some boldness, to analyze a basic nutritional standard using only an approximation of the simplex method. This methodology depended on a technique not fully developed at that time. Though not formally trained, his instincts veered sharply toward the mathematical/statistical direction. However, both Friedman and Stigler rejected the temptation to allow the mathematical (or statistical) tail to wag the theoretical dog. Their argument in this mathematical standoff with a Samuelson or an Arrow lay more with how such tools were used rather than if they were appropriate. They tended to swallow this newly developed passion for mathematization with a good dose of traditional Chicago skepticism. Nor did they ever become entranced by mathematical elegance. "Isn't it because of the excessive mathematization? ... that's sort of utterly peripheral to anything that George [Stigler] was involved with" (Conversation with Milton Friedman, August 1997). Friedman and Stigler continued to prefer testable hypotheses and applicable results to ever more refined theories.

7. In more reflective moments, when intently focused on specific policy issues, Samuelson would acknowledge this older and still deeply ingrained, if often buried, fashion of thinking about such applied matters. Not ironically, an enlivened debate with his old friend, George Stigler, who had only physically left Chicago in the 1940s and 1950s, brought this residue of Classical Liberalism to the fore. "There are no rules concerning the proper role of government that can be established by a priori reasoning" (Samuelson and Stigler 1963: 37).

8. This approach, clearly favored by Simons or Knight, would later be eschewed by their own department and even by Knight's own prize student.

> A second trait was a strong concern for the preservation and enlargement of individual liberty. An interesting thing about this belief is that it was not vividly and continuously reinforced by the skilful demonstration of the efficiency of competitive markets in performing a thousand tasks. There were elements of such an argument in Knight's famous essay on social

cost, but the support was philosophical rather than functional. (Stigler 1976b: 5)

Moreover, a somewhat disillusioned Knight in 1932 would become sufficiently disenchanted, at least temporarily, with his former creed. Seriously disgruntled, he would present a public paper entitled "The Case for Communism: From the Standpoint of an Ex-Liberal." Imagining someone from the later Chicago School delivering an equivalent flag of surrender would require more than a slight flight of fancy. Moreover, Knight never indulged in what might be described as one-sided skepticism. By nature cantankerous, Knight had equally severe reservations about the market mechanism as well, something recognized at least by some of his former students. Skepticism of all views, including one's own, is a hallmark of Classical Liberal methodology. Thus, while he had strong moral beliefs about appropriate policy, he did not require his colleagues to necessarily share those beliefs. Nor was Knight one to equate market outcomes with morality. In later years, his former students would be tempted successfully to migrate toward such a precarious direction. "Frank Knight was conservative. His prime characteristic was that he was a flaming atheist and he just couldn't leave the subject alone. He was an iconoclast, but he was also very critical of simple conservatism. His views were complicated" (Conversation with Paul Samuelson, October 1997).

9. Unlike the founders of the Chicago School who claimed to be strictly Marshallian in spirit (though it could be argued followers more in the breach), Samuelson, despite his defining period as a Chicago student, proved to be consistently immune to Marshall's subtle charms.

> I recently reread all of Marshall for the 1890 *Centennial*. And I read the Whitaker finds. I did not begin with a high opinion of Marshall (he was overpraised by my teachers and I rebelled). But I ended with a diminished opinion. He shows no development, and this from a highly unsatisfactory 1880 state. He never got partial equilibrium right: not only did he fail ever to work out the demand functions for independently-additive utilities, he never shows that he knew how to do so. (Letter from Paul Samuelson to George Stigler, April 11, 1990)

10. A case can be made that Marshall's personality, forged by surviving a rather difficult childhood, transformed him into an invariable hedger and qualifier. The Classical approach would provide him with a suitable and natural home. "Well, that was Marshall's character, which really wasn't very admirable. But it is understandable. I argue it's the way he was brought up by his father. I mean you can always hear the swish of the birch" (Conversation with Ronald Coase, October 1997).

11. The rise of econometrics during this period, (despite Keynes's more classically derived disdain for Tinbergen's work), seemed to provide the scientific toolkit that would facilitate the desired leap from theory to policy prescriptions to take place.

188 NOTES TO CHAPTER 4

Tinbergen's methodology was exceptional at that time and was received sometimes with scepticism. In particular J. M. Keynes (1939), at the time editor of the *Economic Journal*, reviewed "Professor Tinbergen's Method" quite critically, raising as one of the fundamental points that "The method is neither of discovery nor of criticism. It is a means of giving quantitative precision to what, in qualitative terms, we know already as the result of a complete theoretical analysis." Of course the latter criticism illustrates precisely Tinbergen's conviction that knowledge relevant for policy making should preferably be quantitative in nature. As to "discovery," Tinbergen (1940) in his "Reply" indicated that "it sometimes happens that the course of the curves itself suggests that some factor not mentioned in most economic textbooks must be of great importance," and he mentioned some examples. "As to the possibility of ''criticism,' it seems to me," Tinbergen (1940) argued, "that the value found for one or more of the regression coefficients may imply a criticism on one or more of the theories that have been used."

In a "Comment" to Tinbergen's "Reply," Keynes (1940) still held some doubts: "that there is anyone I would trust with it at the present stage or that this brand of statistical alchemy is ripe to become a branch of science, I am not yet persuaded." But Keynes concluded: "No one could be more frank, more painstaking, more free from subjective bias or parti pris than Professor Tinbergen ... But Newton, Boyle and Locke all played with alchemy. So let him continue." And so Tinbergen did. (https://en.wiki quote.org/wiki/Jan_Tinbergen)

Cost-benefit analysis provided yet another precise device for quantifying applied alternatives. By Christmas 1964, George Stigler in his role as incoming AEA president (Stigler 1965) could, like a modern-day Santa bringing gifts to well-behaved infants, lay out a vision of a Brave New World where Marshallian hedging would become a quaint custom relegated to the antiquarian attics of the profession. "It was just that he [George Stigler] was so enthusiastic about quantitative measures. He thought that he was going to change the world. I was sitting with Aaron Director at the time when he gave his Presidential address and we did look at one another at the time to try to see what each one thought about all of this" (Conversation with Ronald Coase, October 1997).

12. Such beliefs may seem surprisingly innocent today, when there is a popular turning away from scientific thought and when expert opinion is routinely scorned. Perhaps today's spirit expresses the antithesis of those more optimistic times. In the 2016 Brexit debate, one of the leaders of the leave campaign, Michael Gove, scorned the analysis offered by economists and other financial experts: "people in this country have had enough of experts."

13. The disaster of the widespread economic black hole that dominated this prewar period generated a collapse of faith in market capitalism. Looking for solutions created an embrace of totalitarianism as well as a less radical embrace of government activism.

14. Notice here the quaint conviction of statistical neutrality. By clutching the scientific method ferociously in its embrace this shared belief managed to install the conviction that operative thought and subsequent policy could be cleansed of the sort of ideology that had plagued the interwar years.

15. An interesting paper by Levy and Peart (2014) demonstrates the way in which the economists at the University of Virginia in 1960 (the Virginia School), including such eminent figures as Buchanan, Coase, and Nutter, were summarily dismissed by the Ford Foundation as being throwbacks to a former time, essentially bogged down by ideological and unscientific prejudices. In fact, the economists at Virginia were not closely aligned to the more restricted viewpoint championed by the Chicago School, but rather reflected the more traditional Classical Liberal approaches identified with such earlier figures as Frank Knight. We will discuss the Virginia approach in more detail in chapter 7.

16. This particular view would gather strength, reaching its zenith during the Kennedy administration. The self-nominated "best and the brightest" believed that they could systematically solve any problem confronting the nation, an attitude best epitomized by Kennedy's pledge to put a man on the moon by the end of the decade, or embedded within Johnson's "Great Society Program" (especially reflected by a pledge to increase the welfare of the poorest of citizens in his "war on poverty"). The disillusionment of the Vietnam War, followed by the seventies stagflation, delivered something of a death knell to those heady dreams, with the term "malaise" entering the consciousness of American society for the first time. To some degree, this paralleled the turn-of-the-century rise of progressivism in the United States and its subsequent fall from grace following the Wilson administration and the slaughter of World War I. This optimism, verging on engineering arrogance, was also reflected in the dominance of the "new economics" that put a definitive stamp on the profession during the 1960s.

> As I [Samuelson] read over my prepared text, I see that I have given some indications of how much fun it was to march with Dorothy, Toto, and the rest on the road to Camelot. I have not, I fear, conveyed well how successful and rational the Kennedy Years 1961–1963 were in terms of economic policy and performance. By a Gresham's Law that bad talk drives out good, history will increasingly remember John F. Kennedy the philanderer and cynic. Predecessors such as Eisenhower and successors such as Nixon and Reagan conspired to make JFK look good in economics. But actually those in the know realize that President Kennedy with Theodore Sorenson's faithful and intelligent loyalty, themselves brought about much of America's good luck. (Samuelson 2011: 962–963)

17. John Maynard Keynes (1963a), playing the part of the provocative pamphleteer, had already attempted to bury the idea of radical individualism in his 1926 essay, "The End of Laissez-Faire." In it, his interpretation of the nature of an appropriate policy agenda remains within what we are willing to classify as the expansive tent comprehending Classical Liberalism. This more traditional

approach, as mentioned, did not forswear the perennial need for government co-ordination. Despite his severe disenchantment with the more questionable sim-plicities of Bentham, Keynes placed himself squarely in the Classical Liberal tra-dition, though one that had evolved from its nineteenth-century incarnation. He raises some of these still relevant political issues in "Am I a Liberal?" (1963b [1925]).

18. The overly naïve assumption strongly suggested that these individual func-tionaries lacked any discernible self-interest. This allowed the Chicago School, spearheaded by George Stigler (1971) (along with Gary Becker, Sam Peltzman, and a number of others) to drive a bulldozer through this enormous logical and psychological gap.

> You know, you could read right through all of George Stigler's stuff, even on industrial organisation, and his implicit endorsement of markets, and the condemnation of all government intervention, which of course even-tually inspired his work on *The Theory of Regulation* [1971]. This proved to be an example where ideology is productive. The trouble with ideology is that it can blind you, but it can also sometimes create a spurt. Who would have thought up *The Theory of Regulation*, unless you were already in-clined to regard all government action with deep suspicion, always in-clined to believe it does more harm than good. (Conversation with Mark Blaug, April 1998)

19. At the end of his term as president (1961), Dwight D. Eisenhower deliv-ered a still memorable speech warning against the perils of this rising military-industrial complex. His words haven't lost their relevance. The speech, in its en-tirety, is available online at http://coursesa.matrix.msu.edu/~hst306/documents/indust.html.

20. As John Maynard Keynes makes clear:

> It is *not* a correct deduction from the Principles of Economics that enlight-ened self-interest always operates in the public interest ... We cannot, therefore, settle on abstract grounds, but must handle on its merits in de-tail, what Burke termed "one of the finest problems in legislation, namely, to determine what the State ought to take upon itself to direct by the pub-lic wisdom, and what it ought to leave, with as little interference as possi-ble, to individual exertion." (Keynes 1963a [1926]: 312–313)

21. The older, Classical Liberal methodology demanded a highly nuanced approach. The certainties and at times simplicities offered by postwar economics proved to contain too potent an appeal for it to be followed, despite the inherent dangers lurking just beneath the surface of its scientific assurances.

> Economic doctrines when expressed in short and handy form generally neglect this element of time: they imply that certain results will follow on certain causes, leaving the common sense of the reader to supply the qualification—"provided no great change, working in a different direction,

sets in before the effect of these causes have time for full development." This qualification being ignored, the dictums are taken to be unconditioned and thus trouble arises. (Marshall 1923: 185)

22. Samuelson's concise 1954 article used an elegant graphical exposition to theoretically justify the case for public goods. Jumping from this grounding, however, to a sweeping Galbraith-type judgment on the need for public goods falls somewhat short of a legitimate leap. Theory fails to perfectly bridge this gap. Similar expositions can be found in the work of Kenneth Arrow as well, if the reader has the patience and forbearance to search for them.

23. There is an important distinction here that Hayek delineated in a paper delivered to his intellectual compatriots of the Mont Pelerin Society. He deliberately distinguished between the objectives and behavior of Liberals as opposed to their erstwhile allies, the more recalcitrant conservatives. Hayek, whether accurately or not, places himself firmly in the Liberal camp. The acid test for him seems to be measured by one's faith in the market mechanism. "Looking forward it [the conservative mind] lacks the faith in the spontaneous forces of adjustment which makes the liberal accept without worry changes even though he does not know how the necessary adaptations will be brought about" (Hayek 1957: 3).

24. In his autobiography, George Stigler (1988b) describes attending that first meeting of the society in a chapter entitled, "The Apprentice Conservative." In many ways that event marked a distinct drift away from, and eventually a more general rejection of, many of Frank Knight's ideas. The suggestion that Friedman and Stigler were heavily influenced by Director might come as a surprise to those not intimate with Director's quiet but highly influential career. (See the work of Van Horn and Mirowski 2009 for a useful analysis of Director's influence.) Yet it was only after the first meeting of the Mont Pelerin Society in 1947 that Friedman and Stigler's views seemed to coalesce and strike out in a discernible direction. It was through the influence of Aaron Director that they managed to attend that meeting. This represented the birthplace of Stigler's subsequent bond with Milton Friedman's brother-in-law. Director would proceed, almost effortlessly, to heavily influence Stigler's subsequent work in Industrial Organization and the Economics of Regulation. In fact, Director (along with Friedman and Becker) remained among the very few that could shape or influence Stigler's views. Director's staunch and unyielding conservativism acted as something of a sheet anchor for the Chicago School. "Dr. Director's conservatism was such that he called Dr. Friedman, long a revered guru to conservative intellectuals, 'my radical brother-in-law'" (Martin 2004).

The close relationship between Milton Friedman and George Stigler is largely taken for granted by more superficial observers. However, fewer academics seem to realize the larger influence that Aaron Director exerted on Stigler's way of thinking.

MILTON FRIEDMAN: Added to that, well a lot of George's attitude came from Aaron. I think you had a lot of influence on what he said.

AARON DIRECTOR: I don't think so.

MILTON FRIEDMAN: Between you and me, you were more influential. But of course, you know, people get into patterns of what they say and it doesn't always correspond to what they do. (Conversation with Milton Friedman, Rose Friedman, and Aaron Director, August 1997)

25. The question remains whether these Chicago-style rebels were conscious of deserting their professed Liberal principals. Certainly, Stigler was no stranger to Liberal economic methodology. There is at least room to conjecture that they were either unbothered or blissfully unaware of any such transgressions. The ability to hold contradictory stances is a very human trait, as individuals seem prone to luxuriate in this realm of cognitive dissonance. Moreover, it can be strongly argued that they really did believe that the world worked in the way their models suggested. Self-doubt was seldom allowed to encroach on their public, or academic, personas.

But as I said, he [Stigler] really believed in the rational mind. You'd show him some example of an irrational behaviour ... there's a lot of this sort of work going on now it just so happens ... and he would show you that it can't be true.

Almost by definition ...

Almost. Almost. It's getting more and more, more and more part of him as he got older actually, this whole view. He insists it's rational. He would tell you, "There is some rational explanation for it. It's just that you haven't looked completely into it and found it." (Conversation with Sam Peltzman, October 1997)

26. No evidence exists to suggest any regret generated by relinquishing the guidelines offered by this traditional methodology. Certainly it is possible to spin a Friedman-like "as if" story to explain their subsequent disregard for Classical Liberal methodology. Such an approach might have unduly constricted their ability to compete with their more interventionist opposition. But formulating such an explanation seems to be more an exercise of relieving them of some of the responsibility for their decision. Without any hard facts that would, to some degree, underwrite such explanations, these thoughts must be labeled more as wishful thinking than as an established explanation.

Chapter 5. What Has Chicago Wrought?

1. It is a misnomer to somehow categorize the interwar Chicago Economics Department as composing a "School" unless that term is extended to include any collection of academics. A facile strategy is to identify economics at Chicago during those years with such luminaries as Knight, Simons, and perhaps Viner and Mints. But the department also included Paul Douglas, at daggers drawn with Frank Knight, the statistician Henry Schultz, and institutionalists such as John

Nef, Chester Wright, and Simeon Leland. A key issue when comparing those eras should be the change in the approach taken by those who self-identified as continuing within the liberal tradition. In contrast to those interwar years, the postwar Chicago School, gaining traction in the 1950s, did reflect the defining characteristics of economics at Chicago during that period. To speak of a first and second Chicago School or even of an old or new one is to dabble in the treacherous waters of false equivalency.

2. According to this approach to theory, it was quite natural to extend this same self-interested basis of human behavior to comprehend an ever-widening sphere of activity. These "rigorously tested, scientific theories" became the only filters through which human experience could be properly sieved and policies accordingly conceived as a direct conclusion from theoretical analysis. "[As] I have studied economic activities in the United States, I have become increasingly impressed with how wide is the range of problems and industries for which it is appropriate to treat the economy as if it were competitive" (Friedman quoted Van Horn 2011: 296).

3. Harvard's economics department during these years had as its chair the somewhat mediocre, but flamingly anti-Semitic, Harold Burbank.

> When I arrived at Harvard in 1935, Harold Hitchings Burbank had been department chairman since time immemorial. Burbank's incompetence as a scholar could not be exaggerated.... Burbank suffered fools gladly, but not Jews. On major departmental appointments, he could count on a near-majority of cronies. Where patronage appointments in the lower ranks were concerned, he was absolute king. (Samuelson 2011: 1086–1087)

4. Paul Samuelson gives the following account of the greater tolerance practiced at Chicago. "What was Chicago's transient advantage? John D. Rockefeller's largesse as a Baptist? Yes, of course. But, also, I give importance to Chicago's monopoly advantage as a place that would hire some extraordinarily able Jews. That made their money go farther. Not that there was no anti-Semitism at Chicago. There was some of that anywhere" (Samuelson 2011: 1084). He elaborated as follows: "Chicago was not free of anti-Semitism, but it was relatively free in those days. And as a result, I think that explains in part, its greater pre-eminence in those years, the early Hutchins years; the years just before Hutchins and up until, say, the end of the 1930s" (Conversation with Paul Samuelson, October 1997). See Reder (2000) for a discussion of anti-Semitism within the economics profession.

5. A towering intellectual figure of the interwar period like Viner, though a strong supporter of markets, remained an eclectic thinker, supporting what were considered to be heresies at the time, and recommending former students viewed in the McCarthy period as fellow travelers, if not outright communists. Though ostensibly exemplifying the "in your face," antagonistic attitude cultivated at Chicago, that stance seemed, to a significant degree, to be the product of his environment. He invoked fear and even terror among graduate students taking his famous Econ 301 graduate class in economic theory. "When one victim alibied, 'I

am beyond my depth,' Viner is supposed to have said, 'Sir, you drown in shallow water'" (Samuelson 2011: 597). Yet once removed to Princeton, his characteristic ferocity largely melted away. "Years later when I discussed with Jacob Viner the legend of his ferocity, he said that the department had given him the function of screening the candidates for higher degrees. It was not work for which he was ill-equipped" (Samuelson 2011: 597).

6. Like Stigler, Director would later break away from the ideas of Knight, who was consistently conservative but never strictly doctrinaire.

> MILTON FRIEDMAN: Well, Frank Knight had a particular influence on the people who came close to him, including Aaron. Aaron was a disciple of Knight's as well, much more so, in a way. Would you say you were more or less so Aaron than George was?
>
> AARON DIRECTOR: Maybe for a while, but not for long.
>
> MILTON FRIEDMAN: For a while I would say you were more so, I would think. Aaron and Knight once jointly owned a farm in Indiana. But Knight had a very peculiar, a very real influence on those who became his disciples, which George broke from in the main. (Conversation with Milton Friedman, Rose Friedman, and Aaron Director, August 1997)

7. Van Horn (2010a, 2010b) presents a compelling case that undermines the notion of any sudden, or even gradual, Knight-induced conversion. In this context, nurturing preexisting tendencies can be succinctly distinguished from a measurable, and especially seismic, turnaround.

8. Gary Becker, who would return to Chicago and, along with his close colleague George Stigler, extend the range of price theory to cover a broad swath of social science issues, was initially drawn to Chicago by the Cowles Commission. As an undergraduate, perhaps still at an impressionable age, Becker didn't seem to fully realize that the Cowles Commission and Milton Friedman had reached the proverbial point of being at "daggers drawn." Admittedly, the task of attempting to visualize a young, impressionable Gary Becker might pose a problem for many readers.

> I knew about two things. I knew about Milton Friedman, and I knew that the Cowles Commission was here. They were here in those days. I was interested in the mathematical aspects of economics. And, I had my choice between Harvard and Chicago, that's where I was thinking of going. I'm not sure I came for very good reasons. I came because of the Cowles Commission and I came out because I was on the East Coast and I wanted to go out to the Midwest. You might say I came for accidental reasons. I'd known Friedman. He'd come to Princeton once, but gave a paper that didn't impress me that much. It was probably my own limitations at the time I think, but the fact was it didn't impress me that much. I didn't talk to him at all when he was there, so I can't say I came for Milton Friedman or the great Chicago traditions. I would say I was interested in the Midwest and the Cowles Commission. (Conversation with Gary Becker, October 1997)

9. Early in his Chicago tenure, Milton Friedman faced a classic exit or loyalty decision which seemed to at least hint that even hard-bitten Chicagoans failed to fit consistently into the prescribed Chicago silhouette. Narrow self-interest (rather than purely ideological considerations) did, at least temporarily, cause Friedman to reconsider his Chicago career.

> Machlup was pressing me to consider Johns Hopkins. As you doubtless know, Smithies turned them down for Harvard. I don't know whether to think about it seriously or not. They would offer 8,000 which with 3,000 to 5,000 from the Bureau makes an enormous differential over the 7,500 plus 4E contract I am scheduled to get next year (7,000 this year). Tell me, from the fullness of your experience, together with my indifference curves, how large a price ought I to pay for the privilege of being at Chicago? (Letter from Milton Friedman to George Stigler, Tuesday, April 7, 1948, Hammond and Hammond 2006: 80)

10. "He [Milton Friedman] had the usual poor immigrant parents, and went to cheap and nearby schools. At Rutgers (where he met, studied under, and formed a durable friendship with Arthur F. Burns) he financed himself by breaking the college bookstore cartel and waiting on tables" (Stigler manuscript of speech on the occasion of Friedman's birthday, February 2, 1969). Friedman was not simply an outsider by birth, but also by disposition. His time spent as a graduate student at Chicago had nurtured his natural combativeness. "Now Milton had certain troubles, because of two things. Anti-Semitism, but also people were afraid of him. His corrosiveness and so forth" (Conversation with Paul Samuelson, October 1997).

11. George Stigler himself could be quite eloquent in his theoretical embrace of diversity. Yet in seeking to appoint the best people to a given position, like tends to be more receptive to like-minded economists. Stigler, for instance considered the terms a "good economist" and a "Marxian economist" to represent mutually exclusive terminology, Though it is far from remarkable for faculty members of all stripes to reserve a higher opinion for those holding similar (and by definition valid) viewpoints rather than opposing ideas or ideologies. Such inbred bias is simply a psychological given when choices are made.

> Let me begin by stating that I believe the ideal university should hire men strictly on the basis of their scientific and teaching capacities. If there is no difference in these basic respects between two men, a university would be wise to seek variety of political viewpoints because (1) variety of faculty views makes it easier to avoid indoctrination, which is no part of a university's function but is a temptation to all men who believe in their own views and think that these views matter, and (2) the conflict of views stimulates re-examination of one's beliefs and helps combat the tendency we all have to become the complacent holders of "the" truth. I hasten to add that often the leading candidates for a position are not even approximately equal in scholarly abilities, and then ideologies should not be considered

> in making appointments. (Letter from George Stigler to the President, Board of Trustees of Stanford University, March 28, 1966)

In practice, however, any judgment levied of an applicant's capabilities can be influenced by one's own entrenched views. Not surprisingly, Stigler and Friedman found certain policy views to be closely correlated to perceived competence. Doing so represents a tendency hardly limited to those two dominant figures. This unconscious version of entrenched prejudice, sadly, is not a phenomenon limited to that earlier, and supposedly less culturally aware, era.

12. The Walgreen Chair represented an attempt by drugstore magnate Walgreen to make something resembling amends to the University for claiming publicly that the academic staff were infiltrated by, or were practically dupes of, communist forces during the interwar years. This heavily funded Chair had been filled sporadically under the more leftward-leaning stewardship of the political science department. Allen Wallis, as Dean of the Business School, ever adept at playing academic politics, gained control of the fund and lured Stigler away from Columbia.

> He had an enormous grant at that time. And his salary was maybe $25,000 in 1958 dollars. That was what I think he was making per year. *It was one of the biggest salaries in economics.* And he had a grant for a full-time research assistant! (Conversation with Claire Friedland, October 1997)

13. In a story told many times, George Stigler had been selected by the department for the position, only to be vetoed at the last moment by the president of Chicago, standing in for Vice Chancellor Hutchins, who was ill on that fateful day. What ideas or sentiments the far from inhibited George Stigler might have voiced during that particular interview have never been revealed. However, he did during his lifetime cultivate a reputation for spontaneously crafting gratuitous insults.

> George has told the story in his *Memoirs,* far better than I can, of his being rejected for a position at Chicago by then President Ernest Colwell because he was too empirical, and of my subsequent appointment to it, presumably because I was not. He claimed thereby that President Colwell and he "had launched the New Chicago School"! (Friedman 1993: 769)

Some light may finally be shed on this mystery in a forthcoming article by David Mitch. Promised are notes made at that fateful interview.

14. Certainly Stigler, born to immigrant parents and raised in Renton, Washington outside Seattle, also fitted this mold. Moreover, he shared Friedman's natural aggressiveness, nurtured in no small part by his study under, and admiration for, Knight. But he resolutely remained an outsider, even after decades of academic and public recognition. His letters sent back to the United States while overseas hark back to Mark Twain's *Innocents Abroad.* "Another story about George, I've always found it to be a problem, which is how incredibly American he was. I used to be shepherding these Latinos through and here they would come to some question in his Price Theory examination. 'Explain something, some-

thing about the Dred Scott Decision'" (Conversation with Arnold Harberger, October 1997).

15. Like his longtime friend and opponent, Paul Samuelson, or his odd couple soulmate, Robert Solow, not only did he know the literature of economics, but he was solidly versed in other fields as well. Although perhaps based on an overly superficial impression, succeeding generations of economists seem to have a much narrower vision of their field and of the arts and sciences in general. No one who wasn't unfairly dismissive, or focused only on point scoring, would ever categorize Stigler as a mere technician.

> Why don't more people take the trouble to write economics gracefully? Why don't you make your students read Hegel, preferably in the original, and point the finger at them? Of course, the destruction of style has something to do with the professionalization you're talking about—I guess you can't have everything. (Letter from Robert Solow to George Stigler, October 20, 1959)
>
> Tell Bobby (Solow's wife) to read (if she doesn't know them by heart) McCauley's Essays. They are wondrous in their prose, their abusiveness, their erudition, and their fundamental lack of insight. The ones on James Mill, Sadler, and the copyright bill are even worth your time. Tell her also that I predict that eventually every nineteenth century figure will experience a revival, and Herbert Spencer's turn is soon. (Letter from George Stigler to Robert Solow, November 6, 1959)

16. A *Reader's Digest* condensed version of Hayek's warning (edited by Max Eastman, former admirer of the Russian Revolution) made it possible for the message to reach a much wider American audience. Among those who embraced this fervently received truth was Harold Luhnow, president of William Volker & Co. (furniture distribution) and accordingly head of the Volker foundation. Mirowski and Van Horn (2009) as well as Caldwell (2011) have described and analyzed the influence of Hayek's publication on the formation of the Chicago School.

> At the meeting Luhnow sought to commission Hayek to write *The American Road to Serfdom*. The original text had been composed with a British audience in mind and perhaps had been pitched at too elevated a level of discourse for American audiences. Subsequently, Hayek in his later book *Hayek on Hayek* claims he did not take Luhnow's offer seriously, but says that he spoke at length with his "great friend" Henry Simons about it in Chicago. (Mirowski and Van Horn 2009: 141)

17. Others were more skeptical of Director's contributions:

> Aaron Director was extremely conservative. Why, I don't know. By the time I knew him he was already like that. And he was an iconoclast. But he didn't develop new data with respect to industrial organisation. He didn't develop any articulate new theories. He just said that the conventional belief wasn't so. (Conversation with Paul Samuelson, November 1997)

18. Those attending the first Mont Pelerin meeting were quite naturally diverse. Discussions often unearthed fierce differences. But they were united in opposition to what they deemed to be a dangerous, collectivist drift in most western societies. As Milton Friedman recollected, "The world was turning to planning" (http://socialdemocracy21stcentury.blogspot.com.au/2011/11/mises-to-friedman-youre-socialist.html). Mises, for instance, deprecated what he perceived as any signs of compromise or deviance by fellow attendees, judging them from his more rigid anti-socialist platform. At one point during a heated debate, Mises stormed out of a meeting, leaving all his fellow delegates with the parting insult, "You're all a bunch of socialists" (http://socialdemocracy21stcentury.blogspot.com.au/2011/11/mises-to-friedman-youre-socialist.html).

19. George Stigler claims that he never bothered looking at his dissertation again, at least not after it was published, considering the work to be too heavily influenced by Knight, who served as his dissertation supervisor. Certainly, much of his early writing still retains the type of Knightian Liberalism from which he would later decisively turn away. For instance, near the start of his career, the influence exerted by Knight was still much in evidence.

> The familiar admonition not to argue over differences in tastes leads not only to dull conversations but also to bad sociology. It is one thing to recognize that we cannot *prove*, by the usual tests of adequacy of proof, the superiority of honesty over deceit or the desirability of a more equal income distribution. But it is quite another thing to conclude that therefore ends of good policy are beyond the realm of scientific discussions. (Stigler 1943: 357)

Such a nuanced statement stands in complete opposition to his later work with Gary Becker (1977), a work which, as Ross Emmett (2006) carefully points out, Knight himself would have found unappealing.

20. The standard story told by Chicago School economists has not sufficiently emphasized the aggressive, *in your face*, dissident tradition that formed a pattern of continuity with the past. Instead, the more common suggestion has conjured a historical tradition of policy views that created an unbroken link with their preferred perspective, in particular by substantiating their theory-based policy. For example, Friedman relentlessly battled Don Patinkin over a fair stretch of years in his quest to construct a bridge tying his formulated quantity theory of money with some ersatz oral tradition that mysteriously thrived in Chicago during the 1930s. (See Freedman 2006 for an investigation of the roots of this creation and the reasons behind it.) Nor were these Chicagoans initially eager to propagate the existence of a distinctive postwar Chicago School entity. Friedman, for instance, refused to be impressed by Miller's (1961) original attempt to define the Chicago School in his JPE article.

> Miller's piece is, as you say fairly innocuous & I cannot for the life of me see why Harry [Johnson] accepted it ... Had Miller been more critical & offensive, I would understand it far better. Even then, such a piece is not

of the kind that should be published in J.P.E. (Letter from Friedman to Stigler, August 2, 1961)

21. However, Lester Telser in conversation (October 1997) distinguished Stigler and Friedman as forming an inner circle within the department, presenting something of a "band of brothers" struggling against a hostile environment. Milton Friedman himself was given to referring to "our kind" (or even as "good eggs") in classifying people who shared his views. "He [Arrigo Levi—journalist for *La Stampa*] is not of our persuasion but also he is not hopeless" (Letter from Milton Friedman to George Stigler, September 20, 1971).

22. As Stigler's coauthor, Jim Kindahl succinctly summed it up: "He would come across empirical work which was contradictory to other empirical work. Somehow it always seemed to him that the empirical work which favoured his side was done better than the empirical work which didn't" (Conversation with Jim Kindahl, October 1997).

23. Such notable economists as Samuelson could be dismissed peremptorily by the exacting standard of this duo. "It may merely be prejudice, but I'm inclined to write him [Samuelson] off as an economist" (Letter from Stigler to Friedman, January 1949, in Hammond and Hammond 2006: 97).

24. Solow himself doubts that he would have found the inherently combative atmosphere characterizing Chicago to be particularly congenial.

> Oh, I don't think it would have much effect ... I'm a very counter-suggestible person. It might have changed me methodologically a little, but I don't think I would have been happy because being involved in intellectual conflict ... in controversy with one's colleagues all the time is never a formula for relaxation. I also think probably I might have been more productive at the University of Chicago, more productive in terms of volume although I'm not so sure in terms of quality. It's the ethic here. It has always been a little more laid back, a little more relaxed. So, I don't think it would have turned me into a conservative, or a monetarist or any of those sorts of things. Or a, you know, a gung-ho free marketeer. (Conversation with Robert Solow, October 1997)

Chicago of course was a contentious arena. For instance, George Stigler's famous industrial organization workshop treated discussion as a "take no prisoners" blood sport.

> People had their knives out. I participated in some of them. I think people were using George's example. No prisoners were taken in other words. And everybody just jumped in. It was just *chaos* those workshops (Conversation with Sherwin Rosen, October 1997).

However, though specific disagreements were fierce, the fundamental tenets defining the Chicago School were never really up for debate. To members of the Chicago School, these pro-market tenets were close to, if not absolutely, self-evident.

25. George Stigler and Robert Solow represent an exceptional case of immediate intellectual attraction that managed to ignore ideological disparities. Solow
possessed the rather rare ability of being able to meet Stigler or Friedman on a
head to head basis. Like Stigler, he was sharp-witted, well read, and possessed of
a remarkable flair for economic insight and analysis. But the two made something
of a mixed match duo to both their friends and colleagues. As described, there
was something of a magnetic attraction, almost a "love at first sight" relationship,
from their first meeting at the Center for Advanced Study in the Behavioral Sciences in Palo Alto during the 1957–1958 academic year.

> George and I just fell for each other. And we just enjoyed each other's
> company, more than I can tell you and we spent a lot of time together. The
> two couples spent a lot of time together. We played bridge together, we
> got to know each other. We got to know the Stigler kids who were older
> than ours, so that I don't know that George ever really got to know our
> kids really well. And I still know Steve Stigler, the oldest son, very well.
> And we just, we just hit it off. We were good friends. (Conversation with
> Robert Solow, October 1997)
>
> There was a sixty-fifth birthday party for George that the University of
> Chicago put on, and my wife and I flew out there to be there and I remem-
> ber that we were all put up in a University building, the Center for Continu-
> ing Education which had bedrooms. And we came in one evening and the
> next morning we walked into the dining room where all the other guests at
> this party were having breakfast and a hush fell over the whole dining room.
> And, finally a friend of mine, I think it was Si Rottenberg from the Univer-
> sity of Massachusetts, came over and said, "We were all wondering 'what
> are you doing here?'" (Conversation with Robert Solow, October 1997)

26. Leading Chicago lights, like Stigler and Friedman, did exude a somewhat
extraordinary sense of unshakable confidence. This unshakable certainty was allied with a remarkable ability to think so quickly on their feet that they left the
less sharp-witted of the profession trailing behind in any sort of face-to-face encounter. Pinning Milton Friedman down would almost always prove a nearly impossible task, one that would become increasingly frustrating. George Stigler's
longtime research associate, Claire Friedland, claimed that if you accepted Milton Friedman's initial assumption, you would be doomed to capitulate eventually
(Conversation with Claire Friedland, October 1997).

> There are a large number of well-known economists who have debated
> with Milton, and I have never known him to lose an argument, although
> in one or two cases I dream that I almost got a draw. Let me advise you on
> how to conduct yourself if you ever have the misfortune to debate with
> Milton. He will begin by asking you to grant, say, three assumptions:
>
> 1. $2 is better than $1.
> 2. The law of diminishing returns.
> 3. Individuals do not have complete and accurate knowledge of the future.

My fundamental advice is: *do not grant these assumptions*. If you do, you will find yourself led, by irresistible logic, to conclusions such as these:

1. The Federal Reserve System should be abolished.
2. The Board of Governors of the Federal Reserve Board should be put on Social Security.
3. Social Security should be abolished. (Stigler 1977: 2–3)

Moreover, both Stigler and Friedman were simply relentless, whatever the subject of a debate might happen to be. The idea of walking back any one of their arguments, or yielding a micro-meter of ground, was simply not a conceivable option for either one. Each of these intellectual warriors also exuded an almost rigid confidence, as though the answers either had been revealed to them or had been unlocked for all eternity. The possibility that a crucial idea or insight might have eluded their grasp never seemed to have entered their argumentative framework. "In debate with Milton Friedman, Bob Solow used to quote Sydney Smith's words to Thomas Babington Macaulay, 'I wish, Babington, I were as sure of anything as you are of everything' (Samuelson 2011: 943).

A similar view of Friedman's style is conveyed by Mark Blaug.

> I [Mark Blaug] was totally opposed to American involvement. Milton was a firm adherent of the bombing of Hanoi. We would have these incredible arguments. Now, I had read quite a lot about Vietnam. I don't think Milton had read anything. I was much better informed. Nevertheless, we would start these arguments at 9:00 o'clock and by 2:00 o'clock in the morning I would say, "Milton, I just can't go on. I'm tired. I just can't take any more." And he would say, "Let me just give you one more argument." He was patiently prepared to spend eight or ten hours trying to persuade me of the error of my ways. He knew nothing at all about Vietnam, or Communism. This was outside his knowledge.
>
> He was always patient, always polite, never got short tempered like I do in an argument, never got nasty. But he was a horrible person to argue with, just a nightmare. My idea of a nightmare is to stand on a stage and debate with him in front of the public. I watched him debating at Cambridge with Joan Robinson on flexible exchange rates. Unbelievable! I mean, Joan Robinson was one of the world's most aggressive, hostile, debaters. He wiped her analytically, he wiped her rhetorically, he had the entire audience eating out of his hand after an hour, an hour and a half. An amazing, amazing guy. But a madman, a madman. One of the few people I could strangle with my bare hands. I feel I could actually do it. (Conversation with Mark Blaug, April 1998)

27. If we take Frank Knight as an apt representative of that older Chicago tradition, then the consensus judgment levied by a noticeably discordant group of economists, namely the choir represented by Gary Becker, Paul Samuelson, Sam Peltzman, and Claire Friedland, is that these three progenitors of the Chicago School broke cleanly away from Knight's more Classical Liberal Economic

posture. Or, as Gary Becker, one of Knight's later students and eventually a close colleague of Stigler, concludes:

> He changed his view about Knight, I think I mentioned that. He changed in his view about Knight, the assessment of Knight's work. I think that his opinion of Knight went way down. He still thought Knight's work was important, but nowhere nearly as important as he did when he was an undergraduate and a young person. (Conversation with Gary Becker, October 1997)

28. The long-standing Chicago tradition cultivated people who were combative by nature. They enjoyed a good fight. Gaining the upper hand was deemed inadequate. Opponents had to be bashed and hammered into a basic pose of submission. Milton Friedman's unconscious use of the term "nonsense" mirrors Knight's own often vituperative language. One of Knight's students, Don Patinkin, examined his copy of *The General Theory of Employment, Interest and Money*, after Knight's death. Voluminous notes were scattered throughout the volume. "[T]he expletive 'Nonsense!'—replaced on occasions by even stronger terms— makes a frequent appearance in these margins" (Patinkin 1981: 299).

29. This *pit bull* aspect, which allowed no room to ever take a step backward, let alone back down, transformed discussion and debate into the type of combat more reflective of the courtroom than the seminar room. In legal battles the objective is never truth or justice but simply which side can triumph by telling the more cogent and convincing story. Marketing under these objectives becomes the essence, at least to some degree, of scholarship. The goal of the debate was not to move closer to the truth; the goal was to win at all costs, using whatever means available. Debate became something of a blood sport, as best reflected in George Stigler's Industrial Organization workshops.

> Well, he was very intimidating in his critical approach. Your biggest fear was that he would make a joke at your expense. So one was always somewhat on guard. He had this workshop.... A paper was never given. It was just discussed. It was taken apart. And it was breathtaking. It was totally breathtaking. (Conversation with Sherwin Rosen, October 1997)

30. Stigler makes this clear by identifying scholars with the storytelling ability and overall persuasiveness of preachers. "The tenacity with which people hold the ideas in which they have a proprietary interest is not due simply to vanity. A scholar is an evangelist seeking to convert his learned brethren to the new enlightenment he is preaching" (Stigler 1988a: 211).

31. In the rare cases when either Friedman or Stigler were willing to retreat from a staunchly defended position, their tactful withdrawal was seldom a matter for the public record.

> I think that's the case with 100% money, which was just a crotchety part of the first Chicago school. Irving Fisher also embraced it. The only thing

> it fits into is Milton's later monistic monetarism where, if you have a 100% reserve ratio by law, then you can't have a variable de facto reserve ratio and therefore you won't get an additional component in the variance of the money supply. And of course getting a variance in the ups and downs of the money supply is the worst thing possible. Gary Becker, I think, cured him of that. Probably he said, "Look. You have barriers to money in the banking system and private banking under one disguise or another will inevitably arise. You will simply make the banking system ineffective with a kind of Gresham's Law arising." And I think Milton quietly changed, he just quietly dropped that. He doesn't particularly announce changes in positions, but instead, lets them just decay away. (Conversation with Paul Samuelson, October 1997)

32. At Chicago, being self-critical translated into the moral and strategic equivalent of unilateral disarmament. Under this unyielding regime, to poke fun at or ridicule one's own endeavors made as much sense as displaying one's wit at airport security checkpoints.

> Some of these traits of intellectual leaders are caught in the statement that they lack a sense of humor. I mean by this, not the inability to laugh at the right point when hearing a joke, but the ability to view oneself with detached candor. Ridicule is a common weapon of attack but amused self-examination is a form of disarmament; one so endowed cannot declaim his beliefs with massive certainty and view opposing opinions as error uncontaminated by truth. (Stigler 1988b: 213–214)

33. Stigler's focus on income distribution goes back to his days preceding Chicago, when he was completing an MBA at Northwestern. This interest mutated into a history of thought dissertation (under the watchful eye of Frank Knight) on theories of distribution (published in 1941 as *Production and Distribution Theories*). Price theory was underwritten by an assumption of perfect competition yielding a John Bates Clark variant of marginal productivity theory. Such an approach allowed a total product to be efficiently shared among factors of production according to their implicit contribution. Thus, any product would be distributed efficiently and equitably. Non-equilibrium or multi-equilibrium systems provided no such validation for any resulting market distribution. A lack of justification on either efficiency or equity grounds immediately excused government intervention as being no more than an attempt to improve on these less than desirable market outcomes. For Stigler, this represented a clear and incipient danger that had to be eradicated at all costs.

34. For both Stigler and Friedman, defeating an opposing theory was never sufficient. Any challenge had to be decimated with only a burned-out carcass left to serve as a warning to other incipient theoretical charlatans. (See Freedman 2008, 2002, and 1995 for further explanation.) In doing so, they were following a well-established Chicago tradition that perhaps would have best been observed in the breech.

35. As we have pointed out throughout this book, while Frank Knight was certainly cantankerous and strong willed, he was not inflexible, or closed-minded. He was always questioning, attempting to integrate his scientific understanding with his philosophical understanding. Economics, for him, had one foot in science and one foot in moral philosophy.

36. This proclivity did not translate into any simple acceptance of theoretical or empirical work that yielded the preferred policy outcomes. However, their large-bore ammunition was typically conserved and used tactically against theories that challenged what they saw as economic wisdom. Moreover, whether to use their scientific work as a platform from which to preach policy measures remained a contentious issue. Stigler parted company with his close friend Milton Friedman in refusing to proselytize policy positions, though it can easily be argued that his work implicitly supplied a foundation for a remarkably consistent strain of approved positions. Though to be more precise, this refusal was based on his insistence that self-interest rather than any intellectual debate determined policy implementation. Stigler came to believe that political markets operated much like the economic variety, with consumer sovereignty holding sway.

37. This is not necessarily a bad thing, at least if one is self-aware of using such a technique. As Stigler's close friend Robert Solow explained, looking over from the opposite side of the fence:

> He was interested, I would say primarily, in a particular sort of puzzle and it's a typical Chicago puzzle. And I don't mean that in any bad way, it's the sort of puzzle that the Chicago School's presuppositions require. Show me an apparent anomaly, something that does not seem to be explicable using the Smithian apparatus and the Marshallian apparatus and I will show you that it can be explained that way. That was exactly the sort of thing that George went looking for. And that's not a bad thing. I'd have to say that it can actually be very good. (Conversation with Robert Solow, October 1997)

It is perhaps only fair to note that Richard Posner in recent times has moved in the direction of a more open Classical Liberal methodological approach. See Posner (2010).

38. Stigler makes this attitude explicit in his 1988 autobiography. If a reader were particularly disingenuous by nature, it might be possible to convince oneself that Stigler is here speaking as a neutral observer of the profession. But this would contradict his consistently sardonic style and his continual recognition of the role of marketing in promoting one's views. Like his friend and compatriot, Milton Friedman, he was one of the discipline's most skillful marketing agents.

> The tenacity with which people hold the ideas in which they have a proprietary interest is not due simply to vanity. A scholar is an evangelist seeking to convert his learned brethren to the new enlightenment he is preaching. New ideas encounter formidable obstacles, the foremost being

indifference, but also the new ideas will often conflict with old ideas or clash with apparently contradictory experience.... Another aspect of this salesmanship is the heavy use of repetition, perhaps the most powerful of arguments. (Stigler 1988b: 211)

39. Part of this stemmed from a firm belief that they acted as the true heirs to the Smithian/Marshallian economic viewpoint. This type of status quo bias meant that alternatives would receive a far fiercer grilling than those in accord with their firmly held doctrine. The tendency to do so was especially true when applied to theories deemed conducive to collectivist policies.

> And then I think he would have said, "It's the better part of wisdom when you come to these really narrow decisions and the data speaks ambiguously, it's the better part of wisdom to accept the long-standing, the long view we've come to accept as knowledge and it's unwise, on the basis of that kind of evidence, to say I should throw over something that has stood us in good stead since 1776." (Conversation with Robert Solow, October 1997)

40. The use of the term "restoring" is hardly accidental. In opposing mainstream Keynesianism and other rationales supporting government intervention, they were posing as counterrevolutionaries. But the beating heart of their movement was what they saw as the restoration of Classic Liberalism, although necessarily modernized for the current age. Thus, in English history, the Restoration under Charles II was an attempt not only to undo the changes and actions initiated by Cromwell's Commonwealth, but to bring back the monarchy and the multitude of traditions attached to that institution. (Though of course to place the reins into more skillful hands, in contrast to those represented by his nitwit and decapitated brother.) In contrast, the Glorious Revolution represents the overturning, to some extent, of the prevailing status quo.

41. This attitude is succinctly summarized by Milton Friedman: "the standard cliché for every social ill has become—more government spending, more government manpower. The result has almost always been that the money ends up being spent for very different purposes than those intended by the do-gooders, and makes the problem worse rather than better" (Friedman 1971: 3).

42. Yet there remains no evidence that they evaluated their tactics as the employment of illiberal means or that they felt forced or obliged to adopt the tactics then gaining vogue within the profession. Embracing illiberal means translates into rejecting those precepts endorsed by Knight or Viner. These approaches were now dismissed as being simply old-fashioned, needing to be discarded if they were going to successfully engineer a modern reconceptualization of Liberalism. Both Friedman and Stigler had embraced empirical methods and research from an early stage of their careers. Nor had they ever proved averse to a measured used of mathematical methods when appropriate. Consequently, sketching a picture of reluctance or being forced by necessity seems fanciful given the lack of evidence to support such flights of whimsy.

Chapter 6. Economic Policy Becomes a Science

1. The movement away from laissez-faire and toward a stronger planning framework, inherent within the New Welfare economic policy model, is relatively easy to understand. The Great Depression, followed by World War II, required government to take an expanded role, at least temporarily, in the economy. The Depression ended with the advent of World War II, in which the allies triumphed. Given these dramatic events, even the strongest Classical Liberal supporters of laissez-faire recognized the indisputable need for government action under such adverse circumstances as the Great Depression. For example, William Hutt, renowned for his virulent anti-Keynesian pose, was forced to conclude, "But once the persistent ignoring of 'classical' precepts has precipitated chaos, and insurmountable political obstacles obviously block the way to noninflationary recovery, only a pedant would oppose inflation" (Hutt 1979: 45).

2. Those interested in the controversy surrounding Pigou's appointment might start with Coase's (1994) succinct analysis.

3. At a Federal Reserve seminar, Lerner outlined his view of functional finance. Keynes dressed him down and told Lerner that his views were incorrect (Colander 1984). According to Alvin Hansen, at a cocktail party later, Lerner confronted Keynes and Keynes, after looking around to see that no reporters were present, told Lerner that the art of statesmanship involves telling lies, but they have to be plausible lies (Colander and Landreth 1996).

> Keynes gave two famous Federal Reserve seminars, which I was not able to attend. However, from accounts at the time—probably from Hansen—I know what happened. At the first one he was utterly charming but was kind of reactionary and, in particular, he jumped on Abba Lerner, who had written about functional finance. One of the things he said—and I can never remember whether it was Aristotle or Plato—was, "Plato said, 'The art of politics is the art of telling plausible lies.' But you know, Abba, those lies have got to be *plausible*," implying that Lerner's weren't. He must have felt, maybe at the time, that Lerner had overdone it: or maybe he came to feel that. But anyway, in the meantime, Lerner's *The Economics of Control* came out. He must have paged through it—he was a very quick reader—and in the second seminar he made redress and went out of his way to say nice things. How Lerner happened to be in Washington on these two occasions I don't know. Lerner was a brilliant mind, and only his lack of *gravitas* limited his influence on actual policy. (Samuelson 2011: 1001)

4. Samuelson's own discussion of the origins and impact of his textbook can be found in Samuelson (1997).

5. Oskar Lange (1938) published his noted model of market socialism, a volume that was based on previous articles and presentations. In doing so, he had been strongly encouraged by Abba Lerner. The result is sometimes referred to as the Lange-Lerner model. According to this model, a planning board could set (at

least in theory) the required marginal conditions that would yield an optimal outcome. Given this theoretical perspective, capitalism would cease to be a necessary requirement to achieve such results.

6. Opposition to this program needed not only to be effectively organized, but also to be indicative of a way forward. It could not rely simply on conservative obstinacy. Hayek's dark vision, as fashioned in *The Road to Serfdom* (1944), came to serve as something of a call to arms for disaffected intellectuals on the right. Partially, if not entirely, inspiring the first meeting of the Mont Pelerin Society in 1947, conservatives, or those who saw themselves acting in the tradition of Classical Liberals, united in a collective attempt to shift intellectual debate away from what they envisioned as the dangerous acceptance of collectivism. (The meeting itself turned out to be more rancorous than united.) Though pledged to the time-honored methodology of Classical Liberalism, a struggle to reformulate and modernize that approach soon became evident.

> In overcoming the failures of laissez-faire, Hayek urged, it would be essential to develop a social philosophy that provided a rich account of the moral dimensions of human existence. Any advocate of capitalism who understood its benefits in purely material terms or prioritized economic concerns over matters of spiritual fulfillment was bound to fail in the court of popular opinion. They would need to cast aside an arid rationalism in favor of humility and, in doing so, heal the "breach between true liberal and religious convictions" that continued to prevent "a revival of literal forces." (Burgin 2012: 103)

7. Essentially, it added another equation that related individual welfare to social welfare, with that equation embodying the needed moral judgments.

8. Bergson (1954: 249) later wrote that his "ethical thinking had evolved" and that it was unclear even theoretically that his social welfare function could serve as an adequate basis for policy.

9. There were numerous attempts to get around the normative nature of policy analysis, but all failed. The reason they failed was that they were trying to do the impossible—to pull normative conclusions from scientific work. Economic policy analysis cannot escape Hume's Dictum that you cannot draw a "should" from an "is." This was recognized by economists such as Robbins and Myrdal in the 1930s and Little and Graaf in the 1960s. Sen (1970b) would later seal the coffin, closing out any hope of developing a practically useful and relevant formal welfare economics.

10. In a review article of economic policy, Selznick (1998) highlighted some of the problems attached to applied policy economics. In it he pointed out that there has been little cross-fertilization between theory and applied policy work. He characterized the standard approach of assuming a representative consumer in applied policy work as being "unappealing both because distributional issues are ignored and because much evidence shows that aggregate demands are inconsistent with the behavior of a single representative agent" (ibid.).

11. Gross Domestic Product (GDP) possessed the all too convenient characteristic of being measurable. Thus, focusing on increasing output in this way was more conducive to the scientific imperative that dominated postwar economics. However, the underlying rationale for using GDP as a useful proxy assumes that when aggregate output as measured by GDP increases, societal welfare increases. That is a complicated connection to make formally. A number of economists have pointed out the inherent weaknesses attached to using GDP as a measurement of welfare, but in most policy discussions, the weaknesses are generally dismissed or simply overlooked.

12. This story has been told nicely by others, especially Burgin (2012), and is not our focus here. Classical Liberal methodology, as characterized by Mill, was committed and open to opposing views. It was not tied closely to any ideological position.

13. As students and one-time admirers of Knight, it would be difficult to conceive that this trio of would-be counterrevolutionaries were unaware of Classical Liberal methodology. But they would have felt little, if any, reluctance in jettisoning this perspective which in their view had outlived its usefulness. Far more important matters were at stake than maintaining respect for an old-fashioned tradition. The need to place economics on a scientific footing, while pushing back the tide of collectivism, would have demanded a far greater priority.

14. The logic here should be clear. From this postwar perspective of these younger academics, the older generation of economists had been forced to rely on their judgment and experience in formulating policy because of their rudimentary knowledge of economic science. Thus, the need for their suggested firewall dissipated with the subsequent postwar improvement in that theoretical base. "In writing their treatises, may not the classical economists have employed an apparatus which is different and in modern eyes inferior, to that which they employed to analyse concrete problems? I shall argue that this is indeed the case" (Stigler 1949b: 26).

15. The impetus behind the first meeting of the Mont Pelerin Society in 1947 should come as no surprise. The clear intention was to shift the terms of intellectual, as well as policy, debate to more congenial grounds. The shared recognition of those attending that gathering perceived a troubling reality where left-wing and dangerous collectivist thought had come to dominate debate within Western democracies. The inherent, but hidden, traps offered by the supposedly well-intentioned leaders who constructed dreams of a better (collectivist) society were broadly formulated decades later by Milton Friedman. "Heaven preserve us from the sincere fanatic who knows what is good for us better than we do, and who knows that it is his duty and his obligation to make us do what is good for us—whether his name is Torquemado, Lenin, or Hitler, or on a minor scale, Marcuse, or Nader" (Friedman 1971: 5).

16. Stigler could appear somewhat obsessed with statistical verification, even though at times his own econometric evidence served to weaken, rather than validate, the logic of an otherwise strongly propounded argument. Thus his 1971

paper on regulation appears let down by his simple statistical analysis despite Stigler's strenuous efforts at spinning his results.

> But George had, regardless of what he did personally, a very deep conviction that we do too much economics without empirical implications. It's not economics without implications. It's very important that there be implications. What I take all that stuff as trying to do is to say, "Look, here's my story. But look again, there's a bottom line that can be appended to this story." He took his empirical work probably more seriously than you or I might. I'm sure he did. But I think that what he's trying to do is, by setting an example, saying, "Look, what you should do is go out and do this sort of work. Go ahead, you do it better. But this is what you've got to do. This is the kind of thing you've got to do. You've got to systematically show me that regulation has an effect on electric prices. You've got to systematically show me what's behind entry control in (whatever he was doing, trucking I think or occupational licensing)" (Conversation with Sam Peltzman, October 1997).

17. Becker took over the core graduate course in price theory from Friedman.

18. The cult-like insistence on the objectivity of empirical evidence was effectively dismissed by Jacob Viner and it has been by Frank Knight before him. It was not an inherent part of neoclassical economics that empirical evidence would be given the central role in "proving theory." Theory didn't have to be proved to be useful in providing a framework for thinking about policy. Viner understood this completely and, had the profession followed his lead, it would have stayed much closer to its Classical Liberal roots. The quotation from Viner that we provided in Chapter 1 is worth repeating.

> I do not think it is practical to write an elaborate work on the working of economic process in modern society on a completely "objective" basis ... Anyone who could do so would be pathological ... In so far as is possible, value-judgements should be labelled as such, but their systematic exclusion is, I am convinced, not in practice either possible or desirable. (Viner quoted in Van Horn 2011: 291fn)

19. Stigler's concoction of the Coase Theorem (loosely based on an article by Ronald Coase) provided ammunition against the welfare economic conclusions derived by theoretically pinpointing market imperfections and externalities.

20. Though ostensibly based on the bedrock of scientific methodology, programs such as Johnson's "War on Poverty" tended to be evaluated from noticeably ideological perspectives. Standards for judging them either failures or successes proved slippery in practice.

21. The lengthy taped conversation of the Chicago counterrevolutionaries recorded and edited by Kitch (1983) which appeared in the *Journal of Law and Economics* has an openly triumphal flavor to it.

22. One of the rationales provided by Stigler for dropping History of Thought from graduate education was the danger of providing young minds with too many plausible alternatives. He required missionary soldiers, not ranks of puzzled philosophers.

> The young economist who reads some of the early controversies with care will surely learn one lesson, and he may learn two. The inevitable lesson is that after studying previous controversies one cannot become quite so engaged in the current controversies—one cannot become quite so convinced of either the correctness or the importance of one's new ideas. The more subtle lesson is that it does not pay to learn the first lesson: the temperate, restrained, utterly fair-minded treatment of one's own theories does a disservice to these theories as well as to one's professional status and salary. The scientist is loath to buy new models which have not been well advertised. (Stigler 1982:111)

23. The realm of science imagined was self-sustaining, an antiseptic campus where economists roamed free to investigate the impact of the outside world and the specifics that were effectively encompassed within those boundaries. Unfortunately, such a free-floating realm existed as only the faintest of whispers. Instead, Stigler described a scientifically validated process that he proposed is, and should be, hermetically sealed.

> The channel through which economic events are reaching economic theorists is undergoing change. Specialization has created the empirical research economist, who collects and systemizes the (some) facts of economic life. He is becoming substantially the only source of information for the specialized theorists: the only things the theoretical economist knows about economic life are those things the empirical economist tells him. All other sources (the theorist must increasingly assume) are unreliable or unrepresentative—in short, unscientific. (Stigler 1960: 41)

24. The Chicago view, best articulated by Stigler, is that specifics are only of rather minor importance since ultimately the players in any economic drama are reacting to market forces.

> Well, because I had the same view as George, on that issue. That I don't think you can talk with restaurant managers, in fact, about such things. You know they are not trained, they know in a certain deep sense, but they are not trained to articulate why things are happening. But any restaurant owner does in fact recognise it's good if you can get customers to come in and you can lose your audience pretty easily. You know there's unstable demand. Even when you're in the door, you can go out. That, they're all aware of, and so, in that sense they would say, "sure this is going on." In terms of pricing and so on. I think that would be a hard thing to get by asking them. So I would have the same view, that yes, I use surveys in labour economics a lot. Surveys may give you suggestions about behaviour

but you can't really take that as the same type of evidence. (Conversation with Gary Becker, October 1997)

Given this starting point, what people intend to do, or say they are doing, may exist only as items of curiosity, rather than as data containing any trace of analytic value.

> Nobody was as empirical as George, considering how good a theorist he was, one of the most empirical economists of his day. There are very few theorists who have that much of an empirical insight into the empirical side of questions. He certainly used all the data he could get, surveys, whatever. Now, I was thinking in the sociological sense where you've got people asking questions to gather census data. This is absolutely essential in my field. And George would use it. If however I saw data based on responses to questions like: "How do you feel this morning? What do you feel about Richard Nixon? Did your wife and you have an argument this morning?" I don't pay attention to *that* kind of data. There is this definite bias in Economics. You see what people *do*, not what they say. Because, you can never competently judge their motives, or what is in it for them. [laughs] You've got to study their behavior, pure and simple. (Conversation with Sherwin Rosen, October 1997)

25. Paul Samuelson, for all his contributions to modernism in economics, would seem to be channeling some classical pragmatism while engaging in a revealing debate with George Stigler. "There are no rules concerning the proper role of government that can be established by a priori reasoning" (Samuelson and Stigler 1963: 37).

In stating this general principle, Samuelson is harking back, whether intentionally or not, to an earlier Classical compatriot. "It appears to me that the most fatal of all errors would be the general admission of the proposition that a government has no right to interfere for any purpose except for that of affording protection, for such an admission would be preventing our profiting from experience and even from acquiring it" (Nassau Senior quoted in Reisman 1990: 55).

26. Stigler, for instance, venerated Adam Smith, yet he directly broke with him (Stigler 1971c) over the preferable role allocated to government. What Adam Smith and his subsequent followers understood was that whether or not government had a role to perform within the operations of a market economy was a non-issue. The more productive terrain of debate disputed the nature of the role necessarily played by government and the limits that could and should be usefully imposed.

As we pointed out in our introductory chapter, Adam Smith was not a doctrinaire advocate of laissez-faire. As Jacob Viner pointed out, he did not trust government and believed that the powerful would use government for their benefit, not for the benefit of society. But he also recognized that society needed government to do all types of tasks that individuals would not do. As such, one could not make blanket statements in favor or against government intervention, but one had to look at each issue on its own and make a decision as to whether government intervention was warranted.

27. As we pointed out in Chapter 3, John Stuart Mill had no doubt about the importance of the debate aimed not at winning, but at understanding one's opponent's position and arriving at a joint understanding of the issues—what we have called argumentation for the sake of heaven. Argumentation for the sake of heaven requires honest engagement by committed proponents of opposing views. This approach would, in Mill's view, most likely achieve the greatest good for the greatest number. Mill wrote, "In the case of any person whose judgment is really deserving of confidence, how has it become so? Because he has kept his mind open to criticism of his opinions and conduct. Because it has been his practice to listen to all that could be said against him…" (Mill 1947 [1859]: 20)

28. Serious argument and discussion inevitably involved the precarious task of trying to demarcate an already ambiguous, gray-shaded boundary.

> Despite the lingering popularity of the idea of laissez-faire and the widely shared assumption that it was the prevailing view of most economists, for more than fifty years [1874–1924] the world's leading practitioners of the profession had applied it only as, in the words of John Elliot Cairnes, a "handy rule of practice" with "no scientific basis whatever." (Burgin 2012: 2)

Chapter 7. Roads Not Taken

1. Buchanan moved to the University of Virginia in 1956. Ronald Coase joined Buchanan there in 1958. Together with William Breit, Warren Nutter, Leland Yeager, and Gordon Tullock, the University of Virginia assembled a group of economists working in a Classical Liberal tradition that rivaled Chicago in terms of its intellectual fire power. Despite its abbreviated span, it did leave a lasting legacy in the form of a journal, *Public Choice*. This endeavor was the brainchild of Gordon Tullock, a project originally titled *Papers on Non-Market Decision Making*.

> Nutter stands squarely in the Virginia School of political economy in that he applied price theory to real world problems with a sharp eye on the institutional setting within which decisions were made. This interest in market process was, as I have indicated, a hallmark of Virginia economics. It had been instilled in Nutter, as in Buchanan, by Frank Knight, Henry Simons and Milton Friedman at the University of Chicago. (Breit 1987: 649)

2. One of us was invited to give a lecture recently at the University of Virginia. During the lecture, the Virginia School was mentioned as having been a distinct school of thought. The young assistant professors present had no idea that such a school of thought had ever existed.

3. Even in his old age (86), Coase remained hopeful that the economics profession would come to embrace some version of his approach.

I've just been involved in the starting of a new society, The International Society for the New Institutional Economics. And the inaugural conference was held last month in St. Louis. I wanted to have a small meeting, but we invited some people and they told other people and they told still other people and in the end we had 200 people come from all over the world. No one from Australia, but someone from New Zealand, and I know there were people from Russia, and China, Taiwan, all the European countries and so on. So there is a lot of dissatisfaction with the present state of economics. It's not dominant, but there's a lot of it and it's widespread. (Conversation with Ronald Coase, October 1997)

4. Following this strategy allowed Coase to dismiss the common Pigouvian approach that zeroed in theoretically on a discerned market shortcoming. In contradistinction, Coase attempted to demonstrate that in the absence of transaction costs, a world deemed conducive to abstract welfare economics, markets intrinsically worked. Contracts, and subsequent exchanges, could be effortlessly negotiated. Consequently, it is not externalities or other theoretical imposts that generate market dysfunction, but the bothersome existence of transaction costs.

5. Keeping with his Classical Liberal approach, Coase claimed that as editor of the *Journal of Law and Economics*, he had received article after article evaluating specific government policy interventions. It was this mountain of evidence that strengthened his support for a more laissez-faire approach (Conversation with Ronald Coase, October 1997). Unfortunately, evidence can be a slippery concept tinged by ideological leanings. Facts after all do not speak freely for themselves. They lack a voice of their own. However, whatever his ultimate judgment, editing the journal and being swayed by evidence was consistent with a Classical Liberal approach. Coase goes as far as to say that it was really the promise of becoming editor in 1964 (taking over from Aaron Director) that induced him to come to Chicago.

> Consequently, when I was approached to fill Aaron Director's place on his retirement, what I found most attractive about coming to Chicago was the opportunity it gave me of editing the Journal. Indeed, it is probable that without the Journal I would not have come to Chicago. I knew nothing of the original aim of the Journal. What I wanted to do was to encourage the type of research which I had advocated in "The Problem of Social Cost," and I used my editorship of the Journal as a means of bringing this about. (Coase 1993: 252)

6. The type of formalism previously described as a mainstay of the postwar move to scientific modernism never exerted much sway over Coase. As George Priest points out: "I agree with Ronald Coase about formalism. I don't think it advances thinking in law and economics. Formalism has made it acceptable to just use maths, because it is easy to make a model, but it doesn't advance the field" (Mordfin and Nagorsky 2011).

7. As early as 1946 (and, as will be demonstrated, even before), Coase took aim at what he saw were basic missteps in understanding the tools economics could provide. Here it might prove convenient to remember Coase's practical turn of mind, which proved not to be overly amenable to purely theoretical efforts. In particular, the modernist spirit in the 1940s had allowed young economists, such as Lerner (1944), to deduce the need for government intervention in markets where firms enjoyed economies of scale. The science displayed was impeccable. Efficient pricing (and production) demanded marginal cost settings. Economies of scale implied falling average costs and therefore marginal costs lying below average unit ones. Since firms would find efficient pricing to be antithetical to survival (covering opportunity costs), governments were scientifically obliged to step in to uphold market requirements (to duplicate optimum resource results). "The amount by which total costs exceed total receipts (the loss, as it is sometimes termed) should be a charge on the Government and should be borne out of taxation" (Coase 1946: 169). The interesting problem raised by this early example of model-based policy is the lack of any concrete examination of what firms actually do (or could do) when faced with exactly this challenge. Even worse, no indication exists either in Lerner's work or that of Hotelling (1938), which hints at the need to consider other potential pricing schemes or the subsequent response of consumers within the relevant market. Policy formation is instead stripped down to the construction of an economic model with policy directly derived from that model's conclusions. But when examined from Coase's perspective, the very logic underpinning this broadly accepted analysis is faulty. "Any actual economic situation is complex and a single economic problem does not exist in isolation. Consequently, confusion is liable to result because economists dealing with an actual situation are attempting to solve several problems at once" (Coase 1946: 170).

For Coase, the methodology and unsubstantiated certainty attached to such policy recommendations have an otherworldly quality attached to them. Historical results are simply dismissed, with markets expected to align themselves to the constraints imposed by economic science. These cleverly stitched together policies carry with them a definite trace of Swift's tailors of Laputa. Imbued with Knight's skepticism of any such all-embracing plans for world improvement, Coase displays little faith that governments, of any stripe or ability, would be capable of implementing such schemes.

> This, he [Hotelling] says, "is an interesting historical question." And he adds later: "When the question arises of building new railroads or new major industries of any kind or of scrapping the old, we shall face, not a historical, but a mathematical and economic problem." Nowhere in Professor Hotelling's article does one find recognition of the fact that it will be more difficult to discover whether to build new railroads or new industries if one does not know whether the creation of past railroads or industries was wise social policy. And it is certainly not absurd to take into account the fact that decisions are likely to be better made if afterwards

there is some test of whether such decisions were wise social policy than if such an enquiry is never made. (Coase 1946: 175–176)

8. The exact properties would become more precisely (and scientifically) defined over the years. Logic, however, insisted—as far as Mill and numerous other economists were concerned—that direct payment for service was so obviously ruled out of existence in the case of the lighthouse that no actual investigation need be undertaken.

> It is a proper office of government to build and maintain lighthouses, establish buoys, etc. for the security of navigation: for since it is impossible that the ships at sea which are benefited by a lighthouse, should be made to pay a toll on the occasion of its use, no one would build lighthouses from motives of personal interest, unless indemnified and rewarded from a compulsory levy made by the state. (Mill quoted in Coase 1974: 357)

In one of his much later papers Ronald Coase would make his working approach to economics and his version of Classical Liberalism quite clear. He stresses the need to understand how things actually work and to avoid the allures offered by what he termed blackboard economics. According to Coase,

> As I see it, progress in understanding the working of the economic system will come from an interplay between theory and empirical work. The theory suggests what empirical work might be fruitful, the subsequent empirical work suggests what modification in the theory or rethinking is needed, which in turn leads to new empirical work. If rightly done, scientific research is a never-ending process, but one that leads to greater understanding at each stage. (The Conduct of Economics: The Example of Fisher Body and General Motors, 2006, https://www.coase.org/about ronaldcoase.htm)

9. In these arguments, Coase laid the groundwork for work by Elinor Ostrom, who would win a Nobel Prize in 2009 for her work on the governance systems of common pool resources.

10. Coase makes this the core of his lighthouse article since its stepping-off point is really focused on Samuelson's approach. By employing marginal cost analysis Samuelson concluded that even if private industry were willing to build lighthouses, doing so would be inefficient and should be prevented. He writes, "It costs society *zero extra cost* to let one extra ship use the service; hence any ships discouraged from those waters by the requirement to pay a positive price will represent a social economic loss—even if the price charged to all is no more than enough to pay the long-run expenses of the lighthouse" (Coase 1974: 359).

11. Pigou was careful to note the limitations of his framework. Later users of his welfare framework, such as Lerner, were less finicky (Pigou 1920; Colander 2016). Coase (1946) seems to have shared the profession's general perception of Pigou. Many of his seminal responses (1946, 1960) could be attributed, in part, to a negative response to Pigou's work on welfare economics.

12. Of course, if there are no transaction costs, then there would be no problem with individuals working through government to solve collective problems. Individuals would simply coordinate their actions to achieve the best possible outcome.

13. Coase understood that he was not putting forth an original argument. He acknowledged that he was simply reflecting the general Classical Liberal methodology learned as an essential part of his studies. He writes:

> In my long life I have known some great economists but I have never counted myself among their number nor walked in their company. I have made no innovations in high theory. My contribution to economics has been to urge the inclusion in our analysis of features of the economic system so obvious that, like the postman in G. K. Chesterton's Father Brown tale, "The Invisible Man," they have tended to be overlooked. Nonetheless, once included in the analysis, they will, I believe, bring about a complete change in the structure of economic theory, at least in what is called price theory or microeconomics. What I have done is to show the importance for the working of the economic system of what may be termed the institutional structure of production. (Coase 1992: 713)

14. Stigler presents the evening as a triumph of market logic over poorly examined textbook verities. But a key to understanding Coase's insight was widely missed. The largely unrecognized impact of that evening's debate remained buried, with the subsequent focus of inquiry being shifted quite sharply. Initially unremarked was Stigler's willingness to jump, from his formulation of a fundamentally ersatz Coase's theorem, directly to a set of implied policy recommendations. Instead, Stigler presents a more romantic historical snapshot where truth triumphs over false belief. "We strongly objected to this heresy. Milton Friedman did most of the talking, as usual. He also did much of the thinking, as usual. In the course of two hours of argument the vote went from twenty against and one for Coase to twenty-one for Coase. What an exhilarating event!" (Stigler 1988a: 76).

15. Given Stigler's search for a unified field theory of economics, his formulation of the Coase theorem allowed an end run around market imperfections. If markets successfully internalized externalities, then the perfectly competitive model could still prevail. Certainly, it was immune from a scientifically based attack. The importance Stigler attached to this insight is signaled by the full chapter he devoted to its discovery and ramifications in his autobiography. "I have spent all of my professional life in the company of first-class scholars but only once have I encountered something like the sudden Archimedian revelation—as an observer" (1988a: 73).

16. Coase recognized that Stigler did not understand the point he was trying to make. Coase recollected that during that fateful dinner, only Arnold Harberger managed to actually understand what he was attempting to do (Conversation with Ronald Coase, October 1997).

> I remember at one stage, Harberger saying, "Well, if you can't say that the marginal cost schedule changes when there's a change in liability, he can run right through." What he meant was that, if this was so, there was no way of stopping me from reaching my conclusions. And of course that was right. I said, "What is the cost schedule if a person is liable, and what is the cost schedule if he isn't liable for damage?" It's the same. The opportunity cost doesn't shift. (Coase 1997: 2)

The habit of thinking in terms of transaction costs, while employing a straightforward application of the marginal cost concept, is not original with the 1960 paper. A similar approach appears in his earlier but equally famous paper on the firm (1937). In his insights and methodology, Coase seemingly remained an unabashed hedgehog throughout his lengthy career. But his focus on institutional specifics makes that simpleminded evaluation somewhat questionable.

17. Care must be exercised at this point to emphasize the total absence of any malevolent objective on Stigler's part. Machiavellian manipulators and creators of spidery conspiracies have no role to play in the unfolding of these described events. No evidence of dishonorable intentions appears ready to be unearthed. Rather, this is the way George Stigler comprehended the world. Given his underlying understanding of Coase's (1960) work, if anything, Stigler was being aboveboard and generous by recognizing Coase as the originator of this famous (if not at times infamous) theorem. "I christened the proposition the 'Coase Theorem' and that is how it is known today. Scientific theories are hardly ever named after their first discoverers (more on this later), so this is a rare example of correct attribution of a priority" (Stigler 1988a: 77).

18. The argument we are making here is well known by historians of thought and methodologists. For example, Mark Blaug clearly recognized the issue at stake. He points out:

> Similarly ideological is the way he [George Stigler] lit on Ron Coase and read the Coase theorem incorrectly, much to Coase's own amazement. Coase never realized there was a theorem there. That's all a wonderful example of ideologically inspired criticism and also a perception of the subtle weakness of economics. This, from an economist who otherwise would, of course, have denied that ideology had any role to play in advancing the role of economics. (Conversation with Mark Blaug, April 1998)

19. The theorem might come equipped with a cinematic tagline: "a theorem inspired by an article written by Ronald Coase."

20. That Stigler chose to title that chapter of his autobiography Eureka!" easily reveals a not so well-hidden agenda. Samuelson also conjectured that a bit of sleight of hand was being performed by the Chicago contingent.

> But Stigler and Friedman jumped on to Ronald Coase and felt that the Coase doctrines about transaction costs and property rights—just get the property rights right then laissez-faire could be relied upon—was the

lifeline that they sought. Now, all that I know about this part of the story is what's called the Coase Theorem. And that's a coinage of Stigler's. I don't think Coase knew what his theorem was. There's great argumentation as to whether there is a theorem. (Conversation with Paul Samuelson, October 1997)

21. Stigler's longtime research associate, Claire Friedland, best sums up Stigler's views on externalities.

George was focused on the way the market marches in to *eliminate* the externalities, to work *around* them to make them a market problem instead of a non-market problem. I think I've quoted him in my memoir as saying something like, "externalities are what the market has not *yet* eliminated." (Conversation with Claire Friedland November 1997)

He described externalities as that for which there are no transactions *at the present time.* (Friedland 1993: 781)

22. Coase continued to evaluate transaction costs as posing a serious problem to the efficient operations of markets. Taking a directly opposite approach, Stigler recognized the existence of such impediments, but when approached from his perspective, their importance tended to be minimized. Markets, for all intents and purposes, mirrored the perfectly competitive models of theory.

23. There was in fact a distinct tendency to criticize the scientific validity of the theorem, in this fashion, nicely avoiding the implied policy issue.

24. Stigler's longtime friend and assistant, Claire Friedland, put it this way:

He liked upsetting people. I told you he wrote that column for *Business Month*. After a year went by, nobody had criticized it. They didn't get any letters to the editor. And you know, he had said so many outrageous things: that insider trading is really okay, that sort of thing. He said things meant to upset people. Well, he gave it up. He wasn't having any fun. He wanted people to criticize his ideas and then he wanted to come back with his rejoinders. You know, he wanted to have a little controversy. (Conversation with Claire Friedland, November 1997)

25. Buchanan entered the University of Chicago, with self-described, "strong socialist leanings." However, under the tutelage of Frank Knight, Buchanan notes that he soon became "a zealous advocate of the market order" (https://econjwatch.org/issues/volume-10-issue-3-september-2013).

26. While there are many different aspects of Public Choice economics, the approach is essentially the economic model of the selfish rational actor applied to politics. In the book that is seen as the origin of Public Choice, *The Calculus of Consent*, Buchanan and Tullock (1962) insisted that for political science to have a strong theoretical foundation, economic rational choice reasoning had to be applied to politics. They argued that Public Choice theory added a rational actor analysis of voting and a profit-maximizing analysis of politicians. When com-

bined, they provided a scientific foundation for the study of politics that was lacking in the standard theories of political scientists.

27. The strongest Chicago-style approach to legislative self-interest is perhaps seen in the work of George Stigler who, along with his close friend Aaron Director, pushed the idea of utility maximization and market efficiency as far as it could go (and perhaps further). Stigler even felt justified in taking Adam Smith to task for not sufficiently incorporating self-interest into the political realm.

> In the political scene no corresponding search is made for the effective principles of behaviour. Therefore reforms must be effected, if effected they can be, by moral suasion. At best this is an extraordinarily slow and uncertain method of changing policy; at worst it may lead to policies which endanger the society. Of course erroneous and undesirable public policies arise out of failures of comprehension as well as out of the efforts of self-serving groups, but there is little reason to accept Smith's implicit assumption that the main source of error is ignorance or "prejudice." Yet Smith's only remedy for erroneous policy is sound analysis, and that remedy is appropriate only to a minority of objectionable policies. (Stigler 1982: 143)

For Stigler, and many of his Chicago colleagues, political markets and political decisions were based on the narrow self-interest of rational economic decision makers. Beneficial government actions then served only as a smokescreen for more selfish objectives.

> So he [George Stigler] would often take, and it got him into trouble, he often would take these very strong positions which he often convinced himself were actually true. Like when he was confronted with some fact about regulation, he would say "Ah, you're going to find some Congressman was bought off. [laughter] You are actually going to find that. That's what you're going to find. Are you sure that you didn't find that this Congressman wasn't on the take?" You know, that kind of writing, that kind of a very strong view. (Conversation with Sam Peltzman, October 1997)

28. In anticipating the worst from government intervention, Buchanan's position was in accord with that held by his Chicago counterparts. "Buchanan—well Buchanan was a Chicago product, and Tullock was, I guess Tullock was too" (Conversation with Milton Friedman, August 1997). None of them invested any faith in the public-spiritedness of government bureaucrats or politicians.

> John Maynard Keynes was a strong believer in the public interest theory of regulation, and in the operation of government. Indeed I think it was his legacy on that subject which was much more damaging than his legacy on economics. (Conversation with Milton Friedman, August 1997)

29. Stigler basically accepted that individuals respond to market price signals, leaving them in a somewhat passive position. What then remains essential

for analysis are not anecdotal deviations from rational self-interest but rather the dominating fact of such decisions.

> However, that cannot be the entire story; human behavior is not so rigorously deterministic as a multiplication table. There are people who do not care for wealth, more who do not reason well, and vastly more who are incompletely informed. These people will not necessarily achieve optimal agreements, and especially is this true in new circumstances. We do not believe that such people govern important markets: Others who love wealth, reason precisely, and buy information in optimal quantities will call the tune. (Stigler 1989: 631)

30. Chicago School economists believed that political forces would not work for the common good as well, but this insight didn't form the sole focus of their formal theoretical model. Rather, it was only one aspect of a broader analysis.

31. Individuals at Chicago worked on such issues and produced theoretical models without situating themselves narrowly within the field of Public Choice. For one example of Stigler's formal modeling, see Stigler (1970). In addition, George Stigler's protégé, Sam Peltzman, often dealt with such issues. See Peltzman (1976, 1980, 1985). These and contributions by others mostly appeared in the house journal that helped to construct the Chicago version of law and economics (*Journal of Law and Economics*).

32. To reiterate and clarify, the Chicago School's handling of the political market was largely an extension and application of the core Chicago model. This approach was pioneered by Gary Becker, who considered rational choice to form a nearly universal model for social science. In the Public Choice field, it formed an intrinsic starting point for the construction of their all-inclusive model.

33. We are not arguing that they should not have developed formal models. As we stated in the text, the tenor of the times, which saw policy following from theory, required it. Had Buchanan or the Chicago School not integrated the insights into formal models, they likely would never have prospered to the degree that they did. In that case, Coase and Buchanan likely would have been two largely forgotten economists.

34. As discussed in chapter 3, James Laughlin, first department chair of economics at the University of Chicago, set the tone for the aggressive style that would later flourish there. This result seems, at least at first glance, to be some combination of nature and nurture.

35. Coase's influence did not rest entirely on one ersatz theorem. Oliver Williamson, inspired by Coase's 1937 article on the firm, attempted to resurrect an almost obsessive focus on transaction costs. This work earned Williamson a Nobel Prize in 2009 (shared with Elinor Ostrom).

36. Other Classical Liberal methodological approaches to economics, such as Austrian or Institutionalist, were also quickly shunted from the mainstream into a broad grouping dubbed heterodox economics. In essence, this labeling strategy allowed most economists to ignore and exile those who dared to reject standard methodological perspectives.

Chapter 8. The Classical Liberal "Argumentation for the Sake of Heaven" Alternative

1. Samuelson and Friedman are used here as something of a collective noun for the development of economic thinking during the 1950s and on through the 1970s. These developments were shaped by MIT and Chicago. In the case of Chicago, we have noted other key players. The same would occur were the MIT/Harvard connection to be equally analyzed.

2. The joke also includes an unacknowledged strain of arrogance. Economists are pictured as somehow shrewder than their other scientific rivals. Only the economist is capable of glimpsing the least cost (least effort) method for gaining an accurate answer. In essence, trading for information trumps those constrained by their own inflexible methods. This is to be expected, since the joke has been formulated by an economist without any input from the worlds of either engineering or physics.

3. There is an aspect here of Hayek's (1937, 1945) notion of spontaneous order which, given a recognized state of limited knowledge, transmutes into a defense of market coordination and a condemnation of central planning.

4. Being cautious when using economic theory doesn't, of course, mean flippantly dismissing it out of hand as providing no real guidelines or information. The issue is a matter of weighting.

> Milton Friedman remarked to me long ago that the study of the stability of general equilibrium is unimportant, first, because it is obvious that the economy is stable, and, second, because if it isn't stable we are wasting our time. He should have known better. In the first place, it is not at all obvious that the actual economy is stable. Apart from the lessons of the past few years, there is the fact that prices do change all the time. Beyond this, however, is a subtler and possibly more important point. Whether or not the actual economy is stable, we *largely lack a convincing theory of why that should be so*. Lacking such a theory, we do not have an adequate theory of value, and there is an important *lacuna* in the center of microeconomic theory. (Fisher 2011: 35)

5. There is a well-known *New Yorker* cartoon showing a bearded economist at a blackboard raising the core economic question: "That may be all very well in practice, but does it work in theory?" The almost Hegelian belief that the real is the ideal is exemplified by Harry Johnson's barbed comments about the Cambridge School of Keynesianism.

> Then along came Roy Harrod with his dynamic growth equation; and Joan Robinson latched on to that and proceeded to create a new confusion which Cambridge has insisted on ever since in the realm of capital theory. It is the mistaken belief that to prove capitalism to be logically impossible is sufficient to dispose of its existence. (Johnson and Johnson 1978: 145)

Elsewhere, Johnson had previously depicted this peculiar failing, which confused theoretical issues with normative or policy considerations.

> Much of the development of economic theory, of course, concerns the separation of the economic logic of prices being attached to things that are scarce from the question of *morality*. That confusion of logic still runs right through the Cambridge Keynesian school (and I will say a little more about that later). (Johnson and Johnson, 1978: 138)

6. As we stated in Chapter 1, Keynes summarized the skills needed to be a top economist. Since it is the combination of skills that define the Classical Liberal method, and since Keynes put it so elegantly, it is worth repeating.

> The study of economics does not seem to require any specialized gifts of an unusually high order. Is it not, intellectually regarded, a very easy subject compared with the higher branches of philosophy or pure science? An easy subject at which few excel! The paradox finds its explanation, perhaps, in that the master-economist must possess a rare combination of gifts. He must be mathematician, historian, statesman, philosopher—in some degree. He must understand symbols and speak in words. He must contemplate the particular in terms of the general and touch abstract and concrete in the same flight of thought. He must study the present in the light of the past for the purposes of the future. No part of man's nature or his institutions must lie entirely outside his regard. He must be purposeful and disinterested in a simultaneous mood; as aloof and incorruptible as an artist, yet sometimes as near to earth as a politician. (Keynes 1924: 321–322)

7. An economist's training tends to be highly technical and focused on theoretical and statistical methods, rather than on case studies. Back in 1987, one of us (Colander and Klamer 1987) did a survey of students at top graduate schools in which we asked how important a knowledge of institutions was to succeeding as an economist. Only 3 percent said it was very important. What was important: 65 percent said a knowledge of mathematics was very important. In response, the AEA set up a commission to study graduate education. The commission agreed that an economist's training was too focused on technical issues. But little has changed since then. Graduate training has become even more technical and more focused on scientific empirical work since then (Colander 2007a).

8. Despite legitimate claims of its subsequent impact and guidance, the examined reality reveals an alternative picture. Methodology texts would seem obliged to either describe how economists actually conduct research or alternatively how they should do so. But the evidence supporting Friedman's formulation tends to crumble if examined closely. It doesn't appear to encapsulate what economists do as economists.

> When I was a graduate student we were taught a paradigm of how you do research. I've got to tell you that it's all wrong. It's not the way we operate.

> We don't sit up here and develop hypotheses and go out and test them. That's just not what we do. George taught me that. Milton taught me that. They're wrong! (Conversation with Sam Peltzman, October 1997)

Nor does this method appear to be what economists should follow.

> If all economists followed Friedman's principles in choosing theories, no economist could be found who believed in a theory until it had been tested, which would have the paradoxical result that no tests would be carried out. This is what I meant when I said that acceptance of Friedman's methodology would result in the paralysis of scientific activity. Work could certainly continue, but no new theories would emerge. (Coase 1994: 24)

Even more perversely, it is not clear that Friedman himself followed his own specified methods.

> Friedman may have won some methodological battles with F53 but he lost the methodological war because he went on to write *A Monetary History of the United States, 1867–1960* ... with Anna Schwartz—a thick examination of the historical evidence for the theory that money causes price and not the other way round—while the rest of the economics profession put its faith in thin corroborations by means of econometric regressions. (Blaug 2009: 353)

9. See for example Hillary Putnam (2002) and John Davis (2014). At the time of constructing his argument, Milton Friedman made no claim to having dived deeply into any methodological literature. It can be convincingly argued that Friedman exhibited little interest in such questions either before or after his 1953 effort. Rather, the objective behind the argument was more likely to be an attempt to forestall and close off any future methodological discussions. During the period in which Friedman wrote his article, heated challenges to price theory orthodoxy raged. One potent attack concentrated on the reality of any underlying assumptions. A focus on assumptions, particularly the requirement that assumptions be tinged at the very least with real content, ran counter to the program championed by both Friedman and Stigler. Such unorthodox reasoning was raised particularly in opposition to the employment of the perfect competition model. Alternatives, such as monopolistic competition, grounded as they were by more realistic assumptions, were savagely attacked by both Friedman (1941) and Stigler (1949b). Their reaction to views condoning monopolistic competition seems to have spurred the correspondence between Friedman and Stigler that led to Friedman's (1953) influential piece.

10. Although the discussion will focus on Friedman, we are referring to what might be called a largely unacknowledged Friedman/Stigler collaboration. It was this collaboration that yielded the methodology solely ascribed to Friedman. Stigler, however, produced a condensed version of this approach in his 1948 LSE lecture on monopolistic competition (Stigler 1949b). Moreover, evidence of that joint effort can be found in letters exchanged between the two during the late 1940s

(Hammond and Hammond 2006). In any case, Friedman and Stigler were not the only Chicago-style economists to opt for a theory-derived policy perspective.

> MILTON FRIEDMAN: I had written the methodology paper, which was later formally published. This preceded, by three or four years, the earlier versions. And he refers in one of those lectures to the fact that we had been talking about it.
>
> *And how influential were you in each other's thinking on this matter?*
>
> MILTON FRIEDMAN: We were very influential. I think there's no doubt that my work would have been different if I hadn't been influenced by George and George's work would have been different if he hadn't been influenced by me. (Conversation with Milton Friedman, Rose Friedman, and Aaron Director, August 1997)

11. Again, we are focusing on Chicago and Friedman as our targeted case study. However, the argument would have been much the same had we used the more mainstream example of Samuelson and MIT as the relevant case study. The MIT approach also accepted that policy debates were to be resolved through scientific methods, not through argumentation for the sake of heaven.

12. In practice, Friedman had never been as tied to this approach as had someone like his close friend and colleague, George Stigler. He had long favored empirical approaches, unlike someone such as Frank Knight. His 1953 piece then does not represent an abrupt break from the past; rather it is more of a public announcement of the position he had supposedly adopted in his work.

13. That which was not resolvable by existing methods would be defined as being outside the realm of science. Although there are times when within the more strictly defined scientific borders there may be an overwhelming consensus, uniformity is never achieved. Moreover, with the passage of time, scientific truths can transform into scientific falsehoods given the accumulation of knowledge.

14. John Stuart Mill serves as our guide for what we mean by argumentation for the sake of heaven. Here is how he described that desired argumentation approach. He writes:

> He who knows only his own side of the case, knows little of that. His reasons may be good, and no one may have been able to refute them. But if he is equally unable to refute the reasons on the opposite side; if he does not so much as know what they are, he has no ground for preferring either opinion. The rational position for him would be suspension of judgment, and unless he contents himself with that, he is either led by authority, or adopts, like the generality of the world, the side to which he feels most inclination. Nor is it enough that he should hear the arguments of adversaries from his own teachers, presented as they state them, and accompanied by what they offer as refutations. That is not the way to do justice to the arguments, or bring them into real contact with his own mind. He must be able to hear them from persons who actually believe them; who

defend them in earnest, and do their very utmost for them. He must know them in their most plausible and persuasive form; he must feel the whole force of the difficulty which the true view of the subject has to encounter and dispose of; else he will never really possess himself of the portion of truth which meets and removes that difficulty. Ninety-nine in a hundred of what are called educated men are in this condition; even of those who can argue fluently for their opinions. Their conclusion may be true, but it might be false for anything they know: they have never thrown themselves into the mental position of those who think differently from them, and considered what such persons may have to say; and consequently they do not, in any proper sense of the word, know the doctrine which they themselves profess. They do not know those parts of it which explain and justify the remainder; the considerations which show that a fact which seemingly conflicts with another is reconcilable with it, or that, of two apparently strong reasons, one and not the other ought to be preferred. All that part of the truth which turns the scale, and decides the judgment of a completely informed mind, they are strangers to; nor is it ever really known, but to those who have attended equally and impartially to both sides, and endeavoured to see the reasons of both in the strongest light. So essential is this discipline to a real understanding of moral and human subjects, that if opponents of all important truths do not exist, it is indispensable to imagine them, and supply them with the strongest arguments which the most skilful devil's advocate can conjure up. (Mill 1859/1947: 35–36)

15. A methodological approach that might be used is to have an "overseer" who comes from a different ideological perspective. Such an individual would review the article or book, providing suggestions as the research is being done, and provide a final assessment that is published as part of the research. One of us played such an "overseeer" role on a research project overseen by Dan Klein (2013).

16. It is only fair to note that David Ricardo was actively lobbying for the repeal of England's Corn Laws. Therefore, to evaluate Ricardo's theoretical framework as, at least, an implicit form of persuasive rhetoric is far from unreasonable. Given his objective, the burnish of scientific inevitability, at a time when the respect for scientific thought was growing, allowed his ostensible theory-building logic to be viewed as an attempt to surreptitiously introduce into the debate a hidden persuader, in the form of scientific impartiality. The extent to which Ricardo actually viewed his policy imperatives as embodying scientific inevitability is highly questionable. The problem with drawing stark contrasts in examining Ricardo, as well as others of that era, is that the reality of the situation will often prove to be much more ambiguous than any simplified account. It was such attempts to strengthen one's policy argument by giving it the imprimatur of science that led economists to advocate a firewall between science and policy in the first place.

17. Schumpeter clarifies the problem of seeking to derive generally applicable principles from the dust of theoretical constructs.

> His (Ricardo's) interest was in the clear-cut result of direct, practical significance ..., he cut that general system to pieces, bundled up as large parts of it as possible, and put them in cold storage—so that as many things as possible should be frozen and "given." He then piled one simplifying assumption upon another ... he set up simple one-way relations so that, in the end, the desired results emerged almost as tautologies. For example (if) ... profits "depend upon" the price of wheat. And under his implicit assumptions ..., this is not only true, but undeniably, in fact trivially, so. Profits could not possibly depend upon anything else, since everything else is "given," that is frozen. It is an excellent theory that can never be refuted and lacks nothing save sense. The habit of applying results of this character to the solution of practical problems we shall call the Ricardian Vice. (Schumpeter 1987/1954: 472–473)

18. This danger becomes clear at times when the practices of the Chicago School are more carefully examined. During their battle over the Chicago antecedents of the "quantity theory of money," Don Patinkin took Milton Friedman to task for his tendency to "let [policy] wag ... theory (Patinkin 1972: 886). He accused Friedman (not without cause) of muddling policy issues with more theoretical matters (whether intentionally or not).

19. Partial concurrence with this position comes, at least on a superficial level, from an unlikely source. George Stigler was almost single-minded in seeing economics as a science. Consequently, this principle led him to be highly suspicious of economists accepting political appointments.

> I conclude—and perhaps I am alone in concluding—that when the economist goes to Washington, he deserves no more credence, and no less, than any other political appointment, and it is mildly deceptive to address him as Doctor or Professor. (Stigler 1988a: 135–136)

He was equally dubious of the role of an economist serving as an expert witness, though his doubts didn't deter him from gaining the benefits available from such performances, especially as his reputation and standing increased.

> Is the expert honest? At very best, probably as honest as is possible in a process in which truth is sought by the vigorous presentations of opposing views, and where any admission by one side is heavily overemphasized by the other side. And that ambiguous answer applies only to the most virtuous of experts. (Stigler 1988a: 133)

20. Deciding on what an impartial spectator would choose is not an easy task, nor does it deliver an unambiguous set of normative judgments. But the procedure likely rules out many normative positions such as "I get everything and everyone else gets nothing." Almost all would agree that an impartial observer

would reject this dictum. This impartial observer approach is likely to lead to general concepts of fairness, such as those formulated by John Rawls (1971), which in some variation would gain widespread support. In the next chapter we consider Amartya Sen's work as an example of how moral philosophy can fit nicely into economic policy analysis. Agreement on policy prescriptions would come about by argument and discussion in reference to that impartial spectator. A desirable policy, one which Classical Liberal economists would argue should be supported, would be one that an impartial spectator would support. It would not necessarily be a policy that an economist as an individual would support. In the methodology defining Classical Liberal policy formation, support was not based solely, or even significantly, on economic science. Instead, it was a function of educated common sense, a transparent moral philosophical position, to which one added relevant scientific facts and insights. For it to be otherwise would once again violate Hume's Dictum that you cannot derive a "should" from an "is."

21. An interesting take on Mill's version of utilitarianism can be found in Persky (2016).

22. This philosophy never purported to be a machine for churning out predictable and automatic policies.

23. In the early 1900s, some neoclassical economists attempted to make utilitarianism more scientific and precise. Instead of serving as a rough guide or an argument for the sake of heaven debate, it became a precise guide of what policy should do. Accomplishing this goal required measuring utility and basing policy on those measurements. Policy would then be directly guided by science. It was that brand of science that Robbins and other Classical Liberals objected to since it would undermine the firewall between economic science and policy. Such a transformation would end up endowing measures of utility with far more importance than they felt they deserved. The goal of policy—the greatest good for the greatest number—could not be determined by science. It had to be determined by discursive argumentation for the sake of heaven. That use of utilitarianism led Lionel Robbins to write his famous methodological treatise arguing that such analysis based on normative value judgments had no place in the science of economics.

Unfortunately, instead of directing economists back to a Classical methodology that possessed a separate branch to deal with policy, Robbins's essay led to values being ostensibly removed from policy analysis. This was definitely not his intention. When Milton Friedman placed policy analysis within the scope of positive economics, the Classical use of utilitarianism as a guide for discursive argumentation was lost. Those arguing for this approach were portrayed as troglodytes who did not understand the need to separate values from theoretical analysis.

24. Even if limited to the scientific context, prescriptive methodology is still suspect. While there are some clear requirements that need to be met in order to qualify as scientific research, there is ample room for ambiguity here. The idea of an average scientist working his or her way through a mechanistic step-by-step procedure doesn't hold up if the actual work of a scientist is carefully monitored. Serendipity, for one, tends to seep in, as do intuitive insights.

25. For Keynes, positive economics involved developing theorems. For example, the following would be a statement in positive economics: If the assumptions of the competitive model hold, and a minimum wage is imposed, unemployment (or, more specifically, non-optimally employed resources represented in a partial equilibrium graph as a difference between the quantity of labor supplied and demanded) will result. The amount of misemployed resources will depend on the elasticity of both the supply and the demand for labor. Such statements, or theorems, were ones that all economists could accept precisely because they did not contain any policy implications. Instead, they provided an organized way of thinking about the issue. Developing and exploring such theorems in logical depth, and then doing so empirically, was what defined positive economics for Keynes. It provided the agreed-upon facts that would be accepted by all economists in any ensuing policy discussion.

Whether a given theorem had any practical relevance for policy matters, such as adopting a minimum wage, did not depend on scientific exploration of a complex model. Instead, it depended on a whole variety of other issues: Was the competitive model the correct one? Were there other side effects of imposing a minimum wage? In what sense would the affected individuals be non-optimally employed? Can we develop precise measures of elasticity, so that we can quantify the effects? Does the wage measure used in the empirical study capture all the dimensions of the work being discussed? What were the alternatives to achieving the normative goal of increasing income for poor people? Fundamentally, no unified labor market exists, but in its theoretical place are a number of specific and very different alternatives that change over time. So, then, is a model that assumes a unified labor market an appropriate one to use? Since many of these considerations are time- and place-specific, there is likely no single, simple, or lasting answer to the minimum wage policy question.

Only after all ancillary issues are examined, and judgments made, can one move from a theorem within positive economics—given the model a minimum wage will cause some unemployment in these cases, and "fact"—empirically our best impartial spectator estimates the amount of unemployment to be—to a precept within the art and craft of economics—the minimum wage law is one that should be supported. Policy guidelines are to be determined in the art of economics, not in the science. This shift can lead to a position that the minimum wage is a policy that should be advocated or one that must be opposed, but any such conclusion represents a decision that is apt to change over time and place.

26. The very nature of Friedman's perspective ultimately eliminates any notion of an "art of economics." If policy is to be directly derived from empirically tested theories then the degree to which judgment is required in formulating policy merely measures a gap in theoretical knowledge. Friedman would reasonably expect that gap to steadily narrow over the years as theory advanced. If then the art of economics essentially reflects an error term, then the art of economics as a field would be expected to wither and die in the future. Again, this is no more than a reasonable implication of Friedman's train of logic, rather than an explicitly stated stance.

27. See Neumark and Wascher (2000) as a fair example of the rebuttal side to this issue.

28. The Card/Krueger controversy inadvertently shined a light on the problem of unacknowledged values creeping into a work meant to fit snugly into the positive economics basket. Card intended to examine a particular question, or set of questions, in the field of labor economics.

> I [David Card] think my research is mischaracterized both by people who propose raising the minimum wage and by people who are opposed to it. What we were trying to do in our research was use the minimum wage as a lever to gain more understanding of how labor markets actually work and, in particular, to address a question that we thought was quite important: To what extent does the simplest model of supply and demand actually describe how employers operate in the labor market? That model says that if an employer wants to hire another worker, he or she can hire as many people as needed at the going wage. Also, workers move freely between firms and, as a result, individual employers have no discretion in the wages that they offer. (Clement 2006)

Card instead became embroiled in a debate so bitterly value-laden that he decided the better part of valor would be a complete withdrawal.

> I think many people are concerned that much of the research they see is biased and has a specific agenda in mind. Some of that concern arises because of the open-ended nature of economic research. To get results, people often have to make assumptions or tweak the data a little bit here or there, and if somebody has an agenda, they can inevitably push the results in one direction or another. Given that, I think that people have a legitimate concern about researchers who are essentially conducting advocacy work. I try to stay away from advocacy of any kind, but that doesn't prevent people from being suspicious that I have an agenda of some kind.
>
> I've subsequently stayed away from the minimum wage literature for a number of reasons. First, it cost me a lot of friends. People that I had known for many years, for instance, some of the ones I met at my first job at the University of Chicago, became very angry or disappointed. They thought that in publishing our work we were being traitors to the cause of economics as a whole. (Clement 2006)

A disarmingly honest evaluation of this debate from a Chicago perspective underlines the importance of drawing the Classical Liberal distinction between economic science and economic policy analysis. "That's right, given my investment, given what I've read over the years. When somebody tells me now that an increase in the minimum wage increases employment, there's just been a study out on that, I'm very skeptical of that claim. I don't believe it!" (Conversation with Sherwin Rosen, October 1997).

29. Ironically, George Stigler's (likely) dismissal of game theory as useful economic science can be aptly applied to Friedman's methodological foray which he

continued to defend on its fiftieth anniversary (during a celebratory session at the 2003 ASSA meetings). The essence of Stigler's objection lay with the accumulation of evidence over time (the test of time). Continuing to insist on a position despite clear contrary evidence would seem to depart from both logic and rationality.

> It's OK to try game theory. But to stick around for twenty years and come up with a result that anything is possible and then to say that this is economics. This is almost the way George would be talking if he was sitting here. "Having you and your six friends argue about a lemma, that's progress!" He wouldn't be indignant. He would be laughing. He would be dismissive. Saying, "You're dopes. You're dopes." What should you do with them George? "Exile them to Samoa." Dismissed with a wave of the hand. Put up, or shut up, and in real time. Don't tell me it's going to happen in the next generation. (Conversation with Sam Peltzman, October 1997)

30. The long-term effect of what many might dismiss as a minor, or even trivial, change should never be underestimated.

> If a physician mishandles a number of patients, there is the danger that they will lose their lives ... If a teacher interprets a poem to his students in an impossible manner, "nothing further happens." But perhaps it is good if we speak more cautiously here. By ignoring the question concerning the thing and by insufficiently interpreting a poem, appears as though nothing further happens. One day, perhaps after fifty or one hundred years, nevertheless something has happened. (Heidegger 1967: 54–55)

Chapter 9. The Art and Craft of Economics

1. The clear attached danger to this theoretical approach is to insist on viewing the world in a fashion that molds it in such a manner that it becomes consistent with a set of carefully cultivated scientific truths. (As previously stated, a classic joke in economics is encapsulated by the statement, "That may be very well in practice, but does it work in theory?")

> What would be the scientific rating of the work of a botanist who should spend his energy in devising ways and means to neutralize the ecological variability of plants, or of a physiologist who conceived it the end of his scientific endeavors to rehabilitate the vermiform appendix or the pineal eye, or to denounce and penalize the imitative coloring of the Viceroy butterfly? ... Those phenomena which Mr. Clark characterizes as "positive perversions" may be distasteful and troublesome perhaps, but "the economic necessity of doing what is legally difficult" is not of the "essentials of theory. (Veblen 1908: 177)

2. Hayek nicely captured how attempts to avoid discussions of value ultimately undermine policy discussions. He writes, "I have arrived at the conviction

that the neglect by economists to discuss seriously what is really the crucial problem of our time is due to a certain timidity about soiling their hands by going from purely scientific questions into value questions" (Hayek 1979: 6).

3. In other work, Colander (Colander and Su 2017) has outlined an "arts and crafts" applied policy approach that is a type of disciplined muddling-through approach that draws heavily on engineering methodology rather than scientific methodology. In it, each branch of economics develops its own state-of-the-art methodology which is constantly changing, as engineers learn by doing, and as analytic technology changes. The methodology is determined by the economists themselves, not by separate methodology specialists.

4. We want to be clear. Our discussion of methodology is about the methodology of applied economics, not about the science of economics. A major reason why the economics profession has moved to a single methodology is that it wants to see itself as a science, judging itself in relation to scientific methodology. We explicitly reject that approach. We believe that economics needs to have multiple methodologies that fit different objectives. Quite different methodologies are appropriate when engaged in applied policy than when exploring economic science. Thus, a Classical Liberal methodology will be consciously multidimensional, with different economists using different methodological approaches. Among and within departments, each different methodological approach would compete for support from the available pool of graduate students. This conception of competition in economics for graduate students closely relates to Lakatos's view of rival research programs. Where we differ from Lakatos is that he discusses scientific, whereas we discuss applied, policy methodology. We have similar differences with Kuhn's analysis and his concept of paradigm shifts. Kuhn's concept of a paradigm, as interpreted by social science methodologists, assumes a close link between theory and policy. Using a Classical Liberal methodology, that close tie is broken. Under these conditions, it becomes unclear what one means by a paradigm. Science and theory operate at the same level. They may have only one methodology; applied policy operates at another level and has multiple methodologies. Economic policy does not follow from given paradigms. Thus, the way a "paradigm" is interpreted and used, much more than the paradigm itself, is where differences in policy exist.

5. We are not beyond writing about the mundane. Elsewhere Colander (1994; Colander and Su 2017) has developed some mundane, obvious, rules. The argument details the idea that a more practical approach would closely follow an engineering, rather than a scientific, methodology. The acceptance that policy models are seen as heuristics, rather than science, is emphasized. A guide to this engineering methodological approach can be found in the work of Billy Vaughn Koen (2003), one of the few engineers who has written about engineering methodology. In defining the engineering method, he explains:

> Everything the engineer does in his role as an engineer is under the control of a heuristic. Engineering has no hint of the absolute, the deterministic, the guaranteed, the true. Instead it fairly reeks of the uncertain, the

provisional and the doubtful. The typical engineer instinctively recognizes this. The ad hoc method is easily labelled, doing the best you can with what you've got (namely "finding a seat of the pants solution," or "just muddling through"). (Koen https://files.eric.ed.gov/fulltext/ED 276572.pdf)

That categorization serves as a good description for what goes on in the basement or the engine room of productive investigations. Unlike economists, who tend to feature themselves as applied scientists, engineers see themselves as problem solvers. They are not limited by any existing scientific methodology. Instead, they use state-of-the-art (SOTA) heuristics. These SOTA heuristics are constantly changing, as engineers learn by doing. Consequently, whereas scientific methodology tends to be rigid and similar across subfields, engineering methodology is looser, evolving, different in different subfields, and in a constant state of flux. For economics this means that policy economists would:

- use a much looser, less scientifically oriented methodology
- see themselves as problem solvers, not truth seekers
- emphasize the ad hoc nature of their models and other heuristics
- add a fudge factor to their policy recommendations
- focus more on creativity in their policy deliberations

See also Colander and Kupers (2014).

6. We have previously warned against cultivating a one-sided skepticism that easily recognizes the flaws in opposing perspectives, but finds it difficult to turn the same critical gaze back on one's own positions.

7. If we were to summarize this respectful attitude, it would include:

- A respect for existing theory, but one that sees it as at best a half-truth in guiding policy. Policy depends on much more than economic theory. Thus any policy discussion must deal with differences in sensibilities that cannot be resolved by science. Argumentation for the sake of heaven is a necessary part of policy analysis.
- Be willing to object to the mainstream view, whenever one believes that mainstream view to be wrong. Classical liberal methodology is by nature skeptical of revealed truths. But do it in a way that encourages constructive debate.
- Be willing to use whatever tools are available that may help resolve the question at hand.
- Separate scientific theory from policy. When you are doing science, focus on searching for the truth and recognize that having policy views related to that science will likely undermine the objectivity required to find that truth. When engaged in policy analysis, use the impartial spectator approach to integrate as objective values as possible into such endeavors. Make those values transparent. Keep as strong a firewall between the pursuits as best one can, recognizing that a complete firewall is impossible.

8. Because of the way in which Classical Liberal methodologies treat scientific theories, the concept of heterodoxy becomes imperceptibly blended in with more mainstream analysis. You can work with a theory, but not believe it, and can have multiple theories when considering policy. There is no orthodoxy. We have suggested that economists following the Classical Liberal methodology can be labeled as representing "inside the mainstream" heterodox economists (see Colander 2010).

9. In simple economic terms, acceptable to the profession, academics will maintain a vested interest in supporting the status quo. Established members especially will resist abandoning time-honored methods. The sunk costs reflected by their research and teaching will make any radical change distinctly unappealing.

10. For example, academic research conducted with the express aim of publication, given standard conventions, will incorporate a strong incentive to arrive at results that meet precise scientific significance measures. These criteria will hold even though those significant measures generally overstate the importance of the particular proxy.

11. This is the best we can do. The methodology of a craft does not exist in any written work on methodology but rather is displayed by the practice of economists. It is passed on from generation to generation as any art and craft is passed on. Here is what worked for successful economists; use it as a guide, modifying it wherever you see fit since problems and technology inevitably change.

12. The economists selected by no means represent a comprehensive list. However, taken together, they demonstrate the range of different ways in which we see the Classical Liberal attitude influencing the way economics is done.

13. After writing this chapter, Ariel Rubinstein (Rubinstein 2017) published comments on Dani Rodrik's new book, *The Rights and Wrongs of the Dismal Science*. It makes many of the same points we make and it discusses the similarities and distinctions between Rodrik's and Rubinstein's methodological approaches. We found nothing in Rubinstein's discussion with which we disagree.

14. The prescribed strategy is for each economist to be given a degree of latitude in finding a method that works best for him or her. By forcing every academic into the same constrictive box, instead of encouraging the employment of his or her strengths, the profession is forcibly denying the core economic idea of comparative advantage.

15. Essentially this means that they are all well-cited economists whose work is also known widely within the discipline. None of them could be considered as dwelling on the periphery of the profession. They are then anything but fringe economists.

16. Whether Leamer's thoughtful objections managed to reroute the way in which economists continued to practice applied econometric research is another matter. McCloskey and Ziliak (1996) would later point out the way in which the profession blurred the difference between economic and statistical significance.

17. For a description of rules that could govern econometrics practices in the basement, see Peter Kennedy (2002).

18. In an insightful book, Abraham Hirsch and Neil de Marchi (1991) make this point in reference to Chicago methodology. This phraseology of focusing on what is actually done has also become a favorite of statesmen and politicians, though life would be simpler if language as subterfuge or camouflage was used neither in economics nor in politics.

19. Deirdre McCloskey is another economist whom we easily could have used as an example of an economist with Classical Liberal attitude. For lack of space, and because her work is sufficiently well known and reviewed, we have not discussed her continued efforts here, other than to say that she exhibits the essence of a Classical Liberal attitude.

20. There seems to be an almost irresistible parallel here to the marked reluctance of men, in former decades, unwilling to come "out of the closet," to "speak the love that dares not breathe its name." In economics as well, pressures to appear mainstream, or orthodox, can easily overwhelm any tendency toward what are seen by the majority to be deviant tendencies.

21. Most economists concentrate on doing economics rather than spending any time talking about the way or means of that doing. As in most professions, those deeply involved in their work are often not given to extensive introspection.

22. See http://fivebooks.com/interview/ariel-rubinstein-on-game-theory.

23. A reviewer emphasized that Rubinstein states that he does not see economics as a science, whereas we argue that Classical Liberals separated out the branches. Thus, from the perspective of that reviewer there remains a question of whether he fits. As we stated in chapter 1, we believe the difference is just semantic. The theoretical work that Rubinstein does involves mathematical logic. It is rigorous and precise, and, depending on one's sematic preferences, one can consider it a part of science or not. Even if mathematics isn't considered science, it is the language of science. The Classical Liberal attitude holds that theoretical work in economics, whether called a science or not, has different methodological rules than does policy work, which is the point Rubinstein is making. Consequently, a discussion on what composes science remains extraneous to our concerns.

24. He also notes that bridge-building needs no scientific component, but that there is a natural relationship between science and engineering. That relationship is not one-way. It is a multifaceted relationship that flows both ways.

25. As we discussed in an earlier chapter, the Keynesian classifier has problems, since it is unclear whether Keynes actually supported the IS/LM approach. For that reason, IS/LM Keynesians are often more accurately referred to as neo-Keynesians. In other words, Keynes may have had no particular problem with Hick's construction of an IS/LM model as a potential scientific construction, without considering it to be a mechanism capable of grinding out policy recommendations.

26. The differences at that time were significant. In a 1980s survey at the Keynesian-based Yale department, 60 percent of graduate students strongly agreed that fiscal policy could be used as an effective economic tool, whereas at Chicago, only 6 percent strongly agreed (Colander and Klamer 1987: 104).

27. An overview of the evolution of macro theory written for non-economists can be found in Colander (2011a: ch. 29, "Thinking Like a Modern Macro Economist").

28. One of us (Colander 1996, 2006; Colander et al. 2008) has been making similar arguments against Dynamic Stochastic General Equilibrium (DSGE) macroeconomics for the past twenty years. Many other economists have done so as well, including Nobel Prize winner Robert Solow (2007, 2008), and a slew of what are usually labeled heterodox economists. Solow (2007, 235–236) called it a "rhetorical swindle" that "seems to lack all credibility." Interesting in this particular case is what a very limited effect on the practice of macroeconomics these critics have exerted over time.

In fact, the simple act of objecting to the DSGE model led critics of that model to be classified as heterodox, since using this "scientific" DSGE model had become a methodological litmus test for acceptable macro methodology. The group of economists Colander worked with did not necessarily oppose the DSGE model as irrelevant. Our argument was not that the DSGE model was logically incorrect, or incorrect insofar as it remained a strictly scientific model. It was, instead, that the model was too far removed from real-world situations to be at all useful in guiding policy. As progress in science, we argued that developing the DSGE model might make sense, but in terms of applied macro policy, it did not.

29. The DSGE version of macroeconomics has been criticized by many outside the mainstream of modern macro. What makes Romer's criticism especially relevant is that he has had an acknowledged seat within the inner circle of mainstream economics for many years.

30. Romer has an interesting, but conventional, history for a mainstream economist. He was an undergraduate mathematics student at the University of Chicago. He then went on to study at MIT before earning a PhD in economics from the University of Chicago. He taught at Berkeley, Chicago, and Stanford, and in 2011 traveled to NYU. His theoretical PhD thesis became the foundation for what would be termed the "new growth" theory. This model attempted to explain the way in which the interactive nature of ideas allowed growth to increase at an increasing rate. However, the model stayed well within the bounds dictated by a standard approach to science. As a result of his dissertation, Romer was soon seen as an up and coming star. But then he stopped engaging in the standard research game and began to approach economics with more of a Classical Liberal attitude. An example of that departure can be seen on his website, where he warns that policy issues exceed narrow economic considerations. Romer writes:

> Growth is intermittent because the most important fluctuations in the rate of human progress depend on the dynamics of rules, which in turn depend on the dynamics of norms. Because our norms are often determined through a process of social interaction in which common norms are reinforced, they tend to be stable. Because this process of social transmission operates through our preferences, outside of conscious awareness, there

is little pressure for inefficient norms to change. (https://paulromer.net/wp-content/uploads/2016/09/WP-Trouble.pdf)

One possible reason for the change is that while at Stanford, Romer embraced what he describes as an entrepreneurial turn. He founded Aplia, an education technology company dedicated to increasing student effort and classroom engagement. In 2007 he sold the firm to Cengage Publishing. During that time, he seems to have lost much of his interest in pursuing purely abstract theory. Instead, Romer became interested in solving real problems posed by urban economics. He came to the conclusion that economic theory was not going to help him solve such problems. In response, he started conducting applied research on the ways in which policy makers in the developing world could use the rapid growth of cities to create economic opportunity and undertake systemic social reform. In 2017, he was appointed the chief economist of the World Bank.

The path followed by Paul Romer is consistent with the history of many top mainstream economists. There are, however, a few differences. He is not just an academic economist, but also a successful entrepreneur, an economist who wants to connect with real-world problems. His decision to shift to urban economics issues, and to involve himself directly with developing a working model of his theories, demonstrates that real-world bent. His particular attitude displays a consistent proclivity that is highly consistent with Classical Liberal methodology.

31. In this sense, the one-sided skepticism that came to embody the Chicago School approach has gradually infected much of the rest of the profession, though it is possible to argue that such tendencies are fundamentally part of evolved human nature (support one's allies, attack one's enemies). The battle as an economist is to struggle against these centrifugal forces.

32. Here are some examples of what we mean: Evolutionary biologists would not give credence to those who promote creation science, nor would astronomers embrace astrologers. This is not to say that creation scientists and astrologers are wrong. The claim instead is that scientists assume they are wrong based on past discussions and arguments. Nor would they consider that such practitioners have employed an acknowledged scientific methodology. Such individuals have put themselves outside accepted scientific conversation. Those views will only be considered by scientists if they develop new arguments and empirical evidence while employing a consistent scientific methodology. The need to make such decisions is justified by expediency. Certain endeavors have to be ruled out of consideration almost by definition.

33. To say that we are not interested in his theoretical work here is not to denigrate or dismiss this seminal research. Sen's work on the normative content of welfare economics guided much of our earlier discussion of the evolution of welfare economics. His writing on moral philosophy and economics represents some of the most insightful writing on the subject. It serves as a useful guide for how to do appropriate work in the broad context of theoretical welfare economics.

34. That Sen's work emphasizes those broader interconnections should come as no surprise. After completing his study of economics, he augmented that work

by investigating moral philosophy. Today he is seen as both an economist and a philosopher. This captures another element of the Classical Liberal approach to applied policy. It will often reflect transdisciplinary investigation and thinking. Such researchers will often find it useful to blend social science specialties.

35. The classic text that definitively tied Classical Liberalism to a specific sense of freedom is Mill's 1859 text *On Liberty*.

> No society in which these liberties are not, on the whole, respected, is free, whatever may be its form of government; and none is completely free in which they do not exist absolute and unqualified. The only freedom which deserves the name, is that of pursuing our own good in our own way, so long as we do not attempt to deprive others of theirs, or impede their efforts to obtain it. Each is the proper guardian of his own health, whether bodily, or mental and spiritual. Mankind are greater gainers by suffering each other to live as seems good to themselves, than by compelling each to live as seems good to the rest. (Mill 1947: 12–13)

36. Another aspect of Sen's policy work that reflects a Classical Liberal attitude is that it involves a deeper consideration of the goals of economic policy. This focus is greater than that accorded by most economists either formally in welfare economics or informally in applied policy analysis. That standard work sees the goal of economic policy as achieving efficiency, which it interprets as producing the most output possible. Put another way, the goal of economic policy is to maximize GDP. Sen challenges that goal, and his challenge has important implications for policy. Specifically, he suggests strongly deemphasizing a GDP measure. In its place Sen offers a focus on capabilities, which are much broader than the standard economic metrics such as growth in GDP per capita. The Capability Approach focuses on what Sen sees as the moral significance of individuals' capability of achieving the kind of lives they have reason to value.

Many capability theorists, and external critics of Sen, express concern that the content and structure of Sen's Capability Approach are "under-theorized," making it unsuitable as a theory of justice. Specifically, Sen does not develop an analysis stating which capabilities are important or how capabilities should be distributed. Those, he argues, are political decisions for society to decide. Sen is not worried by these concerns. He argues that he is not trying to develop a full theory of justice and normative judgments. Sen insists that he is quite content to have only partial rankings. His capabilities approach is meant to guide individuals in struggling with these issues, not to answer questions that societies must answer on their own. This acceptance of only providing guides to policy questions, not answers, is another aspect of the Classical Liberal methodological approach. It does not try to be a full theory. It simply tries to deliver some insights.

37. This way of thinking clashes directly with the marginal productivity thinking characteristic of John Bates Clark. His approach would later be championed by the Chicago School, particularly by George Stigler.

38. To underline the guidance aspect of his work, Sen (2007) emphasized the relationship that the more loosely conceived welfare aspects have to those aspects connected with justice by labeling his recent discussion of these issues *The Idea of Justice*, rather than *The Theory of Justice*. By calling it an "idea," he intended to stress that for him the crucial issue was not developing a full-fledged theory, but rather exploring issues surrounding justice. Sen's intent was to see how such ideas can be integrated into policy proposals even when one lacks a complete theory. This approach is thoroughly consistent with Classical Liberalism.

39. A somewhat different approach to the integration of policy and theory that is consistent with Classical Liberalism can be seen in the work of one of Sen's ongoing coauthors, Jean Drèze. After completing his PhD and teaching at the London School of Economics (LSE) Drèze went to live in India (where he has since become a citizen) and work as a farmer, operating at a farmer's living standard. He did this for years, and layered the insights gained from that physical fieldwork with his theoretical understanding. Doing so led him to develop a number of novel policy proposals for income redistribution that have since become law in India (Drèze and Sen 1989). We are not saying that this is the one and only approach that follows naturally from Classical Liberalism. However, this is an approach that presents a much more open door to different methodological pathways. The perspective adopted by Drèze seeks to understand a given issue particularly with respect to the affected groups. That is quite different than adopting a scientific methodology.

40. https://www.project-syndicate.org/commentary/trump-win-economists-responsible-by-dani-rodrik-2016-11?barrier=accessreg.

41. In his book, *Economics Rules*, Rodrik concludes with ten commandments, which nicely display a Classical Liberal sensibility:

1. Economics is a collection of models; cherish their diversity.
2. It is *a* model, not *the* model.
3. Make your model simple enough to isolate specific causes and how they work, but not so simple that it leaves out key interactions among causes.
4. Unrealistic assumptions are OK; unrealistic critical assumptions are not OK.
5. The world is (almost) always second best.
6. To map a model to the real world you need explicit empirical diagnostics, which is more craft than science.
7. Do not confuse agreement among economists for certainty about how the world works.
8. It's OK to say "I don't know" when asked about the economy or policy.
9. Efficiency is not everything.
10. Substituting your values for the public's is an abuse of your expertise.

42. Our stated purpose here is not to discuss specific policies. However, to provide insight into Rodrik's argument, let's examine one of the qualifications that

might undermine the conclusion that free trade is a policy that should unequivocally be supported. Successful trade requires a harmonization of regulations and property rights. What regulations are chosen and what structure of property rights is selected have enormous distribution effects, for instance the defined intellectual property rights to medicines. (We deliberately dodge the question of whether the prevailing property rights awarded to pharmaceutical companies are in fact publicly beneficial or more accurately an instance of rent seeking.) If a developing country is not part of a constraining free trade agreement (or negotiates an opt-out clause), it could adopt a somewhat looser intellectual property rights regime regarding essential pharmaceuticals. Such an approach would allow companies in its jurisdiction to provide low-cost generics for its citizens. But to join the "free trade" area, it might be required to accept the partner country's intellectual property rights regime, preventing the use of low-cost generics. This is not just a potential problem. The World Trade Organization (WTO) requires developing countries to institute far stronger intellectual property rights prior to joining. Otherwise they need to be willing to forgo the other benefits from a regime of freer trade. The proposed trade-off facing a developing country is difficult to resolve. The obvious conclusion is not that one alternative is better than the other. The point is that global trade is a complex process, a complicated process of negotiation and contracting, of sorting out winners and losers attached to any agreement. Decisions on whether it is to be supported are best made contextually, not in reference to one simple model. That is the essence of Rodrik's argument, which makes it totally consistent with the Classical Liberal methodology we have attempted to explore in this volume.

43. Billy Vaughn Koen has a succinct and relevant discussion of how someone following the arts and crafts methodology we are advocating should respond to critics. It is essentially the view that all is heuristics; now let's get on with the discussion about whether the heuristic being considered is useful (Koen 2003).

REFERENCES

Battalio, Raymond C., John H. Kagel, and Leonard Green (1979). "Labor Supply Behavior for Animal Workers: Towards an Experimental Analysis," in Vernon L. Smith (ed.), *Research in Experimental Economics. Vol. 1*. Greenwich, CT: JAI Press, pp. 231–253.

Baudelaire, Charles (1857). "Le Cygne." *Fleurs du Mal*. Paris: Auguste Poulet-Malassis.

Becker, Gary S. (1968). "Crime and Punishment: An Economic Approach." *Journal of Political Economy* 76(2): 169–217.

Becker, Gary S. (1985). "Public Policies, Pressure Groups, and Dead Weight Costs." *Journal of Public Economics* 28(2): 329–347.

Becker, Gary S. and William M. Landes (eds.). (1974). *Essays in the Economics of Crime and Punishment*. New York: Columbia University Press.

Bergson, Abram (1938). "A Reformulation of Certain Aspects of Welfare Economics." *Quarterly Journal of Economics* 52(2): 310–334.

Bergson, Abram (1954). "On the Concept of Social Welfare." *Quarterly Journal of Economics* 68(2): 233–252.

Blaug, Mark (2009). "The Debate Over F53 After 50 Years," in Uskali Maki (ed.), *The Methodology of Positive Economics: Reflections on the Milton Friedman Legacy*. Cambridge: Cambridge University Press, pp. 349–355.

Boettke, Peter J. (1987). "Virginia Political Economy: A View from Vienna." *Market Process* 5(2): 7–15.

Bornemann, Alfred (1940). *J. Laurence Laughlin*. Washington, DC: American Council on Foreign Affairs.

Breit, William (1987). "Creating the "Virginia School": An Academic Environment in the 1960s." *Economic Inquiry* 25(4): 645–657.

Breit, William and Roger Spencer (1997). *Lives of the Laureates: Thirteen Nobel Economists*. Cambridge, MA: MIT Press.

Bronfenbrenner, Martin (1950). "Contemporary American Economic Thought." *American Journal of Economics and Sociology* 9(4): 483–496.

Bronk, Richard (2009). *The Romantic Economist: Imagination in Economics*. Cambridge: Cambridge University Press.

Brontë, Charlotte (1850). "Letter of April 12th to W. S. Williams," in Clement King Shorter (ed.), *The Brontës Life and Letters: Being an Attempt to Present a*

Full and Final Record of the Lives of the Three Sisters, Charlotte, Emily and Anne Brontë. Cambridge, UK: Cambridge University Press.

Buchanan, James M. (1984). "Rights, Efficiency, and Exchange: The Irrelevance of Transaction Costs," in Manfred Neumann (ed.), *Ansprüche, Eigentums- und Verfügungsrechte*. Berlin: Duncker und Humblot, pp. 9–24.

Buchanan, James M. (1986). *Liberty, Market and State: Political Economy in the 1980s*. New York: New York University Press.

Buchanan, James M. (1997). "Buchanan," in William Breit and Roger W. Spencer (eds.), *Lives of the Laureates–Third Edition*. Cambridge, MA: MIT Press, pp. 165–183.

Buchanan, James M. (1999). "Politics without Romance: A Sketch of Positive Public Choice Theory and Its Normative Implications," in *The Collected Works of James Buchanan*. Indianopolis, IN: Liberty Press, pp. 45–60.

Buchanan, James M. (2000). "The Soul of Classical Liberalism." *Independent Review* 5(1): 111–119.

Buchanan, James M. and Gordon Tullock (1962). *The Calculus of Consent: Logical Foundations of Constitutional Democracy*. Ann Arbor: University of Michigan Press.

Burgin, Angus (2012). *The Great Persuasion*. Cambridge: Cambridge University Press.

Caldwell, Bruce (2011). "The Chicago School, Hayek, and Neoliberalism," in Robert Van Horn, Philip Mirowski, and Thomas A. Stapleford (eds.), *Building Chicago Economics*. Cambridge: Cambridge University Press, pp. 301–335.

Canaan, E. (1903). *A History of the Theories of Distribution and Production in English Political Economy 1776–1848* (second edition). London: P.S. King & Son.

Card, David and Alan B. Krueger (1994). "Minimum Wages and Employment: A Case Study of the Fast-Food Industry in New Jersey and Pennsylvania." *American Economic Review* (84 94): 772–792.

Card, David and Alan B. Krueger (1995). *Myth and Measurement: The New Economics of the Minimum Wage*. Princeton, NJ: Princeton University Press.

Chari, Varadarajan V. and Patrick J. Kehoe (2006). "Modern Macroeconomics in Practice: How Theory Is Shaping Policy." *Journal of Economic Perspectives* 20(4): 3–28.

Cherrier, Beatrice (2011). "The Lucky Consistency of Milton Friedman's Science and Politics, 1933–1963," in Robert Van Horn, Philip Mirowski, and Thomas A. Stapleford (eds.), *Building Chicago Economics*. Cambridge: Cambridge University Press, pp. 335–368.

Cheung, Steven N. S. (1973). "The Fable of the Bees: An Economic Investigation." *Journal of Law & Economics* 16(1): 11–33.

Churchill, Winston S. (November 11, 1947). Speech in the House of Commons, in Robert Rhodes James (ed.), *Winston S. Churchill: His Complete Speeches, 1897–1963*. (1974), vol. 7: 7566.

Clark, John Maurice (1936). "Past Accomplishments and Present Prospects of American Economics." *American Economic Review* 26(2): 1–11.

Clement, Douglas (2006). "Interview with David Card—October 17." *The Region— Federal Reserve Bank of Minneapolis*. December 1–10.

Coase, Ronald H. (1937). "The Nature of the Firm." *Economica* 4 (November): 386–405.

Coase, Ronald H. (1946). "The Marginal Cost Controversy." *Economica* (n.s.) 13(51): 169–182.

Coase, Ronald H. (1954). "The Development of the British Television Service." *Land Economics* 30(3): 207–222.

Coase, Ronald H. (1959). "The Federal Communications Commission." *Journal of Law & Economics* 2(1): 1–41.

Coase, Ronald H. (1960). "The Problem of Social Cost." *Journal of Law & Economics* 3(1): 1–44.

Coase, Ronald H. (1961). "The British Post Office and the Messenger Companies." *Journal of Law & Economics* 4(1): 12–65.

Coase, Ronald H. (1974). "The Lighthouse in Economics." *Journal of Law & Economics* 17(2): 357–376.

Coase, Ronald H. (1988). "The Firm, the Market and the Law," in *The Firm, the Market and the Law*. Chicago: University of Chicago Press, pp. 1–33.

Coase, Ronald H. (1992). "The Institutional Structure of Production: The 1991 Alfred Nobel Memorial Prize Lecture in Economic Sciences." *American Economic Review* 82(4): 713–719.

Coase, Ronald H. (1993). "Law and Economics at Chicago." *Journal of Law & Economics* 36(1): 239–254.

Coase, Ronald H. (1994). *Essays on Economics and Economists*. Chicago: Chicago University Press.

Coase, Ronald H. (1997). "Looking for Results." Reason.com. January 1: 1–8. http://reason.com/archives/1997/01/01/looking-for-results/.

Coase, Ronald H. (2006). "The Conduct of Economics: The Example of Fisher Body and General Motors." *Journal of Economics and Management Strategy* 15(2): 255–278.

Coase, Ronald H. and Ronald F. Fowler (1935a). "Bacon Production and the Pig-Cycle in Great Britain." 2 *Economica* (n.s.): 142–147.

Coase, Ronald H. and Ronald F. Fowler (1935b). "The Pig-Cycle: A Rejoinder." 2 *Economica* (n.s.): 423–428.

Coase, Ronald H. and Ronald F. Fowler (1937a). The Pig-Cycle in Great Britain: An Explanation." 4 *Economica* (n.s.): 55.

Colander, David. (1984). "Was Keynes a Keynesian or a Lernerian?" *Journal of Economics Literature* 22(4): 1572–1575.

Colander, David (1992). "The Lost Art of Economics." *Journal of Economic Perspectives* 6(3): 191–198.

Colander, David (1994). "The Art of Economics by the Numbers," Roger Backhouse (ed.), *New Directions in Economic Methodology*. London and New York: Routledge, pp. 35–50.

Colander, David (ed.) (1996). *Beyond Microfoundations: Post Walrasian Economics*. Cambridge, UK: Cambridge University Press.

Colander, David (2003). "Post Walrasian Economics and the Economics of Muddling Through." *International Journal of Political Economy* 33, no. 2 (Summer): 17–35.

Colander, David (2005). "Making of an Economist Redux." *Journal of Economic Perspectives* 19(1): 175–198.

Colander, David (ed.) (2006). *Post Walrasian Macroeconomics: Beyond the Dynamic Stochastic General Equilibrium Model*. Cambridge, UK: Cambridge University Press.

Colander, David (2007a). *The Making of an Economist Redux*. Princeton, NJ: Princeton University Press.

Colander, David (2007b). "*Edgeworth's Hedonimeter* and the Quest to Measure Utility." *Journal of Economic Perspectives* 21(2): 215–225.

Colander, David (2009). "What Was 'It' That Robbins Was Defining?" *Journal of the History of Economic Thought* 31, no. 4 (December): 437–448.

Colander, David (2010). "Moving Beyond the Rhetoric of Pluralism: Suggestions for an 'Inside-the-Mainstream' Heterodoxy," in William Garnett, Erik Olsen, and Martha Starr (eds.), *Economic Pluralism*. New York: Routledge.

Colander, David (2011a). *Principles of Economics*. New York: McGraw-Hill.

Colander, David (2011b). "Is the Fundamental Science of Macroeconomics Sound?" *Review of Radical Political Economy* 43(3): 302–309.

Colander, David (2016). "Complexity Economics and Workaday Economic Policy," in David Wilson and Alan Kirman (eds.), *Complexity and Evolution: Toward a New Synthesis for Economics*. Cambridge, MA: MIT Press.

Colander, David, Peter Howitt, Alan Kirman, Axel Leijonhufvud, and Perry Mehrling (2008). "Beyond DSGE Models: Toward an Empirically Based Macroeconomics." *American Economic Review* 98(2): 236–240.

Colander, David and Arjo Klamer (1987). "The Making of an Economist." *Journal of Economic Perspectives* 1(2): 95–111.

Colander, David and Roland Kupers (2014). *Complexity and the Art of Economic Policy*. Princeton, NJ: Princeton University Press.

Colander, David and Harry Landreth (1996). *The Coming of Keynesianism to America*. Cheltenham: Edward Elgar.

Colander, David and Casey Rothschild (2010). "Sins of the Sons of Samuelson." *Journal of Economic Behavior and Organization* 74, no. 3 (June): 277–290.

Colander, David and Huei-Chun Su (2013). "A Failure to Communicate: The Fact/Value Divide and the Putnam/Dasgupta Debate." *Erasmus Journal of Economics and Philosophy* 6(2): 1–23.

Colander, David and Huei-Chun Su (2015). "Making Sense of Economist's Positive Normative Distinction." *Journal of Economic Methodology* 22(2): 157–170.

Colander, David and Huei Chen Su (2017). *How Economics Should Be Done: Colander's Essays in Applied Economic Policy*. Cheltenham: Edward Elgar.

Davis, John (2014). "Economists' Odd Stand on the Positive-Normative Distinction: A Behavioural Economics View," In G. DeMartino and D. McCloskey (eds.), *Oxford University Press Handbook on Professional Economic Ethics:*

Views from the Economics Profession and Beyond. Oxford: Oxford University Press.

Demsetz, Harold (1968). "Why Regulate Utilities?" *Journal of Law & Economics* 11(1): 55–65.

Demsetz, Harold (1993). "George J. Stigler: Midcentury Neoclassicalist with a Passion to Quantify." *Journal of Political Economy* 101(5): 793–808.

Douglas, Paul and Aaron Director (1931). *The Problem of Unemployment.* New York: Macmillan.

Drèze, Jean and Amartya Sen (1989). *Hunger and Public Action.* Oxford: Oxford University Press.

Ebenstein, Lanny (2015). *Chicagonomics.* New York: St. Martin's Press.

Emmett, Ross B. (2006). "De Gustibus Est Disputandum: Frank H. Knight's Response to George Stigler and Gary Becker's 'De Gustibus Non Est Disputandum.'" *Journal of Economic Methodology* 13(1): 97–111.

Fisher, Franklin (2011). "The Stability of General Equilibrium—What Do We Know and Why Is It Important?" in Pascal Bridel (ed.), *General Equilibrium Analysis: A Century After Walras.* New York: Routledge, pp. 34–45.

Freedman, Craig F. (1995). "The Economist as Mythmaker—Stigler's Kinky Transformation." *Journal of Economic Issues* (29)1: 175–209.

Freedman, Craig F. (2002). "The Xistence of Definitional Economics: Stigler's and Leibenstein's War of the Words." *Cambridge Journal of Economics* 26(2): 161–179.

Freedman, Craig F. (2006). "Not for Love nor Money: Milton Friedman's Counter-revolution." *History of Economics Review*, 42 (Summer): 87–119.

Freedman, Craig F. (2008). "Five Easy Pieces—George Stigler's Blueprint for a Counter-Revolution," in *Chicago Fundamentalism: Ideology and Methodology in Economics.* Singapore: World Scientific, pp. 71–110.

Friedman, Milton (1941). "Review of *Monopolistic Competition and General Equilibrium Theory* by Robert Triffen," *Journal of Farm Economics* 23(1): 389–391.

Friedman, Milton (1956). "The Quantity Theory of Money—A Restatement," in *Studies in the Quantity Theory of Money.* Chicago: University of Chicago Press, pp. 3–19.

Friedman, Milton (1966/1953). "The Methodology of Positive Economics," in *Essays in Positive Economics.* Chicago: Chicago University of Chicago Press. pp. 3–43.

Friedman, Milton (1971). "Doing Good." Commencement Speech, University of Rochester, June 6: 1–6.

Friedman, Milton (1974). "Schools at Chicago." *University of Chicago Record*, 3–7.

Friedman, Milton (1993). "George Stigler: A Personal Reminiscence." *Journal of Political Economy* 101(5): 768–773.

Fuchs, Victor R., Alan B. Krueger, and James M. Poterba (1998). "Economists' Views about Parameters, Values and Policies: Survey Results in Labor and Public Economics." *Journal of Economic Literature* 36 (September): 1387–1425.

Goodwin, Craufurd (1989). "Doing Good and Spreading the Gospel (Economic)," in David Colander and Bob Coats (ed.), *The Spread of Economic Ideas*. Cambridge: Cambridge University Press, pp. 157–174.

Graaff, Jan de Van (1957). *Theoretical Welfare Economics*. Cambridge: Cambridge University Press.

Guillebaud, Claude William and Milton Friedman (1958). "Introduction to *The Cambridge Economic Handbooks* by the General Editors," in Edward Austin Gossage Robinson, *The Structure of Competitive Industry*. Cambridge: Cambridge University Press, pp. v–vii.

Halberstam, David (1972). *The Best and the Brightest*. New York: Random House.

Hammond, J. Daniel and Claire H. Hammond (2006). *Making Chicago Price Theory: Friedman-Stigler Correspondence 1945–1957*. New York: Routledge.

Hart, Neil (2013). *Alfred Marshall and Modern Economics: Equilibrium Theory and Evolutionary Economics*. Houndmills: Palgrave Macmillan.

Hayek, Friedrich von (1937). "Economics and Knowledge." *Economica* (n.s.): 4 (February): 33–54.

Hayek, Friedrich von (1944). *The Road to Serfdom*. Chicago: University of Chicago Press.

Hayek, Friedrich von (1945). "The Use of Knowledge in Society." *American Economic Review* 35(3): 519–530.

Hayek, Friedrich von (1957). "Why I Am Not a Conservative?" Text of speech presented at Tenth Anniversary Meeting of the Mont Pelerin Society, St. Moritz, September 2 to September 8, pp. 1–10.

Hayek, Friedrich von (1979). *A Conversation with Friedrich A. von Hayek: Science and Socialism*. Washington, DC: American Enterprise Institute for Public Policy Research.

Heidegger, Martin (1967). *What Is a Thing?* Chicago: Henry Regnery.

Hicks, John (1939). "The Foundations of Welfare Economics." *Economic Journal* 49(196): 696–712.

Hirsch, Abraham and Neil Di Marchi (1991). *Milton Friedman: Economics in Theory and Practice*. Ann Arbor: University of Michigan Press.

Hotelling, Harold (1938). "The General Welfare in Relation to Problems of Taxation and of Railway and Utility Rates." *Econometrica* 6(2): 242–269.

Hume, David (1742). *Essays, Moral, Political and Literary*, Eugene F. Miller, ed. 1987. Library of Economics and Liberty. http://econlib.org/library/LFBooks/Hume/hmMPL.html

Hutcheson, Francis (1755). *System of Moral Philosophy*. London: T. Longman.

Hutt, William Harold (1979). *The Keynesian Episode: A Reassessment*. Indianapolis, IN: Liberty Press.

Johnson, Elizabeth S. and Harry G. Johnson (1978). *The Shadow of Keynes*. Chicago: University of Chicago Press.

Kaldor, Nicholas (1934). "A Classificatory Note on the Determination of Equilibrium." *Review of Economic Studies* 1(1): 122–136.

Kaldor, Nicholas (1939). "Welfare Propositions in Economics and Interpersonal Comparisons of Utility." *Economic Journal* 49(195): 549–552.

Kemp, Murray C. and Paul Pezanis-Christou (1999). "Pareto's Compensation Principle." *Social Choice and Welfare* 16(3): 441–444.

Kennedy, Peter (2002). "Sinning in the Basement: What Are the Rules? The Ten Commandments of Applied Econometrics." *Journal of Economic Surveys* 16(4): 569–589.

Keynes, John Maynard (1924). "Alfred Marshall, 1842–1924." *Economic Journal* 34(135): 311–372.

Keynes, John Maynard (1926). "The End of Laissez Faire," in *Pamphlet of the Sidney Ball Lecture*. London: Hogarth Press.

Keynes, John Maynard (1939). "Professor Tinbergen's Method." *Economic Journal* 49(3): 558–568.

Keynes, John Maynard (1940). "Comment." *Economic Journal* 50(1): 154–156.

Keynes, John Maynard (1951/1933). "William Stanley Jevons," in *Essays in Biography*. New York: Horizon, pp. 225–309.

Keynes, John Maynard (1963a) [1926]. "The End of Laissez Faire," in *Essays in Persuasion*. New York: W. W. Norton, pp. 312–323.

Keynes, John Maynard (1963b) [1925]. "Am I a Liberal?," in *Essays in Persuasion*. New York: W. W. Norton, pp. 323–339.

Keynes, John Maynard (1963c). "Economic Possibilities for Our Grandchildren," in *Essays in Persuasion*. New York: W. W. Norton, pp. 358–375.

Keynes, John Maynard (1964/1936). *The General Theory of Employment, Interest, and Money*. New York: Harcourt Brace Jovanovich.

Keynes, John Neville (1891). *The Scope and Method of Political Economy*. London: Macmillan.

Keynes, John Neville (1891); republished 1955. *The Scope and Method of Political Economy*, fourth edition. New York: Kelley and Millman.

Kitch, Edmund W. (1983). "The Fire of Truth: A Remembrance of Law and Economics at Chicago, 1932–1970," *Journal of Law and Economics* 26(1): 163–234.

Klein, Benjamin, Robert G. Crawford, and Armen A. Alchian (1978). "Vertical Integration, Appropriable Rents, and the Competitive Contracting Process." *Journal of Law & Economics* 21(2): 297–326.

Klein, Daniel (2013). "The Ideological Migration of the Economics Laureates: Introduction and Overview." *Econ Journal Watch* 10(3): 218–239.

Knight, Frank (1956). "The Ricardian Theory of Production and Distribution," in *On the History and Method of Economics*. Chicago: University of Chicago Press, pp. 37–89.

Knight, Frank (1971). *Risk, Uncertainty and Profit*. Chicago: University of Chicago Press.

Knight, Frank H. (1935). *The Ethics of Competition*. New York: Harper and Bothers.

Knight, Frank H. (1940). " 'What Is Truth' in Economics?" *Journal of Political Economy* 48(1): 1–32.

Knight, Frank H. (1946). "Immutable Law in Economics: Its Reality and Limitations." *American Economic Review—Papers and Proceedings* 36(2): 93–111.

Knight, Frank H. (1967). "Laissez Faire: Pro and Con." *Journal of Political Economy* 75(6): 782–795.

Knight, Frank H. (1972). *Risk, Uncertainty and Profit*. Chicago: University of Chicago Press.

Koen, Billy Vaughn (2003). *Discussion of the Method: Conducting the Engineer's Approach to Problem Solving*. Oxford: Oxford University Press.

Lange, Oskar (1938). *On the Economic Theory of Socialism*. Minneapolis: B Lippincott edition, University of Minnesota Press.

Leamer, Edward E. (1983). "Let's Take the Con Out of Econometrics." *American Economic Review* 73(1): 31–43.

Leamer, Edward E. (2012). *The Craft of Economics: Lessons from the Heckscher-Ohlin Framework*. Cambridge, MA: MIT Press.

Lerner, Abba (1944). *The Economics of Control: Principles of Welfare Economics*. New York: Macmillan.

Lerner, Abba (1951). *The Economics of Employment*. New York: McGraw-Hill.

Levi, Arrigo (1973). "The Professors of the 'New Wave,'" in *Journey Among the Economists*. London: Alcove Press, pp. 100–106.

Levy, David M. and Sandra J. Peart (2014). "'Almost Wholly Negative': The Ford Foundation's Appraisal of the Virginia School," August 22, pp. 1–48; http://papers.ssrn.com/sol3/papers.cfm?abstract_id=2485695.

Machlup, Fritz (1959). "Statics and Dynamics: Kaleidoscopic Words." *Southern Economic Journal* 26(2): 91–110.

Marshall, Alfred (1890). *Principles of Economics*. London: Macmillan.

Marshall, Alfred (1923). *Industry and Trade*. London: Macmillan.

Marshall, Alfred (1996) [1906]. "Letter to Arthur Lyon Bowley," February 27, 1906, Letter 840 in John K. Whittaker (ed.), *The Correspondence of Alfred Marshall*, Vol. 3. Cambridge: Cambridge University Press, p. 130.

Martin, Douglas (2004). "Aaron Director, Economist, Dies at 102." *New York Times*, September 14, pp. 1–2. http://www.nytimes.com/2004/09/16/national/16directo.html?.

Mayer, Martin (1957). *Young Man in a Hurry. The Story of William Rainey Harper*. Chicago: University of Chicago Alumni Association.

McCloskey, Deirdre N. (1985). *The Rhetoric of Economics*. Madison: University of Wisconsin Press.

McCloskey, Deirdre N. and Stephen T. Ziliak (1996). "The Standard Error of Regressions." *Journal of Economic Literature* 34(1): 97–114.

McGee, John (1958). "Predatory Price Cutting: The Standard Oil (N.J.) Case." *Journal of Law and Economics* 1(October): 136–169.

Medema, Steven G. (2011). "Chicago Price Theory and Chicago Law and Economics: A Tale of Two Transitions," in Robert Van Horn, Philip Mirowski, and Thomas A. Stapleford (eds.), *Building Chicago Economics*. Cambridge: Cambridge University Press, pp. 151–180.

Medema, Steven G. (2014). "On the Origins and Diffusion of the Term, 'Chicago School.'" Becker Friedman Institute, University of Chicago, March 17; https://

bfi.uchicago.edu/sites/default/files/research/Medema_Identifying_a__Chi
cago_School_-Sept_2015.pdf.

Medema, Steven (2009). *The Hesitant Hand*. Princeton, NJ: Princeton University Press.

Mill, John Stuart (1844). *On Some Unsettled Questions of Political Economy*. London: Longmans, Green, Reader and Dyer.

Mill, John Stuart (1848). *Principles of Political Economy with Some of Their Applications to Social Philosophy*. London: Longmans, Green.

Mill, John Stuart (1965). *Principles of Political Economy*. New York: Augustus M. Kelley.

Mill, John Stuart (1968). *Essays on Some Unsettled Questions of Political Economy*. New York: Augustus M. Kelley.

Mill, John Stuart (1859/1947). *On Liberty*. New York: Meredith Publishing.

Miller, H. Laurence, Jr. (1961). "On the 'Chicago School of Economics.'" *Journal of Political Economy* 70(1): 64–69.

Mirowski, Philip and Robert Van Horn (2009). "The Rise of the Chicago School of Economics and the Birth of Neoliberalism." in Philip Mirowski and Dieter Plehwe (eds.), *The Road from Mont Pelerin*. Cambridge, MA: Harvard University Press, pp. 139–181.

Mitch, David (forthcoming). "George Stigler's Early Career," (tentative title) in Craig Freedman (ed.), *Remaking Economics: Eminent Post-War Economists— George Stigler*. London: Palgrave Macmillan.

Mordfin, Robin I. and Marsha Ferziger Nagorsky (2011, Fall). "Chicago and Law and Economics: A History." *The Record* (Alumni Magazine University of Chicago Law School).

Myrdal, Gunnar (1954) [1930]. *The Political Element in the Development of Economic Theory*. New York: Simon & Schuster.

Nef, John U. (1967). "James Laurence Laughlin (1850–1933)." *Journal of Political Economy* 75(6): 779–781.

Neumark, David and William Wascher (2000). "Minimum Wages and Employment: A Case Study of the Fast-Food Industry in New Jersey and Pennsylvania: Comment." *American Economic Review* 90(5): 1362–1396.

Nik-Khah (2011). "Chicago Neoliberalism and the Genesis of the Milton Friedman Institute (2006–2009)," in Robert Van Horn, Philip Mirowski, and Thomas A. Stapleford (eds.), *Building Chicago Economics*. Cambridge: Cambridge University Press, pp. 368–389.

Overtveldt, Johan Van (2007). *The Chicago School*. Chicago: Agate.

Patinkin, Donald (2003) [1969]. "The Chicago Tradition, the Quantity Theory, and Friedman," in Robert Leeson (ed.), *Keynes, Chicago and Friedman*. London: Pickering & Chatto, pp. 87–120.

Patinkin, Donald (1972). "Friedman on the Quantity Theory and Keynesian Economics." *Journal of Political Economy* 80(5): 883–905.

Patinkin, Donald (1981). *Essays On and In the Chicago Tradition*. Durham, NC: Duke University Press.

Peltzman, Sam (1976). "Toward a More General Theory of Regulation." *Journal of Law & Economics* 19(2): 211–240.

Peltzman, Sam (1980). "The Growth of Government." *Journal of Law & Economics* 23(2): 209–287.

Peltzman, Sam (1985). "An Economic Interpretation of the History of Congressional Voting in the Twentieth Century." *American Economic Review* 75(4): 656–675.

Persky, Joseph (2016). *The Political Economy of Progress.* New York: Oxford University Press.

Pigou, Arthur Cecil [1920] 2002. *The Economics of Welfare London.* Reprint. New Brunswick, NJ: Transactions Press.

Posner, Richard (2010). *The Crisis of Capitalist Democracy.* Cambridge, MA: Harvard University Press.

Putnam, Hillary (2002). *The Collapse of the Fact/Value Dichotomy and Other Essays.* Cambridge, MA: Harvard University Press.

Raphael, D. D. (2007). *The Impartial Spectator: Adam Smith's Moral Philosophy.* Oxford: Oxford University Press.

Rawls, John (1971). *A Theory of Justice.* Cambridge, MA: Belknap Press of Harvard University Press.

Rawls, John (1993). *Political Liberalism.* New York: Columbia University Press.

Reder, Melvin W. (1982). "Chicago Economics, Permanence and Change." *Journal of Economic Literature* 20(1): 1–38.

Reder, Melvin W. (2000). "The Anti-Semitism of Some Eminent Economists." *History of Political Economy* 34(4): 833–856.

Reisman, David A. (1990). "The State and Economic Activity," in John Creedy (ed.), *Foundations of Economic Thought.* London: Basil Blackwell, pp. 28–58.

Robbins, Lionel (1927). "Mr. Hawtrey on the Scope of Economics." *Economica* 7: 172–178.

Robbins, Lionel (1981). "Economics and Political Economy." *American Economic Review: Papers and Proceedings* 71(2): 1–10.

Rodrik, Dani (1997). *Has Globalization Gone Too Far?* New York: Columbia University Press.

Rodrik, Dani (2015). *Economics Rules: The Rights and Wrongs of the Dismal Science.* New York: W. W. Norton.

Romer, Paul (2017). "The Trouble with Macroeconomics." New York: Stern School of Business, NYU. https://paulromer.net/wp-content/uploads/2016/09/WP-Trouble.pdf.

Rosenberg, Alexander (1992). *Economics: Mathematical Politics or Science of Diminishing Returns.* Chicago: University of Chicago Press.

Roth, Alvin (2002). "The Economist as Engineer: Game Theory, Experimentations, and Computation as Tools for Design Economics." *Econometrica* 70, no. 4 (July): 1341–1378.

Roth, Alvin E., and E. Peranson (1999). "The Redesign of the Matching Market for American Physicians: Some Engineering Aspects of Economic Design." *American Economic Review* 89(4): 748–778.

Roth, Alvin E., T. Sönmez, and M. U. Ünver (2004). "Kidney Exchange." *Quarterly Journal of Economics* 119(2): 457–488.

Rubinstein, Ariel (2012). *Economic Fables*. Cambridge: Open Book Publishers.

Rubinstein, Ariel (2017). "Comments on Economic Models, Economics, and Economists: Remarks on Economics Rules by Dani Rodrik." *Journal of Economic Literature* 55(1): 162–172.

Samuelson, Paul A. (1954). "The Pure Theory of Public Expenditure." *Review of Economics and Statistics* 36(2): 386–389.

Samuelson, Paul Anthony (1948). *Principles*. New York: McGraw-Hill.

Samuelson, Paul Anthony (1997). "Credo of a Lucky Textbook Author." *Journal of Economic Perspectives* 11(2): 153–160.

Samuelson, Paul Anthony (2011) *The Collected Scientific Papers of Paul Samuelson*, Janice Murray, ed. Cambridge MA: MIT Press.

Samuelson, Paul Anthony and George Joseph Stigler (1963). "A Dialogue on the Proper Economic Role of the State." *Selected Papers No. 7*. Chicago: Graduate School of Business, University of Chicago.

Schumpeter Joseph Alois (1987/1954). *History of Economic Analysis*. New York: Routledge.

Scitovsky, Tibor (1941). "A Note on Welfare Propositions in Economics." *Review of Economic Studies* 9(1): 77–88.

Scott, Walter (1826). "Journal Entry, March 14." Reproduced in *The Journal of Sir Walter Scott*, John Guthrie Tait, ed. Edinburgh: Oliver and Boyd, 1950.

Sen, Amartya (1970a). "The Impossibility of a Paretian Liberal." *Journal of Political Economy* 78(1): 152–157.

Sen, Amartya (1970b). *Collective Choice and Social Welfare* (first edition). San Francisco: Holden-Day.

Sen, Amartya (1977). "Social Choice Theory: A Re-examination." *Econometrica* 45(1): 53–89.

Sen, Amartya (1981). *Poverty and Famines: An Essay on Entitlement and Deprivation*. Oxford: Oxford University Press.

Sen, Amartya (2007). *The Idea of Justice*. Cambridge, MA: Harvard University Press.

Senior, Nassau William (1951) [1836]. *An Outline of the Science of Political Economy*. New York: Augustus M. Kelley.

Slesnick, Daniel. 1998. "Empirical Approaches to the Measurement of Welfare." *Journal of Economic Literature* 36(4): 2108–2165.

Smith, Adam (1776/1937). *An Enquiry into the Nature and Causes of The Wealth of Nations*. Edited, with an introduction, notes, marginal summary, and an enlarged index, by Edwin Cannan. New York: Modern Library.

Smith, Adam (1759/1961). *The Theory of Moral Sentiments*. Oxford: Clarendon Press.

Smolin, Lee (2007). *The Trouble with Physics: The Rise of String Theory, the Fall of a Science, and What Comes Next*. New York: Houghton, Mifflin, Harcourt.

Solow, Robert M. (2007). "Reflections on the Survey," in David Colander, *The Making of an Economist, Redux*. Princeton, NJ: Princeton University Press, pp. 234–238.

Solow, Robert (2008). "The State of Macroeconomics: Comment." *Journal of Economic Perspectives* 22(1): 243–249.

Sowell, Thomas (1993). "A Student's Eye View of George Stigler," *Journal of Political Economy* 101(5): 784–792.

Stapleford, Thomas A. (2011). "Positive Economics for Democratic Policy: Milton Friedman, Institutionalism, and the Science of History," in Robert Van Horn, Philip Mirowski, and Thomas A. Stapleford (eds.), *Building Chicago Economics*. Cambridge: Cambridge University Press, pp. 3–36.

Stigler, George Joseph (1941). *Production and Distribution Theories*. New York: Macmillan.

Stigler, George Joseph (1943). "The New Welfare Economics." *American Economic Review* 33(3): 355–359.

Stigler, George Joseph (1945). "The Cost of Subsistence." *Journal of Farm Economics* 27(2): 303–314.

Stigler, George Joseph (1949a). "A Survey of Contemporary Economics." *Journal of Political Economy* 42(2): 93–105.

Stigler, George Joseph (1949b). "Monopolistic Competition in Retrospect." in *Five Lectures on Economic Problems*. London: Longmans, Green, pp. 12–24.

Stigler, George Joseph (1949c). "The Classical Economists: An Alternative View," in *Five Lectures on Economic Problems*. London: Longmans, Green, pp. 25–36.

Stigler, George Joseph (1955). "Mathematics in Economics: Further Comment." *Review of Economics and Statistics* 37(3): 299–300.

Stigler, George Joseph (1960). "The Influence of Events and Policies on Economic Theory." *American Economic Review, Papers and Proceedings* 50(2): 36–45.

Stigler, George Joseph (1965). "The Economist and the State." *American Economic Review* 55(1): 1–18.

Stigler, George Joseph (1968). "What Is Industrial Organization," in *The Organization of Industry*. Chicago: University of Chicago Press, pp. 1–2.

Stigler, George Joseph (1970). "Director's Law of Public Income Redistribution." *Journal of Law & Economics* 13(1): 1–10.

Stigler, George Joseph (1971a). "The Theory of Economic Regulation." *Bell Journal of Economics and Management Science* 2(1): 3–21.

Stigler, George Joseph (1971b). "Modern Man and His Corporation." *Graduate School Business Selected Papers* 39 (March).

Stigler, George Joseph (1971c). "Smith's Travels on the Ship of State." *History of Political Economy* 3(2): 256–277.

Stigler, George Joseph (1976a). "Birthday Speech." Unpublished

Stigler, George Joseph (1976b). "Do Economists Matter?" *Southern Economic Journal* 42(3): 347–354.

Stigler, George Joseph (1977/mislabeled 1976). "Remarks on the Departure of Milton Friedman from the University of Chicago." *Archival Papers in Regard to Milton Friedman: Box 20*. Special Collections (George Stigler Archive): Regenstein Library (University of Chicago).

Stigler, George Joseph (1982). *The Economist as Preacher, and Other Essays*. Chicago: University of Chicago Press.

Stigler, George Joseph (1984). "Laissez-Faire—Policy-or-Circumstance?" Unpublished *Draft Manuscript*.

Stigler, George Joseph (1988a). *Memoirs of an Unregulated Economist*. New York: Basic Books.

Stigler, George Joseph (1988b). "Draft of Interview with George Stigler." *Archival Papers: Box 19*. Special Collections (George Stigler Archive): Regenstein Library (University of Chicago).

Stigler, George Joseph (1988c). "John Stuart Mill." *Working Paper No. 50*. Chicago: Center for the Study of the Economy and the State, University of Chicago, pp. 1–22.

Stigler, George Joseph (1988d). "The Political Redistribution of Income." *Mimeo*. Stigler Papers: Regenstein Library: University of Chicago, pp. 1–14.

Stigler, George Joseph (1988e). "The Effect of Government on Economic Efficiency." *Business Economics* 23(1): 7–13.

Stigler, George Joseph. (1989). "Two Notes on the Coase Theorem," *Yale Law Journal* 99(December): 631–633.

Stigler, George Joseph (1991). "Memorial Service for Ethel Verry." *Mimeo*. October 28: 1–2.

Stigler, George Joseph and Gary Stanley Becker (1977). "De Gustibus Non Est Disputandum." *American Economic Review* 67(2): 76–90.

Stigler, George Joseph and Claire Friedland (1962). "What Can Regulators Regulate? The Case of Electricity." *Journal of Law & Economics* 5(1): 1–16.

Su, Hieu-Chun and David Colander (2013). "A Failure to Communicate: The Fact/Value Divide and the Putnam/Dasgupta Debate." *Erasmus Journal of Economics and Philosophy* 6(2): 1–23.

Tarbell, Ida (1905). *The History of the Standard Oil Company*. New York: McClure, Phillips.

Tinbergen, Jan (1940). "On a Method of Statistical Business Cycle Research. A Reply." *Economic Journal* 50(1): 141–154.

Van Horn, Rob (2010a). "Aaron Director," in Emmett, Ross (ed.), *The Elgar Companion to the Chicago School of Economics*. Northampton, MA: Edward Elgar, pp. 265–270.

Van Horn, Robert (2010b). "Harry Aaron Director: The Coming of Age of a Reformer Skeptic." *History of Political Economy* 42(4): 601–630.

Van Horn, Robert (2011). "Jacob Viner's Critique of Chicago Neoliberalism," in Robert Van Horn, Philip Mirowski, and Thomas A. Stapleford (eds.), *Building Chicago Economics*. Cambridge: Cambridge University Press, pp. 279–301.

Van Horn, Robert and Philip Mirowski (2009). "The Rise of the Chicago School of Economics and the Birth of Neoliberalism," in Philip Mirowski and Dieter Plehwe (eds.), *The Road from Mont Pelerin*. Cambridge, MA: Harvard University Press, pp. 139–180.

Van Horn, Robert, Philip Mirowski, and Thomas A. Stapleford (2011). "Blue-prints," in Van Horn, Mirowski, and Stapleford (eds.), *Building Chicago Economics*. Cambridge: Cambridge University Press, pp. xv–xxv.

Veblen, Thorstein B. (1908). "Professor Clark's Economics." *Quarterly Journal of Economics* 22(2): 147–195.

INDEX

abstraction: Becker and, 173n19; Buchanan and, 117–18; Chicago School and, 66–67; Coase and, 174n27; economic policy and, 21–22, 26, 31; economic theory and, 28, 30, 32; efficiency and, 29; freedom and, 23; Friedman and, 171n13, 172n16, 174n27, 174n29; impartial spectator and, 24, 28, 30–31; interventions and, 25, 31; Knight and, 27, 30; laissez-faire and, 24–28; limited value of, 21–22; Mill and, 170n1, 170n5, 170n7, 171n13, 172n15, 172n16, 173n20; moral philosophy and, 22–24; paternalism and, 28–31, 172n16, 172n17; political economy and, 22; rationality assumption and, 31–35; social science and, 23; statistics and, 27

American Economic Association, 38, 166n17, 176n6, 222n7

anti-Semitism, 42, 67, 179n18, 193n3, 195n10

argumentation: art of economics and, 23, 26, 130, 121–24, 128, 134–35, 137–38, 171n14, 228n25, 228n26; Buchanan and, 117–18, 120; Chicago School and, ix, 10, 41, 76–81, 98, 110, 125–26, 193n5, 198n20, 199n24, 202n28, 203n34, 224n11; Classical Liberals and, 8, 10, 14, 30, 41, 98, 120, 126, 131; Coase and, 110, 120, 217n20, 222n8; competition and, 223n9, 223n10, 231n4; Director and, 223n10; discursive, 6, 9, 11–12, 30, 55, 166n20, 227n23; economic policy and, 122–25, 132–33, 135, 138, 226n20, 229n28; economic science and, 121–24, 127, 130–31, 134, 136–37, 226n20, 227n23, 228n28, 229n29; economic theory and, 120–22, 138, 221n4, 221n5; economists' place and, 129–31; efficiency and, 120; equilibrium and, 123, 221n4, 228n25; Friedman and, 120–21, 124–26, 132–39, 200n26, 202n31, 203n34, 204n38, 221n1, 223n9, 223n10, 224n11, 224n12, 226n18, 229n29; Harvard and,

126, 221n1; Hayek and, 221n3; impartial spectator and, 131; Keynes and, 120, 130, 133–35, 221n5, 222n6, 228n25; Knight and, 224n12; Laughlin and, 39–41, 62, 118; Marshall and, 120, 222n6; mathematics and, 222n6, 222n7; Mill and, 39, 62, 120, 128, 212n27, 224n14, 227n21; MIT and, 121, 126; monopolies and, 223n9, 223n10; moral philosophy and, 127, 131; pit bull, ix, 77, 80, 125, 202n29; positive economics and, 124–29, 132, 135–38, 227n23, 228n5, 229n28; postwar methodology and, 127, 129; resolving policy debates through, 125–27; for the sake of heaven, 8, 10, 30, 39, 62, 92, 118, 120, 125–28, 131, 142, 164, 164n10, 224n11, 224n14, 227n23, 232n7; Samuelson and, 120–21, 221n1, 224n11; Sen and, 226n20; separation of theory from policy and, 127–29; Smith and, 12, 14, 120, 131; South Side policy and, 76–81; statistics and, 128–29, 222n7, 233n16; Stigler and, 177n13, 200n26, 202n31, 203n34, 204n38, 223n9, 223n10, 224n12, 229n29; utilitarianism and, 227n23; value-transparent theory and, 131–33; Viner and, 120, 193n5

Arrow, Kenneth, 9, 48, 54, 153, 184n2, 186n6, 191n22

art and craft methodology: argumentation and, 121–24, 128; Chicago School and, 49; Classical Liberals and, 1–2, 4, 11, 139–62; econometrics and, 8, 41, 53, 55, 75, 144–45, 149, 187n11, 208n16, 222n8, 233n16, 233n17; economic science and, 121–24, 139–62; economic theory as fable and, 146–47; economist as engineer and, 148–49; income distribution policy and, 152–56; international trade and, 156–59; macroeconomics and, 149–52; mathematics and, 163n2

255

Pigou, Arthur C. (*continued*)
33, 83; general equilibrium and, 33;
Lerner and, 215n11; Marshall and, 33, 51,
83–84, 174n28; mathematics and, 51;
political economy and, 83; rationality
assumption and, 33–34; Welfare Economics and, 33, 83–84, 86, 111, 213n4,
215n11
political economy: abstraction and, 22,
171n12, 171n14, 175n2; Buchanan and, 103,
112–18, 212n1; Chicago School and, 38,
46, 176n9; Classical Liberals and, 133–34,
167n26, 169n34, 171n12, 171n14; *Journal
of Political Economy* and, 38, 46, 176n9;
Marshall and, 83; Pigou and, 83; Stigler
and, 46, 103; Virginia School and, 103,
112–18, 212n1; Welfare Economics and,
83
political markets, 204n36, 219n27, 220n32
positive economics, 124–29, 132, 135–38,
159, 171n14, 227n23, 228n5, 229n28
Posner, Richard, 204n37
poverty, 54, 136, 154, 156, 189n16, 209n20
Poverty and Famines (Sen), 156
pragmatism, 26, 29, 45, 58–59, 90, 100–1,
106, 109, 127, 132, 163n6, 165n16, 178n17,
211n25
precepts: Chicago School and, 4, 7, 49;
Classical Liberals and, 4, 7–8, 16, 18, 24,
34–35, 49, 91, 164n8, 205n42, 206n1;
laissez-faire, 4, 7, 14, 16, 24–28, 34, 91,
170n7, 206n1
price theory, 46, 78, 110–11, 174n27, 194n8,
196n14, 203n33, 209n17, 212n1, 216n13,
223n9
Priest, George, 213n6
Princeton, 42, 179n22, 193n5, 194n8
probabilities, 10, 31, 116
"Problem of Social Cost, The" (Coase), 105,
213n5
Problem of Unemployment, The (Douglas
and Director), 68
Progressive Era, 166n17
pro-market approach, 5, 49, 59, 67, 69–70,
75, 80, 99, 167n25, 199n24, 212n1
psychology, 176n4, 184n39, 190n18, 195n11
Public Choice: Buchanan and, 103, 112–19,
173n22, 212n1, 218n26; Virginia School
and, 102–3, 112–19, 212n1, 218n26,
220n31, 220n32
Putnam, Hillary, 3, 223n9

Quarterly Journal of Economics, 38, 176n9

rationality, 26, 31–35, 114–15, 150, 183n37,
229n29
Rawls, John, 226n20
Reder, Melvin, 49, 67, 179n18, 183n37, 193n4
refugees, 42, 67
Review of Economic Studies, 166n20
Ricardo, David, 12, 15, 33, 120, 128, 158,
167n26, 169n32, 170n1, 225n16, 226n17
"Rights, Efficiency and Exchange: The
Irrelevance of Transaction Costs"
(Buchanan), 113
Rights and Wrongs of the Dismal Science, The
(Rodrik), 233n13
Road to Serfdom (Hayek), 47, 72, 182n32,
197n16, 207n6
Robbins, Lionel, 43, 132–33, 136, 227n23
Rockefeller, John D., 175n1, 193n4
Rodrik, Dani, 144, 156–57, 159, 233n13,
238n41, 238n42
Romer, Paul, 144, 151–52, 235n29, 235n30
Rosen, Sherwin, 62, 174n27, 199n24,
202n29, 210n24, 229n28
Rosenberg, Alexander, 3
Roth, Alvin, 148–49
Rothbard, Murray, 34, 167n25
Rousseau, Jean Jacques, 169n33
Rubinstein, Ariel, 144, 146–48, 233n13,
234n23

Samuelson, Paul, ix; anti-Semitism and,
193n4; argumentation and, 120–21, 221n1,
224n11; Chicago tradition and, 42–50,
176n3, 176n9, 177n11, 178n17, 179n23,
179n24, 180n25, 181n29; Classical Liberals
and, 7, 9–10, 120–21, 164n12, 167n23,
221n1, 224n11; Coase and, 215n10; economic policy and, 52, 64, 70, 189n16,
193n4, 193n5, 195n10, 197n15, 197n17,
199n23, 200n26, 201n27, 202n31; economics of control and, 64; *Foundations
of Economics* and, 46; Harvard and, 7,
46, 52, 64, 185n4, 193n3, 221n1; influence
of, 46–47; Marshall and, 187n9; mathematics and, 7, 51–52, 167n23, 185n2,
185n3, 185n4, 186n6; MIT and, 7, 10, 121,
176n9, 185n4, 221n1, 224n11; as polymath,
51; rise of Chicago School and, 51–56, 64,
185n2, 185n3, 185n4, 186n6, 186n7, 187n9,
189n16, 191n22; science/policy firewall
and, 9–10; Stigler and, 217n20; Virginia
School and, 108, 215n10, 217n20; Welfare
Economics and, 86, 206n3, 206n4,
211n25

208n16; Stigler and, 103–5, 109–15, 118–19; transaction costs and, 103–14, 213n4, 216n12, 216n16, 217n20, 218n22, 220n35
Volker Fund, 72, 197n16

Walgreen Chair, 71, 196n12
Wallis, Allen, 42, 71, 98, 180n25, 186n6, 196n12
Walras, Léon, 46, 52, 85, 89, 120, 181n30, 185n3
wealth, 103, 148, 155, 219n29
Wealth of Nations, The (Smith), 14, 50, 184n39
Welfare Economics: Coase and, 85, 97, 206n2, 209n19; Director and, 93, 95; economic policy and, 82, 84, 89–94, 99, 101, 206n1, 207n10; economic science and, 82, 96, 208n14; economics of control and, 85–89, 206n3; economic theory and, 82–83, 85, 91, 93; efficiency and, 95, 98; empirical work on, 96–101; equilibrium and, 83–85, 89; freedom and, 91–92, 98; Friedman and, 93–98; functional finance and, 87–88, 206n3; Graaff and, 138; Harvard and, 94, 98, 100; Hayek and, 207n6; impartial spectator and, 98; interventions and, 84–88, 92–93, 101;

Keynes and, 87–88, 91–92, 94, 206n1, 206n3, 219n28; Knight and, 93–98, 208n13; laissez-faire and, 88, 91, 98, 101; Lerner and, 85–89, 91; Marshall and, 83–85, 89; mathematics and, 6, 85–86, 96; Mill and, 95, 101, 208n12, 212n27; MIT and, 94, 98, 100; moral philosophy and, 6, 90; New, 83–85, 89, 91, 93–94, 206n1; New New, 89–92; optimality and, 30, 82, 86–88, 206n5; Pigou and, 33, 83–84, 86, 111, 213n4, 215n11; political economy and, 83; postwar methodology and, 82, 93, 97, 208n11, 208n14, 213n6; Samuelson and, 86, 206n3, 206n4, 211n25; scientific policy and, 82; Sen and, 207n9; Simons and, 95; Smith and, 97, 211n26; social welfare function and, 30, 57, 89–92, 207n8; statistics and, 95, 98; Stigler and, 93–100; Viner and, 209n18, 211n26; Virginia School and, 115
Williamson, Oliver, 220n35
World Trade Organization (WTO), 158, 238n42
Wright, Chester, 183n36, 192n1

Yale, 42, 181n28, 234n26
Yeager, Leland, 212n1

A NOTE ON THE TYPE

This book has been composed in Adobe Text and Gotham. Adobe Text, designed by Robert Slimbach for Adobe, bridges the gap between fifteenth- and sixteenth-century calligraphic and eighteenth-century Modern styles. Gotham, inspired by New York street signs, was designed by Tobias Frere-Jones for Hoefler & Co.